FUNDAMENTALS OF FRESHWATER FISHING

FUNDAMENTALS OF FRESHWATER FISHING

Charles Bingham
and
Tony Allen

SWAN·HILL
PRESS

Dedication
To Frances, my ever patient wife.

Dedication
To the memory of my father-in-law Bill Waldron. He cast his fly on many waters, in particular the rivers of Tierra del Fuego and Southern Patagonia where he farmed and fished extensively

Acknowledgements

First and foremost my thanks go to Charles Bingham for inviting me to write the coarse fishing section of this book. To Brian and Lindsay Parker for allowing my grandsons, Nicholas and Philip, to accompany me on fishing trips to help with the photography, and especially Brian in his capacity of Head River Keeper on the Bossington Estate for permitting me to fish on his lovely stretch of the River Test. To Shakespeare for providing rods and helping me in the choice of equipment. To *Tight Lines* of Totton for lending me various items of fishing tackle for illustrations.

Tony Allen

Acknowledgements

My thanks to David James and Michael Malyon of the River Test tributaries Anton and Bourne for permission to fish for trout with my daughter, Lara, on their streams. Also to Bob Beard, riparian owner on the Dart, for productive salmon and sea trout fishing, and to The Duchy of Cornwall for access to the moorland reaches of that river.

The River Test photographs were taken on days generously given to Tony and me by John Grose, and by permission from the Bossington Estate Head River Keeper, Brian Parker.

I gratefully acknowledge the welcome given to me and my fly-fishing pupils by Abigail Underhill, owner of the Tavistock Trout Fishery, and to Bruce & Walker who provided me with superb fly-fishing rods.

I have fished with Tony Allen for over 45 seasons, benefiting on each outing from his knowledge and enthusiasm.

Charles Bingham

First published in the UK in 1999
by Swan Hill Press, an imprint of Airlife Publishing Ltd

British Library Cataloguing-in-Publication Data
A catalogue record for this book
is available from the British Library

ISBN 1 85310 996 7

The information in this book is true and complete to the best of our knowledge. All recommendations are made without any guarantee on the part of the Publisher, who also disclaims any liability incurred in connection with the use of this data or specific details.

Typeset by Servis Filmsetting Ltd
Printed in Hong Kong

Swan Hill Press
an imprint of Airlife Publishing Ltd
101 Longden Road, Shrewsbury, SY3 9EB, England
E-mail: sales@airlifebooks.com
Website: www.airlifebooks.com

Contents

PART ONE
COARSE FISHING

INTRODUCTION

Angling is a wonderfully relaxing and healthy recreation open to both the young and old. I have a dear friend aged 90 years who still casts a fly with expertise and cunning. He catches his fair share of fish, probably enjoying his fishing now even more than he did in his young days.

At the other end of the scale, I remember my first experience of fishing which took place at a local lake near my home. I was always pestering my parents to be taken out, and so I was given a little fishing set for my fourth birthday. The set comprised a tiny rod, line, a winder with a float and a No. 20 hook. The whole could be put together in a jiffy.

So, proudly carrying this outfit and wearing my wellies, I arrived at the lake with my long-suffering aunt who often took me for walks. I waded out a few feet with the water perilously close to the top of my wellies. I pinched on a minute piece of dough and fished. I caught minnows. Soon the summer evening was coming to a close, but that 'just one more go' continued. Finally my aunt, in despair, waylaid a lady walking by and persuaded her to keep watch while she 'phoned my mother, who arrived equipped to wade out and drag me away from my shoal of minnows. I was 'hooked' and to this day, some 72 years later, my love of river and lake has only grown.

So poles are not very new, these young hopefuls were fishing on the Cemetery Lake on Southampton Common in the hot summer of 1936. This is where I had my introduction to fishing many years earlier.

There is not only fishing to be enjoyed when you visit the river or lake, nature supplies non-stop entertainment throughout the year. When spring arrives, everything becomes green as nature sheds her sombre winter coat. Swans, ducks, moorhens, coots and all the river birds are busy building nests. Moorhens carry nest-building materials on to reed and mud-beds, away from predators. Coots set about the same activity 'knocking in nails', the peculiar sound made by this bird. Swans hiss if you go too near their nesting places close to the river bank.

Rooks caw in the rookery, dropping sticks and nest-building materials while they argue noisily. Tiny reed warblers suspend their fragile nests in the tops of Cooper's reeds which sway precariously. Skylarks hover overhead singing encouragement. Primroses and daffodils peep out, and there is the sweet smell of wild garlic on the soft wind.

Then May arrives, full of beauty and interest. This is in the coarse fish close season of March to June, but you should be there, walking and observing, for now comes mayfly time – Duffer's Fortnight for the game fisherman. You should still be there to observe large chub swimming lazily near the surface, enjoying the feast of these large flies as they sail down the river like an armada of ships – note where these record-breaking chub swim and return when the season starts. Then the water birds are out swimming with their broods, the young frantically trying to keep up with their parents, and scooting over the water to have their share of the mayflies.

Summer arrives and you are back on the river with rod and line in search of chub, or out with the fly rod for a try at grayling. For the next few months the balmy days of summer give much pleasure. Carp patrolling the margins set your nerves tingling as they swim round your floating crusts, the float nodding and sliding away as the water ripples.

As dusk grows at the waterside of a lake, rats rustle in the bushes and steal your bread or groundbait. Water voles swim along the water's edge, watching and then diving out of sight. Year in and year out these pleasurable times are repeated while you pursue your hobby.

Autumn arrives and the countryside assumes its golden cloak, reeds fade, and before you know it winter is here. It too has excitement and charm: pike are hungry, reeds have rotted, spinning is possible, and the flash as a pike turns to take your spinner sets your pulse racing.

Even snow has its charm with tracks telling a story. Observe the footprints of water birds, rabbits, rats and voles, and the

This is a sign on the Ancient Bridge at White Mill, Sturminster Marshall, Dorset. It reads 'Any person wilfully injuring any part of this county bridge will be guilty of a felony and upon conviction liable to be transported for life by the court. T. Fooks'.

---

paw marks of mink which plunder our fish stocks and cause havoc among the water birds. Deer also leave their tell-tale marks.

Do not expect to see photographs of record-breaking fish or a heap of fish in a keep net in this book. I am not a lover of keep nets, for they damage fish if overcrowded. This book's intention is to give you photographs to identify each species and help you to catch them.

I must impress on you that this is a book giving basic instruction to start a wonderful hobby. There are many books specialising on all aspects of fishing in great detail. These you can read later to improve your knowledge.

By now I hope I have whetted your appetite. Carry on reading to gain the basic knowledge enabling you to enjoy your fishing to the full.

Tony Allen

CHAPTER 1

RODS AND REELS

Rods

GENERAL FLOAT FISHING

These rods can be in two or three pieces and vary between 10–13ft, the variations in length accommodating different species of fish. The length must also suit the venue, whether tree-lined or open meadows, and whether lake or river. In a river, consideration must be given to the required casting distance, and the rod's ability to handle a bait in slow or fast water. Ponds and lakes have similar variations such as whether they are tree-lined, if they have lily beds to fish over, and the type of fish present.

LEDGER RODS

These are usually of two-piece construction and 9ft in length. They can have more than one top to allow quiver-tip and swing-tip fishing. The rod needs a screwed top ring for attaching either of these tips. The rod may also be used for float fishing in a small tree-lined river.

CARP RODS

These are usually 12ft, in a two-piece construction with a $1^3/_4$–$2^1/_2$lb test curve. They must be capable of dealing with the violent rushes of carp weighing up to 40lb hooked on 12-lb nylon.

PIKE RODS

The carp rod may be used for these heavy fish, whether fishing by spinning or bait.

POLES

These can either be telescopic, each section sliding into the next as a fish is played to the net, or can be taken apart as they are fed back on a roller rod rest.

ROD DESIGNS

Some coarse fishing rods are built with a flexible tip action, meaning that the top joint has a flexible tip to facilitate delicate handling and a quick strike. Bait casting rods have an all-through action for long casting and to handle heavier baits such as spinners and dead baits. The carp/pike rod is suitable for this purpose. Spinning rods usually have a double-handed, long handle. General coarse fishing rods have a long handle which can be tucked under the arm, alleviating fatigue and making the striking and playing of fish easier.

ROD RINGS

These are also known as line guides. Float fishing is usually done with fine nylon which in wet weather tends to stick to the rod. Such rods are fitted with stand-off rings which keep the line away from the rod. Ledgering does not have this problem as there is always a tight line from bait to reel.

Carp and pike rods have heavier rings which are usually lined with one of the 'space age', hard-wearing materials, to cope with fast and continuous line passage during spinning. Butt rings should be large to prevent line from a fixed spool reel bunching between the reel and the butt ring. Tip and butt rings should be ceramic-lined to prevent the formation of ridges due to wear from line passage.

ROD PURCHASE

When buying your first rod it is necessary to take an experienced angler with you, as you will be confronted with rack upon rack of rods. If the shop assistant is not an experienced angler, and many are not, you may be landed with a rod for which you have paid far too much and which will not suit your requirements.

There are a number of different categories of rods, although there is no such thing as a general purpose rod to cover all types of fish. There are carp rods, two types of pike rods (spinning and bait), ledgering rods, and general purpose float fishing rods. When you become expert, the extravagance of a match fishing rod may be considered! I suggest a three-piece general purpose float fishing rod of 13ft be your first purchase. This should have a flexible tip action to enable nylons of 3–6-lb to be fished. The reel fittings will be sliding, enabling you to fix the reel anywhere on the long butt to suit personal comfort.

A centre pin reel by Grice & Young of Christchurch, Hants.

REELS

These are either fixed spools or centre pin. For a single purchase I advise the former as they are cheaper and more versatile. I have always used a Mitchell 300 with four line spools of nylon: 18-lb, 12-lb, 6-lb and 3-lb. The 18-lb line spool being used for pike.

Operating a fixed spool reel stage by stage. The reel is a full bail type, the bail arm functioning by capturing the line after a cast and preparing it for the retrieve. There is an auto reverse lever (A) which prevents the handle from turning backwards. Preparing to cast, the lure is reeled in until it is 6–12in from the tip of the rod (B); heavy lures are cast better if they are slightly closer to the tip of the rod. The tip of your finger engages the line as it comes over the line guard (C). The bail arm is pulled back (D) until it is open (E). The cast is made and the line released (F) until the bait is where you have aimed it and on the water. You wind (G) to close the bail arm and the line is retrieved.

When casting, if you release the line too soon as the rod comes forward the cast will have high trajectory, but if too late it will hit the water at your feet. The reel mounted on the rod ready for use (H).

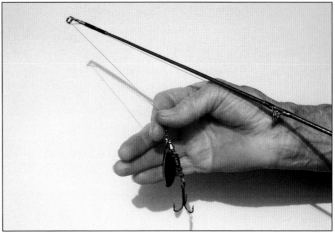

B

C

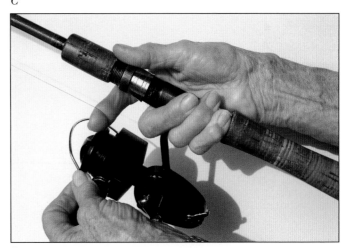

D

A

I also have a centre pin for long trotting. This has two spools for 3-lb and 5-lb nylon to cover all requirements. A centre pin reel needs skill to achieve distance when casting. It is so free-running that one has to beware of creating 'birds nests' due to overrunning if the spool is not delicately controlled by finger pressure.

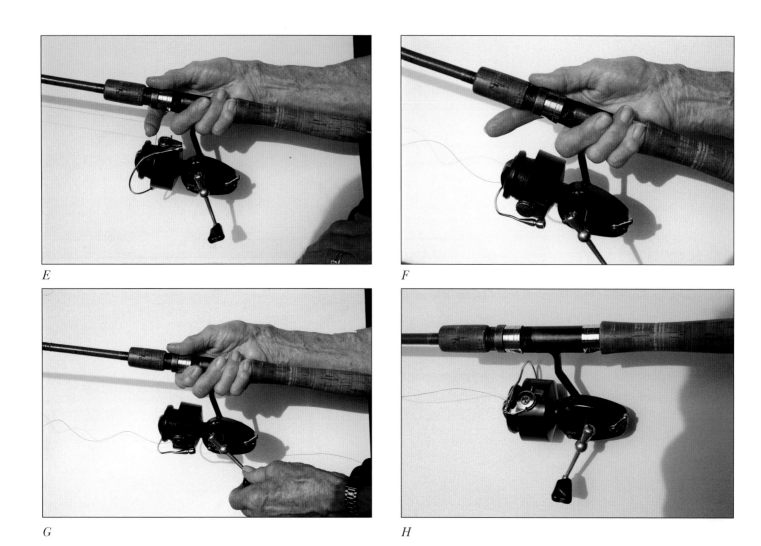

E

F

G

H

An overhead cast with a fixed spool reel.

An underhand cast with a fixed spool reel.

REEL FITTINGS

The outfit must be balanced between the weights of the rod and reel. Where there are fixed reel fittings, as in most fly and spinning rods, the relative weights of the rod and reel must be chosen with care. Where reel fittings are sliding, a finger should be placed just above the handle and underneath the rod tube, and the reel position finalised when the rod balances horizontally. This positioning ensures that the rod can be held all day and you will not have an aching arm to take home!

Sometimes a short 8ft single-handed rod may be used for light bait casting in pike fishing. This rod, as with the 11ft carp

and pike rod, should have screw winch fittings to save the embarrassment of the reel falling into the water. If this happens, it will not reappear above the water until you have pulled in all the line to the fixed end on the reel spool. Such an experience is bad for your temper, and bad if a fish is on the other end. Additionally, mud and silt do not do a reel any good.

NYLON

The tackle shop stocks many different brands of nylon in many breaking strains. All manufacturers state that their brand is best for: smallest diameter-to-breaking strain, wet and dry knot strength, anti-glitter so as not to frighten fish, coloured so that it may be seen by the angler, better floating/sinking than competitors, and so on. I have always chosen Platil or Maxima.

Some monofilaments of the 'fine for breaking strain' type are pre-stretched, lacking elasticity, whilst others stretch a great deal. A hefty strike is needed if a big fish takes at a long distance on stretch nylon, but in keeping with the strength of the nylon in use. I find that pre-stretched nylon becomes weaker after landing a heavy fish. This is a personal observation which may be questioned by fellow anglers.

It is advisable to keep your reel and spare spools in a bag as nylon deteriorates if subjected to heat or light over a long period of time, so check your breaking strains regularly. Also, with very fine monofilaments, examine for tiny knots which can be overlooked.

Nylon is a slippery material, so be sure to use the recommended knots and check them carefully. Remember when tying a knot to moisten it before pulling tight. This will ensure you have almost the full strength as the knot strength is always less than the nylon breaking strain, especially when wet.

Care of tackle

Tackle lasts longer if it is looked after. Dry your rods and care for them, revarnishing where applicable annually in the close season. Check whippings and rod rings for wear and tear. Replace top and butt rings on spinning rods as a groove can be worn by line passage, even in lined rings. Store the rod in its bag and hang from a wall hook in a cool, dry place.

Dry reels and remove the spools. Clean them with a soft cloth and put grease on cog wheels and fine oil on the check and spindle handles. Lubrication makes them a pleasure to use and eliminates squeaks from dry bearings and handles. Run your nylon across the garden and rewind regularly on the spool, checking for rough places which may have appeared, and even knots. Your reel should then go into its bag for storage in a cool place.

The cost of major items

The prices quoted prevailed at the time of writing. To make a start need not be expensive.

PIKE AND CARP ROD

One rod suffices for both fish.
Cat. 1851/360   Shakespeare Zenith pike 12ft 2-piece

A collection of coarse fishing rods and reels.

Left to right: a carbon fibre trout fly rod by Bruce & Walker with an Intrepid multiplying fly reel; a split cane fly rod by Hardy with a fly reel by W.H. Hughes of Cork, both dated about 1930; a Greenheart trout fly rod by A. Carter of London with a Hardy Perfect fly reel; a whole cane pike rod with a Star Back Nottingham centre pin reel; an original Crosswind Threadline reel, one of the first with a fixed spool; a split cane float fishing rod by Seeley of Redditch with a Golden Eagle centre pin reel by Grice & Young of Christchurch, Hants; a Tag Barnes Super carp rod by Pegley Davis with a Mitchell 300 fixed spool reel; a centre pin reel by Crossle circa 1911 and a very old single handle fly reel, maker unknown. Also in the picture are a box of wet flies, my coarse fishing tackle box and a box of spinners and lures for pike fishing.

Test curve 2¹/₂lb   (£46.99)

FLOAT FISHING

For barbel, tench, roach, grayling, chub, perch and dace.
Cat. 1821/390   Shakespeare Zenith match 13ft 3-piece
                                                    (£45.99)

LEDGER FISHING

Cat. 1801/285   Shakespeare Cosmos ledger rod 9¹/₂ft 2-piece.
Threaded tip   (£31.99)

LIGHT SPINNING FOR PERCH

Cat. 1506/180   Shakespeare Europa XL Spin 6ft 2-piece
                                                    (£14.99)

REELS

Carp and pike – Mitchell 260 fixed spool   (£30.00)
All other coarse fish – Mitchell 240 fixed spool (£30.00)
Cat. 2900/400   Shakespeare Eagle centre pin 4¹/₄in diameter
⁹/₁₆in wide spool taking 4–6-lb Maxima or Platil nylon
                                                    (£53.99)

The centre pin is suitable for all fish other than pike.

FLY-FISHING TACKLE FOR DACE AND CHUB

Cat. 1640/270   Zenith fly rod 9ft 2-piece taking AFTM 6/7
fly line   (£30.99)
Cat. 2530   Shakespeare Zenith fly reel 3¹/₂in diameter
Capacity for DT7F line and backing   (£12.99)
Cat. 3226   Shakespeare DT6F green fly line   (£11.99)

CHAPTER 2
HOOK BAITS

Maggots

Of the multitude of hook baits the one which really comes to the fore is the maggot. You can buy many types from the tackle shop: yellow maggots, pinkies, red and white maggots, bronze pinkies, mixed-colour maggots, large whites, squatts and bronze maggots. They are available throughout the year and are not expensive, costing in the region of £1.50 to £2.00 per pint.

The product of the bluebottle fly, these maggots are lively larvae. To check for quality and freshness, put one in the palm of someone else's hand to see that it is a lively wriggler! The other point to discern is that it has a dark patch which is a remnant of the food it has been eating.

Half a dozen maggots flicked into your swim will hold your fish as long as you keep the supply going. Do not overdo the quantity as they are very filling. You may start fishing and get little or no response. Keep going with a very small trickle of maggots – it may be an hour or more before there is activity. Be patient, sometimes a small response builds up to a fish a cast.

In flowing water you must be sure to place your feed upstream in the right place, or maggots washed downstream may take fish out of your swim to an area below. Remember to keep feeding or your fish will look elsewhere for food.

Maggots should be kept in damp sawdust. This can be changed by putting them in a sieve to get rid of the used dust. At the same time take the chance to pick out the dead and any unwanted rubbish.

Squatts, small maggots of the house fly, should be kept in the brown foundry sand in which they are sold. They are to be obtained in natural or red colours and are mainly used for close loose feeding. They are not as active as maggots, staying on the bed of the river rather than burying themselves. They are also good to put in groundbait, or to mix with groundbait in a feeder as they are less active and filter out slowly as the groundbait disperses in the current.

Hook maggots will keep in a cool place for up to two weeks, even in the bottom of a refrigerator (if allowed). They need a good supply of air, so the fridge is really only an overnight way

Assorted baits on a tackle box.

of keeping them fresh. They should be hooked through the 'beard', which is on the blunt (tail) end, with a very sharp hook or they will burst.

Casters

If maggots are kept for several days they gradually turn into chrysalids. Their first stage is to turn light bronze, then brown and eventually black. In this stage they are called casters. It is difficult to buy perfect casters and, when purchased, they will be more expensive than maggots. Those which are going sour should be picked out and disposed of as they will deter fish.

A box of casters.

Casters are excellent to use in groundbait in balls, or in a mixture in an open-ended swim feeder. This is because they do not crawl away like maggots but are washed out slowly by the current. It is important that they do not float. Floaters will go off in the current and not only encourage your fish out of the swim but will bait the river for anyone downstream – not a good policy in a competition!

One wonders if producing casters is worth the effort and expense, but they are effective as groundbait and deadly on the hook, which must be completely concealed in the caster. A double caster for chub, tench, bream and carp on a size 14 hook is very effective. A single one on a size 16 or 18 hook is attractive to smaller fish, and for large fish as well with a little more care in playing and landing. There are special long-shanked fine wire hooks for casters, but they must be treated gently on a heavy fish or they will straighten.

Casters in their early stage tend to float. Some anglers avoid them in this condition, but they can be effective for carp if two or three are mounted in a bunch on a size 14 hook on a long hook link. In reasonably shallow water the rig can be made up so that the casters float to the surface and cruising carp will take them. If the casters tend to sink after a while they do so very slowly and carp will take them on the drop.

To bait a caster the hook should be entered at the blunt end, turned and pushed inside, including the eye or spade end of the hook so that it is buried and out of sight. Sometimes baiting can be achieved on a small sharp hook inserted through the blunt end, as with a maggot.

Bread

Bread is the next main bait. It is available in any household and is, without doubt, the cheapest and most versatile bait. It can be used as crust, flake and paste, the final form in several variations.

BREAD CRUST

Bread crust is cut from a new loaf, sliced into small squares and put in a bag ready for use. A size 14 hook is pushed in through the crust and brought back. Morsels can also be torn off a loaf at the riverside.

Crust swells in the water so allowance must be made for this when preparing or breaking off crust. Some anglers go to considerable trouble in their preparations. They cut thin strips from the bottom of a loaf, cover them with a damp cloth and press them between two pieces of board overnight. (The boards can be clamped together or held under a heavy weight.) The strips are then cut into small pieces of varying shapes. It does not matter if the outline is ragged as this makes them move attractively in the water. With this bait it is advisable to have a tiny shot quite close to the hook as bread tends to float.

Crust is one of the most popular baits for carp when they are working the margins of a lake on a hot summer's day or evening. This time large pieces can be broken off a loaf, even the size of a small match box, and cast out on a free line with no weight attached. It is nerve-racking to watch a big carp circling round a crust, having a good look, and sometimes nibbling all round the edge until the bare hook sinks out of sight.

BREAD FLAKE

Bread flake is one of my favourite baits on which I have taken many roach weighing more than 2lb. Pinch out a piece from a *new* loaf, the size really depending on the fish you are after: large for big fish and smaller for small fish. Double the flake around the hook and pinch at the top of the shank. The hook size should not be smaller than 14 as bread swells and is relatively soft.

BREAD PASTE

Bread paste can be made in many forms. I remember using it as a very small boy on a lake near my home. A tiny size 20 hook and a small piece of cork or a feather quill found by the lake used as a float made up the rig. Hapless minnows were caught and transported home in a jamjar, but after watching their distress in their new surroundings I was always persuaded to take them back to the lake and set them free. If one died in the process my conscience was pricked for many days thereafter.

To prepare bread paste is to tempt the appetites of the most fastidious fish on hook sizes between 18 and 14, the crust should firstly be cut off a stale loaf. Soak it in water and wrap it in a clean cloth. Then squeeze the water out and knead it into a doughy consistency in the cloth. This is now the basic bread bait which can be used on the hook without further preparation.

Flavourings of your choice can be added, together with sausage or luncheon meat moulded into the bread. They all make excellent and tempting baits, a cheese flavour in the paste being especially favoured by chub. Food colouring may be added as sometimes a change of colour can persuade a disinterested fish to feed.

Another way of presenting bread is by using a new thin-cut white loaf and punching out small hard pellets with a bread punch. These punches can be bought in varying sizes from the tackle dealer. Punched bread on a very small hook is an excellent bait for roach and dace.

Another bait associated with bread is a paste made with flour. Put plain flour in a bowl, add water and mix to a stiff paste. This can be coloured with food dyes and custard powder can also be added. Basic bread from the loaf can be given extra attraction by a sprinkling of sugar.

A worm tail and a whole worm mounted at the head end and above the ring. Maggots are hooked at the 'thick' end by gently squeezing when the 'beard' protrudes, allowing fine skin hooking not to burst it. Sweetcorn is just hooked through and with luncheon meat the hook is inserted, turned and drawn back with just the eye showing.

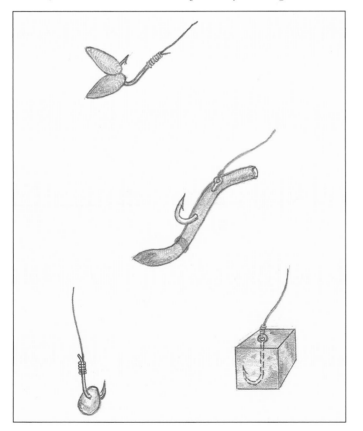

Worms

These are the last of the three main baits and there are many different types. Worms are all-purpose, suitable for any fishery, any fish and, unfortunately, any eel which is in the vicinity.

There are three really useful species. The first is the garden ranger or lob worm. They can be caught on a hot damp summer's night if you go out on to your lawn with a torch. You have to be quick, as they sense heat and vibration and will disappear in a flash. Roach in particular like a lob's tail.

The next in line are the brandling and the small red worm. The red worm is the next in popularity. It is a rich colour with a pale saddle and is found in the compost heap. It is an excellent bait for bream, and favoured by all fish whether ledgered or fished off a float. The brandling is said to have a scent. This is no wonder as it lives in manure heaps. It too is an excellent bait.

There is one other worm, the marsh worm, sometimes dug out of the soft ground in the lower reaches of the Hampshire Avon. This worm is used when float fishing for sea trout.

Red worms should be hooked near the head or, if using more than one, through the middle. Tench and especially perch favour a worm bait – any of the three species can be tried on a size 8 or 12 hook.

A 'wormery' can be made to give a constant supply to combat dry or wintry weather. The best receptacle is a large plastic drum filled with earth and compost. To this, after your worms have been put in, add vegetable rubbish and be sure to keep the wormery damp. Old lettuce leaves, fruit, and left-over cooked vegetables from the table will all be eaten.

Sweetcorn

Sweetcorn is a favourite bait, being readily available in small tins. It is accepted by all fish in lakes and rivers. Hook sizes can be from 10–14 according to the fish for which you are angling.

When using sweetcorn a few pieces should frequently be thrown in to the river to make the fish aware of the offering, and then keen to take the piece containing the hook.

Baiting up with sweetcorn.

Luncheon meat

Luncheon meat is a popular bait, especially for carp, chub and barbel. A size 10 or 12 hook should be used. As the meat is soft it will stay on the hook better if it is cut into cubes the night before and left out on a plate. It is acceptable to use it from a freshly-opened tin on the river bank if necessary.

The best way to keep this soft meat on the hook is to push the hook through the cube of meat, turn it, and then pull it back. As a groundbait, an open-ended swim feeder should be used. Add cubes of meat and then fill each end with normal groundbait.

Hemp-seed

Hemp has the reputation of being a great attractor, and is used as loose feed with casters or maggots throughout the year. It has to be soaked in water for a day or two until it bursts to reveal the white streak. Alternatively place it in a saucepan of water, bring it to the boil and simmer for half an hour or more, until the seeds burst, exposing the white streak. If overcooked it will not stay on the hook. Hemp must be used whilst fresh as it will turn sour after two or three days and be useless.

Hemp is deadly as a bait, especially in fast runs between weeds. Its effectiveness may be due to its resemblance to a fresh-water snail on which fish feed avidly. Summer and autumn are favourite times for its use, roach and dace being particularly susceptible. For these fish, press a size 12 or 14 hook into the white split.

Hemp-seed should be used very sparingly as groundbait. On some fisheries it is not allowed, as fish fed on it as groundbait have been known to refuse anything else.

Macaroni

If boiled in milk, macaroni becomes a good chub bait. Use the fine tube type and cut into short lengths.

Pearl barley

Pearl barley will catch dace if stewed until it is soft and presented on a size 14 hook. At first glance the fish probably mistakes it for bread or a maggot.

Potato

Small new parboiled potatoes fished whole are a good carp bait. Today, the 'boilie' has probably taken its place.

Boilies

This is a fairly modern innovation. Anglers experimenting with various bread baits, parboiled new potatoes and cheese mixes discovered carp responded to a high protein diet. The anglers then invaded their wives' domain and made all sorts of recipes in the kitchen to attract more and larger carp, and so the boilie was born.

Making boilies is a complicated, messy and time-consuming game. The choice of colours is endless, as are some of the ingredients used: sea foods of all sorts, soft fruits, peaches and melons, and exotic and expensive tropical fruits. A fairly easy home mix is (if you have friends who breed fish) $1/2$lb of finely ground trout pellets, 3 eggs, and the flavouring of your choice from the tackle shop. Beat up the eggs and flavouring, add the trout pellets and make into a paste with the consistency of dough. Roll out a long sausage about $3/4$in in diameter and cut into $3/4$in lengths. Roll each piece into a ball and then place in boiling water for five to ten minutes until fairly solid. Drain, cool and dry on kitchen paper. They are then ready for use.

You can buy boilies unflavoured. These you spray with the flavour of your choice and put in a bag ready for the next day. Tackle shops also sell frozen boilies and sealed packs which must be used within six months. On fisheries where boilies have not been used, it takes a while for the fish to know them as food. Where they are used regularly it is good policy to enquire from local anglers the flavour they find successful, as if this particular boilie is used universally on the fishery the fish will not be very interested in any other flavour. Having gained this knowledge, you ought to go to the tackle shop and decide which flavour is worth buying to enable you to wipe the eye of your fellow anglers. There is another side to the selection of a boilie – if fish are being caught again and again they may become wary of that particular bait and be more receptive to a different colour or flavour.

Whenever boilies are mentioned, carp come to mind, also tench and bream. Discussions with a fellow angler pointed to seasons having an influence: savouries in the autumn; sweet flavours in the summer.

Other baits

There are a number of other baits such as wasp grubs and caddis larvae. These may be too dangerous or tedious to collect.

Bait chart

Bait	Species of fish	Hook size and number of baits
Maggot	bream, carp, dace, chub	single 18–22
	perch, roach, tench, gudgeon	double 14–18
	barbel, rudd, grayling	multiple 8–12
Casters	bream, carp, dace, chub	single 16–20
	roach, tench, barbel	double 14–18
	rudd	multiple 12
Worm	bream, carp, chub	lobs 6–12
	perch, roach, tench	brandlings 10–16
	barbel, eel	brandlings 10–16
Red worm	bream, gudgeon, perch, roach, rudd, tench, grayling	12–16
Bread flake and crust	carp, bream, tench, chub, roach, barbel, rudd	12–16 (carp 4–10)
Bread punch	bream, roach, rudd, gudgeon	16–20
Luncheon meat	carp, chub, barbel, tench	8–12
Hemp	chub, dace, roach, barbel	14–20
Boilies	carp, tench, chub, bream, barbel	8–14
Sweetcorn	carp, chub, bream, roach, rudd, tench, barbel, grayling	10–16

CHAPTER 3
GROUNDBAIT

In coarse fishing under some conditions fish can be caught without using groundbait, perhaps because you pick on a swim where a shoal of fish are feeding. However, after landing one or two the shoal may become suspicious and move away. If groundbait is then used the shoal will become absorbed in feeding and other fish will join them, not having been made suspicious or frightened. So the pattern is of groundbait attracting a shoal (tempting them to partake of the morsels), holding them and persuading them that your swim is a good place to feed and stay.

The main principle is that groundbait is just a pre-dinner offering and not a full meal. The maxim is not too much and not too little of a fresh mix made with scrupulously clean hands. Groundbaiting, to be successfully applied, depends on certain factors: the type of fish you hope to catch, the situation and condition of the water, and the make-up of the bait.

Roach time is dusk time. They always come on the feed, weather conditions permitting, about one hour before dark and continue whilst you can see a float or bite indicator. They respond to a constant sprinkle of ground or hook bait to keep them interested and on the feed.

A system I have never tried, but which has been recommended to me by a fellow enthusiast, is to crush some white eggshell and add it to the groundbait mix. This mixture is seen by the fish which find the groundbait and home in on it.

A procedure to avoid is to groundbait with worms and fish with maggots. This confuses fish and is of little benefit to the angler. Of course, if you are fishing worms or maggots, the addition of your hook bait to the conventional groundbait can be an advantage.

Quantity of groundbait
The quantity of groundbait required is determined by the flow of water. In a lake a handful may be adequate, whereas in a fast-flowing stream you must consider bucketfuls, because much will be washed downstream.

Tench and carp in a lake need a fair amount of bait initially to encourage them to come to the swim. After that, use frequent very small offerings, often after every cast. Even when playing a fish a handful of groundbait keeps the swim interesting to the next fish to come to your net.

A swim which is heavily fished can be completely fouled-up by over-baiting. One must study all the conditions and decide on the best policy. Often, in a heavily fished swim, this means using little or no groundbait if the fish are present and showing interest in the hook bait.

Placing the groundbait
The devoted and thinking angler always considers the current and eddy before casting out handfuls of groundbait, because no angler wishes to groundbait for a friend downstream or draw the fish away from his proposed swim.

In a lake there is no problem in placing groundbait, or following it exactly with a baited hook, but where a fast-flowing river is being fished the groundbait must be a stiff mix. Such a mix might even be wrapped around a large stone to take it to the bottom before it breaks up.

One has to consider the area over which it is wise to spread the bait. In still-water a yard or two may be sufficient. If trotting the stream, several yards may be the most rewarding pattern. If a small area is to be covered, or it is favourable to keep the hook bait in amongst the groundbait, one of several types of swim feeders should be used.

SWIM FEEDERS
Some types of swim feeders are open at both ends and are usually filled with groundbait. Others are closed at both ends but have holes in the sides; these are filled with a mixture of maggots and bread, the maggots escaping through the holes. Another type is simply an open wire cage around which groundbait is moulded and which breaks up gradually in the water. There are a number of ways of distributing groundbait, but all should cause as little commotion as possible in the swim. Groundbait can also be squeezed around the shot on the line from which it will flake off as the bait is trotted down a swim.

Preparing groundbait
To make groundbait you need three main ingredients: bread, bran and wheat. To this mix can be added a portion of the hook bait you are using such as ground hemp, maggots and squatts.

One way of making groundbait is to mix the ingredients together in a dry state. Then, when you reach the river, dampen and work the mix until it holds together in a ball without being too wet. Then throw small balls in accurately to bait the area you wish to fish. The bread in this instance can be either bread crumbs, which I prefer, or a stale loaf of bread soaked the night before, then drained and squeezed into a lump-free pulp. Add to this any other ingredient you favour. If the crust is cut from the bread (I always use a white loaf), this can then be cut into tiny cubes for hook bait, a brilliant roach attractor.

Bread and bran are the most popular groundbaits. Boiled wheat can be used when also serving as a hook bait, and hemp likewise. There are other less common additions such as brewer's grains, boiled rice, oil cake, mashed potatoes and

An assortment of groundbait.

barley meal. Cheese is useful, mainly when fishing for chub with cheese as the hook bait.

When using wheat it should be soaked and then left for several hours in hot water, the grains being ready when they have burst to expose the white centre. To save time, wheat may be simmered. Brewer's grains should be soaked well until soft to the touch. Oil cake is not commonly used. It should be soaked, mashed and mixed with bran or bread. Barley should be stewed

until soft and used by itself. I have not tried the system, but the grains are said to be good when fishing for dace.

Cloud bait attracts inquisitive fish to the swim, but scarcely feeds them. When perch fishing, cloud bait is popular as it attracts small fry and minnows – a favourite snack of perch! Cloud bait is made by drying bread crumbs in the oven and then mashing them into a powder. This is dampened at the river bank and thrown out in small balls in a routine manner. To add a little more attraction to cloud bait, add portions of hook bait or any favoured ingredient.

All these baits can be made up in advance and kept in polythene boxes ready for finalising their composition at the water's edge.

Some time ago I used to fish for flounders with a baited hook tied a few inches from a spoon bait, in a shallow bay at the seaside. The way to catch fish was to move the spoon intermittently by reeling in, causing a cloud of sand to rise. The cloud attracted flounders to appear next morning on the breakfast table. I have read of this method of attraction being used on a river when conditions were not good. A shallow area is needed above the area to be fished. The shallow is then raked and scuffed-up, sending mud, silt and various goodies down to the swim to be fished. Repeated at intervals, this was found to be productive.

Table of groundbaits

Fish	Groundbait quantities	Type of groundbait
Carp	Medium to heavy	Bread and bran, bread and bran plus hookbaits, lobworms or maggots
Chub	Light	Bread and bran, bread and bran plus hook baits and worms, maggots, cheese mixes, sweetcorn
Dace	Light	Bread, bread and bran plus hook baits, hempseed, maggots, boiled wheat, worms, cloud bait
Roach	Light to medium	As for dace
Tench	Medium to heavy	Bread and bran, bread and bran plus hook baits, worms and maggots
Perch	Very light	Mainly cloud bait to attract minnows and fry, worms

Cloud bait is universally attractive as all fish are inquisitive. It should be considered on all visits to the river bank.

CHAPTER 4

FLOATS

When buying floats there are three important factors to consider, or you will end up with a box full of attractive floats you will never use.

- If the river you intend to fish is fast-flowing, your float must be able to take enough weight to sink your bait quickly to the level at which the fish are feeding.
- It should be buoyant enough and sufficiently long to combat the elements and eddies, yet not too long and thus scare fish.
- It must carry enough shot to enable you to cast the distance you require to cover the fish.

Having considered these factors, there are three important and basic designs: balsa floats, stick floats, and wagglers.

Assorted floats and plastic float attachments.

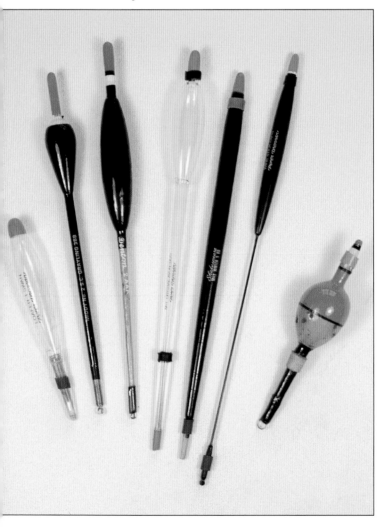

Balsa floats

The balsa float designs embrace the Avon and Chubber. These floats come into their own when the stick and waggler are defeated by heavy, turbulent water and do not carry enough weight to cast the distance you require.

The balsa float has two types of stem to stabilise it: cane and wire. The wire stem is less susceptible to influence by surface turbulence than the cane design. Some of the balsa floats are large and bulbous in order to carry heavy bread baits or large lobworms, and combat strong conditions of wind, weather and water.

Stick floats

The stick float in all its forms is a pleasure to use, and much favoured by all coarse anglers. They are made with wood, wire or plastic stems and, unlike the waggler type, are fixed to the line with two or three rubber bands, three usually being used on the wire stem type.

A wooden stem gives weight and stability to the float. This helps casting and makes trotting a bait more efficient as the float has less tendency to lift out of the water when it is held back or the line is mended. The float settles in the water right at the beginning of the cast and has a solid appearance trotting down the flow, whilst controlled to your liking. The wire stem is not so influenced by turbulence and gives more stability as it has weight without bulk. This has the beneficial action of cocking the float when it hits the water and before the shotting has effect. I recommend it for ease of use.

The shotting pattern of this versatile float is important. It can be varied and experimented with to fish the level at which your quarry is feeding. If weather conditions are mild and fish are feeding off the bottom, several small shot evenly spaced will enable the bait to sink down slowly, thus reaching every level until you determine where the fish are. You can then alter the shotting pattern.

On a cold day one would expect the fish to be feeding near the bottom, so a bunch of heavy shot near the bait with, say, a couple of small shot below the float will get the bait down quickly to the feeding level.

Waggler float

The delicate waggler has three forms: the straight waggler, the insert waggler, and the bodied waggler. The wagglers cover a multitude of conditions, although I feel they are more for the exacting expert than the beginner. They have one great asset – it is possible to change the type very quickly as they are attached at the base by a float adaptor, which is a small socket with a flattened end to take the line. Once you have threaded this on

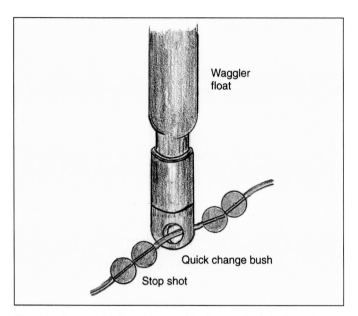

Shotting of a waggler float with a quick-change plastic bush on the stem. It is important to have some play between the bush and the shotting for the float to work efficiently.

and placed a stop shot, any float can be pushed quickly into the socket, and thus all three waggler types can be interchanged.

BODIED WAGGLER

The bodied waggler has a bulbous base and is ideal where currents are fast and turbulent. It can be loaded by varying the weight of the stop shot to make distance casting easier. It will also combat difficult wind and weather conditions better than its fellows.

STRAIGHT WAGGLER

This waggler will perform in conditions a little less difficult than those taken on by the bodied waggler. It has good buoyancy and is ideal for quieter waters where the flow is not vigorous or turbulent.

INSERT WAGGLER

This is the ultimate sensitive float to defeat those 'on the drop pirates' which madden the angler by snaffling the bait with little or no indication on the float. A delicate balance of shotting will make even the most surreptitious bites give a warning, enabling timid feeders to be brought to the net.

Slider float

This is a float which comes into its own when you are fishing a deep river, lake or reservoir where the distance from the surface to the bottom is more than the length of your rod. The depth is determined and a float stop fixed on the line in the form of a stop knot. The float is then placed on the line between the stop knot and the first shot which is, perhaps, 3ft from the hook. For fishing such depths it is usual to have three or four heavy shot below the float stop shot, and one light shot about 12in from the bait.

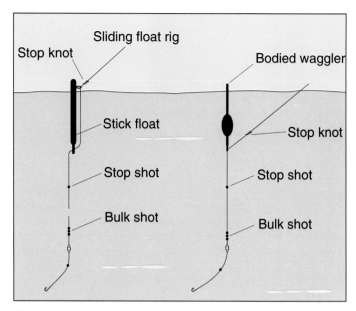

Tackle set up for a sliding float using a 'stick' float and a 'bodied waggler'. The left-hand sketch shows the 'stop knot' above the float with the first shot below the float being the 'stop shot'. Three further shots below are used for correct weighting. The right-hand tackle uses a 'bodied waggler', with the 'stop knot' and 'stop shot' being placed as shown along with further shotting. I always put a very small shot a few inches from the hook. A sliding float is used when fishing water deeper than the rod length. It is especially useful in overgrown waters where trees obstruct the angler from casting, so the float can be only a few feet or less from the rod top.

If you are fishing a river or lake which is deep and heavily overhung with trees which limit casting room, your float stop can be placed in a position near the top ring. This provides room to swing the rod far enough to get the distance required to cover the fish.

Bubble floats

These are bubble-shaped plastic floats. They are used for trotting a bait in very shallow water inhabited by dace and grayling.

A sliding float showing the small ring on the side to take nylon line.

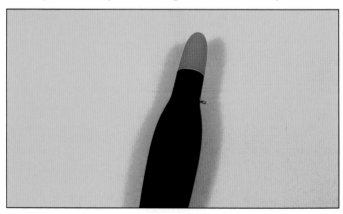

Fishing Gazette float

This is a large turnip-shaped float used when pursuing pike with a fish bait on a snap tackle, or a dead bait rig. It is usually made of cork with a slot in one side to open up the central hole through the float. A split hollow quill is inserted through the central hole and the line inserted through the split. The quill is then turned to close the slot. A tapered peg in the central hole sets the depth of the bait.

Avon float

I look upon this float as being one of the 'big boys' that fights its way around a turbulent weir pool with its head held high, defying anything to drown it other than a fish! This float was born on the Bristol Avon and lives up to its name equally on the Hampshire Avon where I fish. It is a versatile float for deep or shallow water and is rigged with the bulk of shotting just above the hook link. This leaves the link free except for a tiny shot near the bait which enables it to have the freedom to ride over minor obstacles and snags.

The quill protrudes at least $^1/_2$in or $^3/_4$in above the balsa or wood body which should be weighted so that all the quill and the top of the body are showing. Undulations at the bed of the river do not pull the float under as the bait trundles along.

Home-made floats

Search the countryside for materials to make your own floats. It is a simple and rewarding occupation similar to that of tying your own flies and catching fish on them. There are all sorts of bird feathers for the taking. Chief amongst these are the unfortunate swans that hit power cables. This bird supplies a great selection, the big wing feathers all being usable.

Consider also crow quills and those from a pheasant wing. Peacock quills are favoured and can often be begged from an aviary. Duck and goose wing feathers are also suitable. The construction is a simple operation: strip off the sides with a sharp razor blade, taking care not to cut the quill. Clean the stem with fine sandpaper until it is smooth, then cut to the required length by trimming the end of the feather.

If you want to make the Avon or bodied type, tackle shops sell balsa already trimmed to shape. Drill the central hole, insert your quill and fix with Araldite or instant glue. Paint on two or three coats of varnish to seal the quill, then paint a bright colour of your choice at the top.

Peacock quills make first-class wagglers, and you can make the insert waggler by using the fine part of a quill at one end. A porcupine quill is one of the very best as it only requires a coat of varnish and a coloured top.

For attachment, float adaptors can be bought to slip on the end to make a waggler, and all you need for the stick, Avon and others are two or three small elastic bands to slip over the float at the top and bottom. Sometimes a band in the middle will do no harm.

Float colour

All floats have a coloured tip. Whether to choose white, yellow or fluorescent orange depends upon the type of reflection you are going to get on your pond or river. To save eye strain if you are fishing with a white float in a bright reflection, carry felt-tipped pens in red and black to modify the tip.

CHAPTER 5

FLOAT FISHING

Bait and tackle

There is a thrill to watching a float lazily bobbing in the current, nodding or dipping when a fish investigates. You hand hovers over the rod whilst your nerves are on edge and your pulse races. The float then lifts, slides away and disappears, followed by thumps on the other end of the line. Anticipation follows – how big, what is it, and will it be landed? For me, the excitement has grown over the years.

As with many hobbies, success comes through reading books written by experts, watching fellow anglers and gleaning tips. Above all, keep notes on your observations (and especially details of your fishing trips) on weather, water, fish caught and how you succeeded, even to the hook size and the time of day. I read my fishing diaries at the beginning of every season to remind me of that special occasion when I succeeded in my efforts, whatever the fish.

Visit your local tackle dealer frequently and make friends with him. He has local knowledge, which bait is popular for which fish, and knows all about the new rigs or rods which have been dreamed-up by the experts. Also, if you are looking for tackle he will, no doubt, have some second-hand equipment as anglers are always changing tackle for something different or better than they already possess. The old saying 'the grass is greener on the other side of the fence' applies if you have a glass fibre rod, now almost a thing of the past. You will be desperate to acquire one like that used by a friend made of carbon fibre or boron, which is only a fraction of the weight of your present rod.

Tackle

RODS
There is a huge array of rods to choose from, varying in price from £20 to £180. For both the beginner and the expert, you get what you pay for. Club rods and match rods in carbon fibre and graphite vary in length from 10–14ft, usually in three sections. There are practical telescopic rods, one I have seen

advertised is in six sections and some of the telescopics are in five sections.

Shakespeare market two amazingly cheap rods for the beginner: a 10ft at about £20, and a 12ft at about £26, which are certainly worth considering. They also offer a general coarse fishing rod of 13ft with a stiffish action and flexible tip, a good choice for the beginner. In a better range they supply a Clubmaster match rod in the lengths 12ft, 13ft and 14ft, all are 3-piece and made of carbon fibre. They will cover any size of river or lake. Bear in mind when choosing the length to picture the sort of obstructions to be overcome when casting, and how far you will need to cast to cover the fish. Also remember, if trotting, the further out your float goes the more power you will need when striking to set the hook in the fish.

There is a range of super-sensitive match rods which are constructed to deal with fine lines. One such rod is the Beta Graphite Match by Shakespeare which can be purchased in 12ft, 13ft and 14ft models with a 24in butt for ease of handling. One of those rods will cover all float fishing needs.

Glass fibre rods are still on the market and are far cheaper than the latest materials. One good starter model is the Firebird coarse range which comes in three sections in 10ft, 11ft and 12ft lengths.

FIXED SPOOL REEL
I favour a Mitchell 300 fixed spool reel with spare spools to cover all my float fishing, ledgering and spinning for pike and game fish. I have had one for many decades and it has never let me down. The only part to fail through use is the bail arm spring. Consequently, I always carry a spare spring which only needs a small screwdriver and several minutes to replace. With fixed spool reels it is very important not to bend the bail arm. It is quite flimsy and if bent does not return freely when casting and retrieving.

The Mitchell AB Automatic is a finger dab reel, the bail arm opening automatically at the touch of a finger. The only point to watch is when your rod is in the rod rest and you pick it up suddenly to strike. Then, if you accidentally touch the bail arm it will fly open, you will have a free line and miss the fish. With practice this becomes an avoidable mistake. It is a top-price reel well worth buying.

The Mitchell 200 series is a beginner's reel. The bail arm is pulled back by a finger, there is an anti-reverse switch, you can buy spare spools, and it is easy to use. The Mitchell 240 reel comes in a comprehensive kit of a spare spool, reel bag and a spool of line, all in a carrying case. The reel will take 656ft (200m) of 8-lb line and operates in the same manner as the 200 series.

CENTRE PIN REEL

I have had a beautiful walnut centre pin reel with brass fittings for nearly sixty years. As mentioned in Chapter 7 'Ledgering', it works as well today as it did when it was given to me by a friend and even then it was not new.

A centre pin is a dream to use for trotting the stream as it runs very freely and can be controlled by light finger pressure on the rim. You are always in contact with the float, and on striking your finger pressure will hold the reel. Some are fitted with a check which is flipped on by a lever. Distance casting is difficult, needing lots of practice and heavy float rigs to provide weight.

A centre pin should eventually find a place in your tackle box with as many spare spools as you need. I find one for 3-lb line and one for 6-lb line is quite adequate for most uses, unless you fancy one to use with your carp rod when 12-lb nylon is required.

LINES OF NYLON

There is a large choice to be made from catalogues or by examining the selection in the tackle shop and asking the assistant, if he is an angler! I have found over the years that Maxima, which is a camouflaged nylon, and Platil are excellent and very reliable. I caught my heaviest roach of 2lb 7½oz on a 1-lb Maxima bottom to a size 14 gilt crystal hook, and that was in a fairly turbulent rising flood on bread flake.

Some nylons have a better wet strength than others, and some claim a finer diameter-to-breaking strain. You must beware the latter type which is pre-stretched, for I find that after playing a heavy fish, and taxing the line to its ultimate breaking strain, it does lose strength. Nylons are supplied in 100yd spools, usually joined together. Thus, if you want a continuous length of 200yd, buy two spools. I usually buy 25yd spools of nylon for hook links or bottoms, the length to which you attach a hook. They are available in 1-lb or more breaking strains. I can then tie a hook on to a 12-in looped length of fine nylon. By this arrangement, if you are snagged or broken on a fish, you only lose your hook and not the float.

WEIGHTS

The most useful and really the only weighting you use in float fishing is split shot. All the modern floats are marked with the recommended number of shot you need to cock the float, ensuring it just shows its head above water enabling you to see the tiniest bite.

You can buy a dispenser of shot. This is a small round plastic box with a rotating lid. The top of the lid has a single hole which may be positioned over the selected division containing the size of shot you require. The sizes are usually, going from heavy to light, SSG, AAA, BB, 1, 4, 6, and 8.

Shot today is made from non-toxic materials due to mortality in waterbirds. Birds grubbing on the river bank inadvertently ate lead shot left by anglers. Please respect nature and try not to clutter the bank with tackle and left-overs. No doubt robins and wrens appreciate spare maggots and bread crumbs, as will other birds. If you have a cast-off length of nylon wind it around your fingers, chop it into small lengths, take it home and put it in the dustbin. Nylon and nylon bottle tops can kill. I have found a dead mallard with its head trapped in the nylon ring from a bottle and other dead waterbirds entangled in nylon.

Carry lead substitute wire. It can be bought in fine, medium and heavy sizes and is always useful and easy to add to your rig if a little extra weight is needed.

BAITS

There is a comprehensive list of baits and how to prepare them in the Chapter 'Hook Baits'.

GROUNDBAIT

There is a Chapter on how to make and use groundbait, but here is some additional information. I emphasise that often and little is good practice. If you overfeed a swim your shoal will be too full to take interest in the hook bait.

The purpose of groundbaiting is to encourage fish to your swim. The perch is a predator which swims around looking for its main diet of small fry and minnows. To attract perch into the swim where it can find your worm or float-fished minnow, a dose of cloud bait will draw the minnows. Cooked bread crumbs ground to a dust, dampened at the river bank and rolled into a ball, provide an interesting cloud when cast out which any fish in the vicinity will investigate, especially small fry and minnows.

When fishing still-water locations the ball of groundbait you have thrown in will stay put, there being no current to take it away into the eddies. When fishing a river you need to throw a lot of groundbait upstream to wash down into the stretch where your bait is being trotted. When fishing maggots, a sprinkling of them thrown out at every other cast will suffice to bring the shoal to you.

FLOATS

These are fully described in the Chapter 'Floats'.

TACKLE RIGS

The positioning of shot on the different floats varies to cope with water depths and temperatures, and where fish are feeding

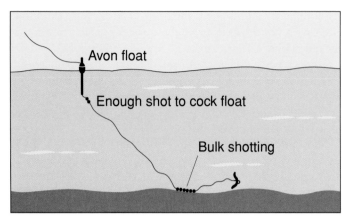

'Stret pegging' is a style of 'laying on' so the bait has free movement in the current. The depth of tackle should be greater than the water depth.

(mid-water, the bottom or at variable depths). Where fish may be taking on the drop, equal spacing of shot between float and hook will do the trick; where they are bottom-feeding and the water is fairly fast, bulk the shot above the hook line and place one small shot below the loop.

You must experiment, as this is very general advice. Make notes of what you do on the day, and the success achieved. Then have a look at the experts' ideas, and study videos and fishing programmes on television. We never cease to learn. I am still learning, looking and listening, even if unsolicited advice is basic.

SWIM FEEDERS

An open-ended feeder can be attached to your hook to dump groundbait, then retrieved and detached for the next load. There is another type of feeder with a plunger at the bottom which, when it touches the river-bed, retracts and dumps a load of groundbait. This is excellent in a fast-flowing stream where you may lose all your groundbait in the current.

Plumbing the correct depth by using a 'plumbob' which is in fact just a ledger weight with a cork insert in the bottom. Three stages are shown, 'too shallow', 'too deep' and 'correct'. It is important to have a minimal part of the float showing to detect the shyest bite, especially when fishing for dace.

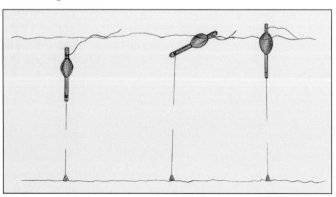

PLUMBOB

This is a conical-shaped weight with a brass loop at the point and a cork insert in the bottom. The hook is fed through the loop and fixed into the cork insert. You guess the depth and cast out your rig. If the float disappears it is set too shallow; if it lies flat it is set too deep. You then adjust the depth to your requirement, remove the plumbob and bait-up.

Techniques

MOUNTING THE BAIT

I have described in detail how to do this in the Chapter 'Hook Baits', but a summary in respect of float fishing is useful.

- Maggots – grip the pointed end between your finger and thumb and gently squeeze. The 'beard' at the blunt end will now be visible and your hook, which should be sharp, is then carefully pushed through the skin.
- Worms – hook by the head and middle.
- Flake bread – tear a small piece off the soft part of a new loaf, wrap around the hook and firmly squeeze the top.
- Bread crust – insert the hook in the soft side, through the crust, and back again.

My home-made tackle box is small and basic, holding all I need. It holds scissors, pliers, a large darning needle (useful for undoing knots), a scalpel blade, disgorger and a few eyed hooks. There is a long partition for floats and four small ones for holding float caps, swivels, split links and ledger weights. It also holds a selection of hooks connected to short lengths of nylon looped at one end and each size wound on a separate card for easy replacement if a hook is lost. One partition holds an assortment of lead substitute shot.

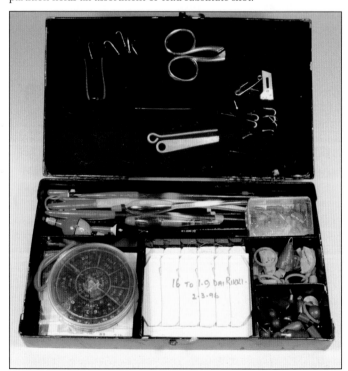

- Casters – insert the hook in the blunt end and push down into the caster until the hook is invisible except for the very end of the spade or loop.
- Hemp-seed – press the bend of the hook into the white part where the seed has split. The seed clips on to the bend of the hook.
- Paste mixtures – mould around the hook.
- Luncheon meat – the hook is pushed into the meat and turned.

There are other morsels of food you may try and the hooking process will be self evident, like sweetcorn – just hook it on!

PLAYING AND NETTING

The process of playing varies. Carp will give you a problem, as will pike. Keep the rod up in an effort to raise them to the surface. If they rush for weeds, turn the rod sharply in the opposite direction to the run and it will often put them off balance. The real danger moment is when they see you and the net. That last bid for freedom may leave you with an empty hook or a broken line. Chub, dace, roach and perch are not usually a problem, only the chub may beat you by weeding or snagging.

It is not recommended to lift fish out of the water unless they

The correct way to use a keepnet is to have it flowing downstream, preferably supported at both ends to allow fish to swim without being cramped which results in scale damage.

My personal opinion is that keep nets should only be used in competitions as misuse damages fish. Keep nets should be placed so that they flow downstream with the current, preferably supported by a net stick at each end, and not just thrown across the river giving the fish no room. In still-water it is important to support the net to prevent it collapsing.

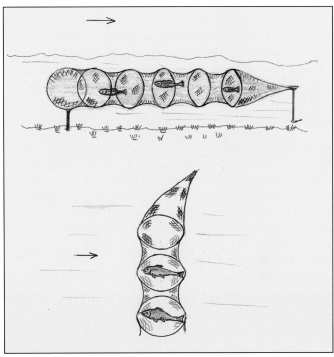

are very small. They also flap about on the ground and can easily come off the hook by tearing their mouths, which encourages disease and, no doubt, a great deal of discomfort to the fish. Always wet your hands before unhooking, and have artery forceps and a disgorger ready to cope with deep unhooking.

KEEP NETS

If you must use a keep net be sure it is large enough and placed in the swim so that it extends downstream to its full length. Fish can then swim without damaging their scales, for such damage causes disease. Do not put grayling in a keep net as they die very easily. They should be held in the water, head to the current, until they swim away, otherwise they will float away upside-down and drown. Care for your fish at all times.

WHERE TO FISH

This depends entirely on the type of fish you are expecting to catch, and weather and water conditions. It is no good going to a river in full flood, or to a summer river which is solid with weed. The only weed clearance which takes place is usually on trout streams, or clearance by the Water Authority in order to avoid flooding where a tree has fallen in and a build-up of flotsam halts the water flow.

If you are fishing a weedy stream with runs between the weeds, trotting a float will often bring excellent results. Fishing a gravelly shallow with a bubble float for grayling or dace can give excellent and exciting sport, and you may pull up a good chub. If using fine tackle, trust not to run into a barbel which you would have little chance of landing.

Pond fishing where there are lily beds, and the accompanying roots, demands fishing with a float as you can plumb the depth and keep away from the roots, although it is well known that float fishing, joyful as it is, lags behind ledgering for the number of fish caught.

When fishing a dead bait for pike you must seek quiet weedy spots, or places where lilies grow or fallen trees rot. These are favoured lairs for this lazy predator which lies in wait for food to drift by in both lake and river.

Roach can be found everywhere from lakes to mill-pools. Tench and carp are inhabitants of ponds and reservoirs. Both fish like swimming in the margins, amongst lily pads and reed-beds, and muddy areas where their favourite foods are found.

Perch live in shoals in ponds and rivers. Heavy specimens tend to be solitary and even feed on their small relatives. So, where small fry thrive in mill-ponds and still-waters you can expect to find perch.

A small bag of roach, dace and perch.

Chapter 6

Pole Fishing

The history of pole fishing

Fishing with a pole is not a new idea. Historically, fishing with an 'angle', the old name for a hook, was done with a wooden pole and a line of any material attached at the top. My 'pole' at the early age of 6 years was a piece of nut bush, a length of strong material and a hook. In summer, wearing shorts, I waded into a pond and caught minnows.

I have a copy of the book *The Compleat Angler*, a discourse on rivers, fish ponds, fish and fishing by Izaak Walton and Charles Cotton written in 1653, in which rod and line-making is described in detail. A passage reads, 'For fishing at the bottom, whether with a running line or float, the reed or cane rod is, on account of its lightness and elasticity, the best, especially if you angle for those fish which bite tenderly, such as roach and dace'. Perhaps Izaak also fished illicitly at times, 'And of these there are rods that put-up, and make a walking stick'. Rods were also made of lengths of hazel which were spliced and bound.

Lines were made of horse hair which was fixed to the tip to make an early model of the present-day pole. The passage describing lines reads, 'for a well chosen, even, clear, round hair, of a kind of glass colour . . . you seldom find a black hair but it is round, but many white are flat and uneven'. The twisting of the hair was a complicated matter, and for barbel 'it must be strong silk'.

Tackle

POLES

Today, poles made of space age materials can be purchased as long as $14^{1}/_{2}$ metres, although a practical and comfortable length is between 7–11 metres. Some poles are telescopic and some can be taken apart; some tie the line direct to the tip whilst others are bushed at the tip to accept high-stretch elastic; many variations are available. On the cheap side of the market there are hollow glass telescopic poles of 5–6 metres in length to which you attach a line at the tip, or cut the tip back carefully to accept a PTFE bush and elastic as explained overleaf. There are also lightweight whips of around 6 metres which are excellent for catching small fish, and these can be held comfortably without a great deal of fatigue. These are telescopic models, a

Pole fisherman on a Hampshire stream.

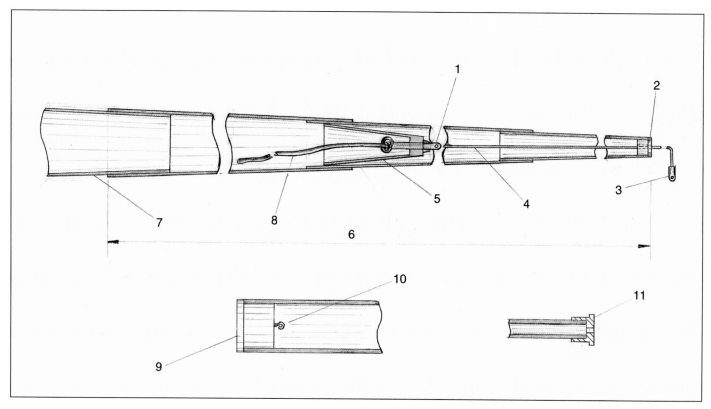

Above: The elastic is fitted to the top two sections of the pole. All three top sections are telescopic. Pole fishermen often carry spare sets with different strengths of elastic which can be substituted at the water's edge. The plastic insert (1) in the Unibung (5) has a tail (8) about 18in long attached to enable the Unibung to be removed. The elastic (4) is attached to the other end (1).

The elastic is threaded through the PTFE bush (2) also shown in detail (11) and is knotted to the connector (3) to which the fishing line is then knotted. The three telescopic sections are illustrated (6) and the rest of the pole lengths are inserted as required (7).
An alternative to the Unibung is shown (9) and the attachment point for the elastic (10).

loop of heavy nylon being whipped to the tip for attaching the nylon line. The line itself should be a little shorter than the rod to allow a fish to be brought easily to the net.

ELASTIC

No. 4 High Stretch is one type of elastic available, but there are more than half a dozen sizes. If you use fine elastic on a large fish there is no hope of landing it. The same principle applies to strong elastic which would tear the hook out of a small fish. A colour-coded table with the various sizes is available from the makers. A pole with a raw-cut top will fray and jam elastic, so PTFE bushes can be bought to fit and obviate this problem.

To assemble and anchor the elastic a tapered bung is placed inside the first or second joint, and a length of elastic is attached to it with an overhand knot. The elastic is threaded through the joints to the tip of the first section of the rod and joined to a plastic connector with an overhand knot. The nylon fishing line is then attached to the connector. The first two or three sections of most good poles are telescopic for easy transport.

Pole elastic on winders, colour-coded in breaking strains.

Now, you may wonder how can you change your elastic at the water's edge. The answer is 'with great difficulty'. So, if your pocket allows, you should have a set of telescopic top sections already made up with different strengths of elastic.

It must be made clear that only the top sections are telescopic and slide over each other, the rest of the pole sections insert into each other for the full length. Poles and accessories are usually accompanied by detailed instructions.

FLOATS

Pole floats are different from those used with rod and line, the latter provide weight for casting whilst the former do not need weight and as a consequence are very light and far more sensitive. Again, you face the float choice problem between those made to do the job efficiently, and those made to catch the angler's eye and fill his tackle box to no avail. Pole floats are small and bulbous with long thin stems and a 'bristle' in the top

made of nylon or wire, the latter being very popular. The long thin stem can be of cane or wire, the latter being favoured for making the float more stable if there is a wind and a chop on the water. When I generalise by calling the shape of a pole float 'bulbous', there is a little more to it than that: some are pear-shaped and all are of buoyant balsa or polystyrene. I find the upside-down pear shape is excellent in flowing water and a little turbulence; the right-way-up pear is better for still, or nearly still, water. There are many shapes for varied situations, but I find upside-down and right-way-up pears are best.

SHOTTING

Very complicated patterns can be read about in some books, but I feel the pattern need differ little from that for conventional float fishing. If the water is deep or heavy and the fish are deep, the bait needs to be sunk quickly so the shot bulk should be well down. If the fish are taking on the drop or off the bottom, whether in still or flowing water, I always spread the shot evenly between the bait and float. If trotting, hold back a little to let the bait precede the float. Bear in mind that your objective is to find your fish. If the water flow is strong and you are after fish in deep water, there is nothing against using a small Arlesley Bomb and a ledger set-up.

ROD RESTS

As a pole is tiring to handle, a pole rest has two supports: an inverted 'U'-shaped hook at the back, and an upright 'U' at the front. In addition, for long and short poles, a roller rest is needed behind the angler. As he draws the pole in the roller rest takes over and the angler merely detaches the number of top sections he requires.

Pole floats are very delicate and specially designed.

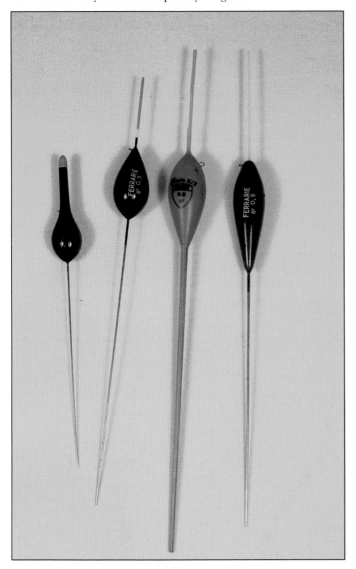

Pole on roller rest.

Pole fisherman demonstrating a pole groundbait dropper.

SWIM FEEDERS

A small cup full of groundbait is clipped on to the top of the pole. When the pole is slid out to the fishing position it is turned over to tip out the groundbait. The cup is easily detached.

Techniques

PLUMBING THE DEPTH

This is very important. When the pole rig is set up attach a plummet and have a guess at the depth. Lower it in the fishing place and adjust accordingly. It is a good idea to mark the pole with a dab of Tippex to record the depth of that swim, and also check that your float has not slipped.

BAIT

Baits and groundbait are conventional for the fish being pursued. Apply groundbait a little at a time and not more than half a dozen maggots.

STRIKING

This should be diagonal to avoid a miss sending your rig into space or the treetops.

PLAYING

If you encounter a large fish whilst fishing for smaller species have confidence in your elastic, which is very strong. As the fish runs away tension will increase and nine times out of ten you will win. If your fish is running to the right, try to overtake it with your rod tip. Slacken, and then reverse the pressure, pulling the fish – more often than not it will turn and run the other way.

When bringing in the fish, detach rod sections until you have the length you require, or run the pole back on the roller. **Remember, high tension electric cables are deadly – do not fish under them.**

Pole fishing is a specialised, delicate and efficient way of placing your bait in difficult places where casting a float would put tackle in the trees or the far bank. Once, I experienced a strong wind blowing against a high bank overhung by bushes. This caused a back eddy, sweeping food off the submerged bank to the delight of a shoal of roach. It was possible to poke the pole under the bushes to drop a bait on their heads, resulting in a bag of a dozen good roach and crucian carp. Those fish were being fed by a dozen or so maggots from a catapult.

I like to arrive at a swim ready to fish and so on a wet day or evening spend time making up a selection of pole rigs, shotting them with the help of a bucket of water, and putting them on winders ready for use. This saves much fishing time, especially if you have a break and need a complete rig.

Kingfisher sitting on a branch

CHAPTER 7

LEDGERING

Ledgering is a system of fishing, with or without a float, in which the bait rests on the bottom of the river or lake. It is kept there by one or more weights. It is an art in its own right and one of the most successful ways to catch fish. Famous anglers will verify this statement in admitting that most of their best fish have been caught on a ledger. At one time, not more than three decades ago, ledgering was thought of as a method of fishing only suited to the angler who took a deck chair to the water's edge, set up his ledger rod and watched a lump of dough suspended on the line above his reel. When the dough twitched or lifted, he had a bite. Today, it is an art, with the choice of many rods, baits, bite detectors to wake up a snoozing angler, and expensive accessories such as a bivouac tent or tilting umbrella to shelter him from the wind.

The excitement of watching a float has not been eclipsed. You can tell the sort of fish after the bait by the behaviour of your float. Equally, you can tell from the movement of the swing tip or quiver tip of your ledger rod what is happening in the depths and who is causing the excitement. You may have a good idea by putting all the signs together, but until you strike, or even draw your fish over the net, you will never know.

Timid bites on a swing or quiver tip can go on for ages as there is probably less resistance felt at the bait end on a ledger than the fish feels when it pulls down a float. This is especially so when the float lifts and drops over tiny waves caused by the wind, especially in a still-water situation.

Ledgering is better than float fishing when using a swim feeder because the hook is always not far away from the groundbait provided, whereas landing your bait where you have *thrown* your balls of groundbait is rather chuck it and chance it. This applies even more so in running water where the current, which is unpredictable on the river-bed, may take your groundbait to a completely different area. When fishing for pike, spinning may not be practical due to river conditions, and live baiting may be banned on many waters. In such cases ledgering a dead bait among the weeds, an area not fishable by any other method, can provide exciting and rewarding fishing. Very big pike are known to be lazy; they are not keen on using up much energy looking for food, especially after a period of flood conditions. One real and basic reason for using a ledger is on a windy day when a float is hopeless. Another reason is when you know the position of your shoal of fish is far out in a lake or river. Plenty of weight can then be used for casting, and the line submerged so that wind or rain cannot disguise or hide the bite of a fish.

The beneficial points of ledgering are:

- You do not have to plumb the depth.
- The bait stays in one place and can be located by a fish searching the river-bed for food.
- Any amount of weight can be used, the more the better as the weight will stay put when a fish tugs at the line, and it is easier to cast a bait long distances.
- It enables the angler to combat windy conditions when casting, and to sink the line below the waves.

These beneficial points outweigh the disadvantages:

- Trying to ledger among weeds is useless except for pike with a dead bait.
- If fish are feeding mid-water they will not find the bait.

Tackle

RODS

One rod will suffice to make a start. There are several basic designs at both cheap and expensive prices. Where I make

A ledger-rig with a Dexter weight and a plastic ledger stop.

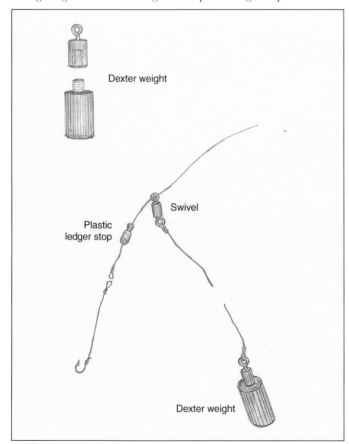

Dexter weight

Swivel

Plastic ledger stop

Dexter weight

suggestions on tackle, they are in the middle range. The basic rod is 9ft with a top ring which has a screwed socket to take quiver or swing tips. This is ideal as the rod can be used adequately for float fishing in a small river or a lake where over-hanging foliage makes casting difficult. Ledger rods can vary from 9–12ft and be of varying weights; most are made of carbon fibre or boron. I suggest a 12ft medium feeder rod with two spare tips, one medium and the other heavy. When fishing for carp, barbel, bream and chub this rod gives the power to cast long distances. A fine tip is for still and slow waters and the stiff tip where the water is fast or you are troubled by turbulent air conditions.

Other suggestions are:

- A 10ft rod with a screw-in top ring for attaching your swing and quiver tips. Short and stiff, this will cope with big fish.
- A 10ft light ledger rod which the makers supply with three tips of varying length and flexibility to make it of general use.
- A 9ft 6in ledger rod with two top sections, one with a detachable quiver tip, and the other a standard ledger top section with a threaded top ring to take various tips.
- A 9ft 6in ledger rod with a detachable tip to take medium weight swim feeders.

Also available are a 10ft feeder rod with a spliced-in quiver tip, and a 9ft ledger rod with a screwed top ring to take tips of your choice.

FIXED SPOOL REELS

My favourite reel for many decades has been the Mitchell 300 fixed spool with spare spools to accommodate lines from 2–20-lb breaking strain. Most fixed spool reels have a single handle on the left or right; some are changeable to right or left-hand wind. Most have a winding handle anti-reverse lever which compels the fish to run against the adjustable drag on the spool. It is important when playing a fish that you do not continue to wind the handle at the same time as the drag allows the spool to unwind, as this twists but does not recover line. If a fish has stopped whilst being played, lower the rod tip and wind in as you do so then, with a forefinger on the rim of the spool to prevent it unwinding. Raise the rod tip and pump the fish towards you. Repeat the pumping process, encouraging the fish towards the net, at the same time being alert to take your fore-finger off the spool rim to allow the spool to unwind if the fish makes a run.

Some fixed spool reels for big fish have a two-tension drag system which can be set to your requirement at the start of the day. If a large fish is hooked and you need more tension there is a separate lever with which the tension may be increased or decreased. Such reels are especially suitable for carp. Other reels have a fast wind facility and closed face to the line spool, and are suitable for match fishing. I recommend a simple model with two spare spools. At the base of the bail arm the line should pass over a roller to prevent wear.

Always carry a spare bail arm spring and a small screwdriver, or you may be stopped in the middle of a day's fishing when the spring breaks and the bail arm will not return to allow you to retrieve line. An important inclusion is a reel pouch with a zip. This keeps your reel clean in your tackle box or bag, and also prevents the bail arm becoming bent. The pouch also stops sun and light rotting your nylon line. A small can of 3-in-1 or similar fine oil should be carried to lubricate the moving parts at regular intervals.

THE CENTRE PIN REEL

The design has not varied much for many decades. I have had a wooden centre pin reel for nearly sixty years and it runs as sweetly today as when new. The spindle is finely ground and polished and the check still works perfectly. Centre pins are made today with or without a ratchet, sometimes having a drag system instead. Most have line guards and spare spools and are a joy to use when trotting a bait. Do not substitute them for a fixed spool, but take them as well when you are out for a day using a float and trotting the stream, or a ledger when distance casting is not required.

A good centre pin reel is expensive, perhaps £100 or more, but as they say about buying puppy dogs 'they are for life'. For all reels there is always a repairer and dealer who specialises in spare parts. Do not attempt to dismantle a fixed spool reel – you will be unable to put it back together! You cannot damage a centre pin as the spool comes off by actuating a lever and then you can go to work with the fine oil.

NYLON

Described in the Chapter 'Float Fishing'.

WEIGHTS

It is illegal to use lead weights between 0.06g and 28.35g to prevent wildfowl being poisoned. A variety of weights are avail-able:

Box of assorted shot, pliers, float adaptors, disgorger and ledger stops.

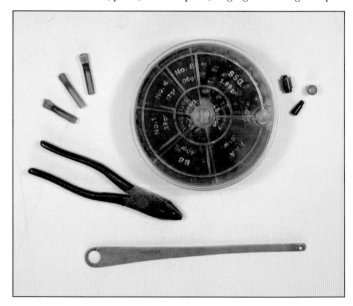

Split shot – sold in boxes and dispensers which have a labelled assortment. A full range is usually SSG, SG, AAA, BB, 1, 4, 6 and 8. (No. 8 being the smallest in this selection.) Smaller dispensers can be purchased as well as boxes of split shot in one size. These items are more widely used by float fisherman, but are also essential for those using a ledger.

Arlesley Bomb – a pear-shaped weight with a swivel attachment, available at weights of $1/8$–$1^1/2$oz.

Black Carp Bombs – similar to the Arlesley but slightly more pointed, also with a swivel. Weights $1^1/4$–3oz.

Dumpsy Pear Weight – has a small metal loop for attachment, weights from 2–5oz.

Korda Distance Casting Weight – long, slim and pear-shaped to defeat wind interference, it has a swivel attachment.

Coffin weight – shaped as the name suggests. It has a hole through the middle, and being flat does not roll along the river-bed with the current.

Drilled bullet – a round weight with a hole through the middle. Diameters $5/16$in to $5/8$in in $1/16$in increments. It is the original ledger weight and excellent for rolling a worm over the shallows for any fish present.

Barrel weight – in the shape of a slim barrel with a hole through the middle. Sold by length from 1–$1^1/2$in.

Wye weight – a shallow half-moon shaped weight with a loop of metal at one end for reel line attachment and a swivel at the other for trace or link attachment. It is mainly used for spinning, having an anti-kink effect, but can be used as a sliding ledger with the line through the swivel.

Lead substitute wire – supplied in fine, medium and heavy rolls on cardboard. Useful in ledgering to weigh down a swing tip in a strong wind.

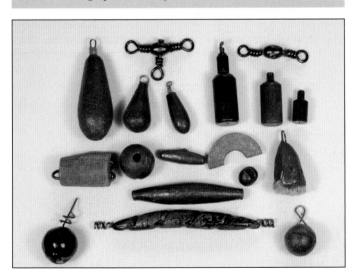

BAIT
Described in the Chapter 'Hook Baits'.

GROUNDBAIT
Described in the Chapter 'Groundbait'.

ROD RESTS
These are many and various, some taking multiples of rods. Rods are often supported by two rests, the front being a 'Y' shape and the rear an inverted 'U' hooked over the back end of the rod butt. An International Rod Lok is also available which is adjustable to take any rod handle and hold it rigid under the roughest of conditions. I use single rests for ease of carrying, and do not have two rods out at once unless carp fishing.

SWING TIPS
Loaded swing tips are either light ($9^1/2$in in length), medium ($10^1/2$in), or heavy ($11^1/2$in in length). Long swing tips are usually used in deep lakes. They are fine for detecting bites as the bait sinks 'on the drop' in deep water. Your bait may take many seconds to descend slowly to the bottom. With a short tip you have to keep tightening-up until the ledger weight reaches the bed of the swim. It is useful in turbulent conditions and streamy water.

There are several types of swing tips varying in length, weighting, and the material used between the tip and the fixing point into the rod top. The top ring of the tip should just touch the water with the line submerged when fishing. As the tip lifts when you get a bite (due to the ledger weight being lifted or moved), it is best for the rod to be positoned in two rests, one as near to the swing tip as possible. The swing tip is used mainly on lakes and still-waters and is an efficient visual bite detector.

The swing tip needs to be set up with care, rod position being important, and as near as possible parallel to the water. The angler should view the swing tip from the side, so that if it lifts the movement will be clearly visible. If the rod is at right angles to the bank (pointing directly away from the angler), a dip of the point will not be easily seen, whilst it will be clearly seen if parallel to the bank. If there is flotsam on the water it is beneficial to just submerge the tip, then the line will not be interfered with by flotsam, giving you a 'rubbish bite'.

There will be the usual line bites caused by fish brushing across the line. These have a certain pattern which may be recognised with practice. The good normal bite will allow your tip to rise almost parallel, and is almost certain to place a fish in the net. Bites have varying amounts of lift – you sometimes have to be 'quick on the draw'. Fish at times 'feel' a swing tip, especially if they are small and timid biters.

Left: Assorted weights for ledgering: two bombs, an Arlesley Bomb with swivel and three Dexter weights, one with a removeable screw cap to enable a variety of different size weights to be attached; a roll of sheet lead; a barrel lead and a plummet with a core insert in the bottom to take the hook when plumbing the depth; a spiral lead for use with a wire trace when float fishing for pike with a dead bait.

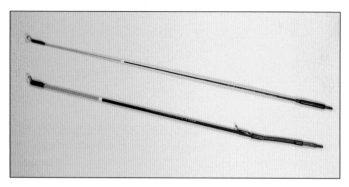

Swing tip (top), quiver tip (bottom), both with screwed ends to attach to a ledger rod.

There are advantages and disadvantages for both swing and quiver tips. If conditions allow I prefer the latter with a bright red fluorescent tip.

QUIVER TIPS

Quiver tips are purchased according to their test curve which can be from $1^1/2$–$3^1/2$oz, in $^1/2$oz increments. They have proved to be the most popular bite indicator and are the Rolls-Royce way of watching your rod tip dip when you have a bite. For many years I used my 12ft coarse fishing rod and just watched the tip, which produced good results but a lot of eye strain.

As previously described in my notes on ledger rods, more sensitive and stiffer tips may be screwed in to the top joint of the rod. The test curves of tips define sensitive and less sensitive tips. Weather and water are the influencing factors in making a choice. On a windy day you need a less sensitive tip. This is also the case if the water flow is turbulent. Still-water fishing, a quiet day and a more gentle water flow may benefit from a sensitive tip.

If you find your screw-in tips end up unaligned with the rod rings, you can put washers on the threaded end to align them. This is an operation you can do at home, fixing the washers in place with a drop of Loktite. Be careful not to get the Loktite on the thread or it may jam in the rod top.

With a quiver tip the rod sits nearly upright on the rod rest at right angles to the water, to which the line slants down. The line is then tightened until sufficient bend is in the tip, when it will be easy to see even the tiniest bite. A good bite will not necessarily be a sharp pull at the tip, often a slow draw is a good indication that you should strike.

When fishing a ledger, if things are slow, be sure to add a constant trickle of hook baits and wind in a few feet of line to stir up the bottom of the swim. This will often attract a fish which is starting to show interest in the bait.

BITE INDICATORS

Bite indicators are many and vary in price. The cheapest is a lump of dough moulded on to the line between the reel and the butt ring. Others work in the same position, the Monkey Hanger having an adjustable load. The Butt Hanger is a flexible arm that clips on the rod and hangs down with a hook over the line, the arm lifting to indicate a bite. It is one of the less sensitive indicators, being useful in rough conditions. To use the Butt Hanger, the rod tip is pushed under the water and the line submerged. This position ensures no interference from flotsam or wind waves. When in position the arm should hang at about 45°. As the rod is in a horizontal position striking upwards is the most efficient way of hooking a fish.

There are other drop arm indicators and a wide range of electronic types which give off a warning sound when a fish bites. They are favoured in particular by anglers who pursue carp at night.

TIGHT CORKING

Tight corking is ledgering with a conventional rig, but adding a float. To ledger in 10ft of water, set the float at 15ft and tighten until just the tip of the float shows. A bite is indicated in the same manner as float fishing.

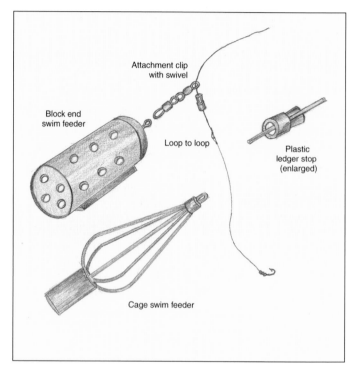

Block end and cage type swim feeders. The former is just filled with groundbait and hook bait, the latter has groundbait moulded round it.

SWIM FEEDERS

There are three types of swim feeders: open end for groundbait and casters (chrysalids), block end for hook baits mixed with groundbait, and wire cage feeders around which you mould a ball of groundbait which gradually disperses in the current. It pays to have more than one of each as you may be unfortunate enough to lose one in a snag.

ACCESSORIES

Accessories are the same as for float fishing: artery forceps, scissors, a needle for undoing knots, assorted swivels, landing net, keep net, a towel for your hands, bait boxes and ledger stops.

Filling an open-ended swim feeder with groundbait.

Techniques

WHETHER TO FISH QUIVER OR SWING TIP

If the weather is inclement and the water covered with floating weed, use a swing tip as the point may be poked into the water and the line sunk. It is also the answer in bad light conditions and when fish are taking on the drop.

A quiver tip is better for shy biting fish and for ledgering in good weather and water conditions.

There are three basic rigs:

- A round bullet sliding free on the line and stopped 18in from the hook with a ledger stop.
- An Arlesley Bomb in the same position as the bullet.
- A swim feeder on the line in place of the bullet or the Bomb.

In all my rigs I always tie a loop in the line and have a looped hook link, or bottom, of weaker breaking strain. This link can easily be replaced and, if snagged or broken, all you lose is the hook, and the fish does not go off attached to a long length of nylon. Remember, in all fishing, to treat fish with care and respect so that they live to fight another day.

ADVANTAGES AND DISADVANTAGES OF LEDGERING

Many anglers have to be weaned off the attraction of watching a float after commencing their fishing careers in that way, as was my case. The thrill is still there to see the quiver tip lift, then drop back at a light bite. Then down it goes and you are in business, the line tightening and cutting through the water.

Another advantage is when dusk turns to dark, with the consequent eye strain, a ledger will still give you fishing time with a luminous bite detector. Even a lump of dough shows up in the dimmest conditions and, if all else fails, a modern electronic bite detector will give you a buzz in more ways than one when a fish takes.

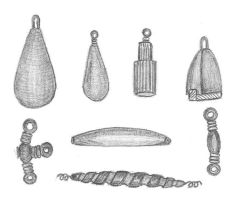
Assorted ledger weights and swivels. An Arlesley Bomb with swivel, a Dexter weight with detachable top, plumbob, a barrel lead, a spiral lead for use with a wire trace and barrel swivels.

CHAPTER 8

CARP

Carp swimming under lily pads

Description

The carp in its native state is the common carp. From this has evolved two varieties, the mirror carp and the leather carp, collectively named king carp and generally known as wild carp. The fish is king-like and sought after by a devoted band of fishermen.

It has a great bronze back with large golden scales, deep flanks and a wide, powerful tail which is responsible for those very determined and sometimes devastating rushes when hooked. The manner in which you handle this fish in the first few seconds determines the ultimate result.

Distribution

The carp is not indigenous to this country. It came from the European mainland as far back as 1496, where it was bred by monks for food. Today, carp species can be found in many streams and ponds throughout the British Isles and, believe it or not, you probably have one in your goldfish bowl.

Habitat

Some rivers sport the occasional carp but they are usually escapees from coarse fishing lakes where they are often bred to provide sport among all the other species. Wherever gravel has been dug, the old pits are almost always converted into profitable coarse or trout fisheries, some holding carp.

Carp thrive where there is nourishing food in muddy lakes or reservoirs. They love snaggy locations where lily pads, reed-beds and rotting lilies abound, in fact any corner into which they can dive in an effort to gain freedom from the angler's hook. It is unwise and unsporting to use finer tackle than you need as a 30-lb fish may one day fall for your baited hook, break free and go off with hook and nylon trailing. This must be painful and may even prove fatal.

Spawning

Carp spawn between the months of May and June depending on the weather conditions. If it is cold, spawning may drag on into the next month. Water temperature is of the utmost importance, for if it drops after the carp has spawned, eggs or carp fry suffer heavy mortality. Today, carp are bred in many areas in fish farms to ensure a stock is available for coarse fisheries.

The courting habits are different from other coarse fish in that carp gather over their spawning beds and a hen fish is served by several cocks. During the rest of the season carp tend to keep to themselves. Eggs are deposited in small numbers or even singly and adhere to weeds, water plants and other material on the river-bed. Hatching time of the several thousand eggs is about ten days. This large number is necessary to offset a heavy mortality rate in both eggs and fry.

Feeding habits

Carp are said to be more intelligent than any other fish, and this is probably the reason why they are so difficult to catch. Their vulnerability to a lack of oxygen and their concentration on spawning also affect their interest in feeding.

When feeding and seeking food they are at their most aggressive and will drive other bottom-feeders, including the tench, away from the feeding ground. This action justifies their reputation of being one of the greediest fish. Their diet consists of vegetable matter, larvae, daphnia, shrimps, snails and other small organisms. They have four super-sensitive barbules which resemble whiskers, a short pair on the upper lip and longer ones on the lower lip.

A carp will plunge its head into the muddy bottom of the lake to seek its favourite foods, thus silty lakes with an abundance of this food are haunts where you are most likely to find them. If the lake has shallows you should visit it first thing in the morning or at dusk, at which times you may see carp working in the shallows, stirring up the silt whilst looking for food. Sometimes lilies and rushes move as they are knocked by a foraging carp. In this mode a carp often cannot be tempted to show interest in a bait, being intent on finding small morsels. The location of carp is often given away by trails of bubbles, some caused by gases released from the disturbed silt or rotting vegetation, and some by the carp as it grinds up food, ejecting the unwanted particles. They have keen eyesight for close objects, able to observe distant movements and silhouettes well enough to be warned when something alien is present.

Carp are very difficult to catch especially if they have been caught before, when they will become suspicious of the same bait. They are sensitive to vibrations and shadows cast over the water, so your approach to the lake edge must be very stealthy. Do not walk up in full view and peer into the water.

Tackle

RODS
Carp are very powerful fish needing a rod with a $2^1/_2$-lb test curve to combat the first powerful rush and put the fish under control. Shakespeare have a good range of rods 11–12ft in length. The two-piece Zenith 11ft rod with a $2^1/_2$-lb test curve is

A carp angler setting up his rods in the early morning sun.

excellent for mid-range fishing and working the margins. It has a butt action, giving the angler good control, and locking reel fittings. The 12ft model makes for easy and precise casting, providing control to strike a fish at long range.

LINES
Again, my preference is for Platil or Maxima, the latter is a camouflaged line of good wet strength. I never use less than 12-lb breaking strain and in weedy lily ponds think it wise to go even stronger. Remember that carp have very good eyesight and can be frightened by too heavy nylon if they have been caught before – many have, probably several times.

WEIGHTS
Most carp fishing is by ledgering and using the hook bait as the sole source of weight. If an angler likes to use a float, a small Arlesley Bomb can be stopped about 4–5ft from the bait, and a waggler-type float attached to the line by the bottom attachment point which is thus free to slide on the line. On casting, the line should be tightened until the float starts to cock and then lift. A bite will be registered by the float and the strike can then be made.

REELS

For carp I have always used a Mitchell 300 fixed spool reel with spare spools. There is also the Mitchell 200 series which is cheap at under £30. If you prefer a centre pin reel, it will be more difficult to cast a long distance but fine for fishing the margins. You should always purchase a reel bag to keep grit, dust, and nylon-rotting light away from your reel. Before putting it away also give it a careful wipe with a soft rag.

BAIT

Bread is a major bait for most fish and the carp is no exception. Bread mixes with various flavours are popular, and bread crust is a must for margin and surface fishing. There is a detailed account of hook baits in the Chapter of the same name, but I must mention boilies as a new favourite.

GROUNDBAIT

Groundbait is essential for carp and should be provided in medium to heavy quantities, providing a carpet of food to attract fish and get them nosing around your hook bait. The groundbait should be similar to the hook bait. If the groundbait is cooked potato, bait with chopped up cooked potato; if it's bread, bait with bread.

You also have to consider the fish other than carp that are in the lake. If your groundbait attracts shoals of the opposition, carp may go away having become tired of competing. In this case, try to locate your carp and groundbait in balls to attract it. Then offer the hook bait. If you are throwing out crust and it starts to take an interest, out goes your baited crust among the other floaters. Then, you sit and wait in hope.

HOOKS

I prefer an eyed hook tied directly to the reel line. The hook size I use depends on the size of the bait, but is generally between No. 4 and No. 8 and I always recommend a reverse bend or sneck bend point.

Techniques

Ledgering is the most popular way of fishing for carp. The hook line is tied directly to the hook, and sometimes no additional weight is used other than the hook bait. When the bait is one of the bread mixtures, or a parboiled potato, the weight is sufficient to cast the required distance. Remember, it is a good idea to cast out as far as possible because the carp is sensitive to

Fisherman holding a fine common carp.

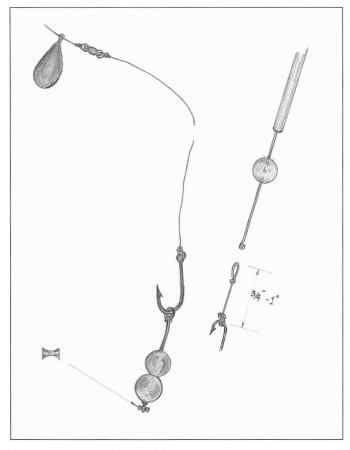

A running rig for boilies is made by sliding an Arlesley Bomb up the reel line, attaching a barrel swivel to the line and then a short length of nylon to an eyed carp hook. The boilies are threaded to a hair which is tied to the bend of the hook. A small 'dumb bell' stop is attached to keep the boilie on the hair.

moving objects and vibrations. A lob worm is a good bait and may be heavy enough to cast without additional weight, as are boilies which today catch more carp than any other hook bait. For light hook baits use an Arlesley Bomb located about 3–4ft from the hook bait in the conventional ledgering manner.

Fishing with floating crust is a successful method, especially in summer when carp swim tantalisingly on the surface with their backs out of the water. A few samples should first be thrown out to give the fish a taste of the bait and allow them to gain confidence. Then your crust should be cast as gently and close to the fish as possible.

In the warm months, and in the evenings, carp patrol the margins of lakes and this is the time and place to try your crust. If there is enough cover and carp are moving very close in, a good method is to position the rod right on the water's edge on two rod rests high off the bank. The crust may then hang down straight from the top ring until it floats on the water. The line should be placed on the ground, or preferably a sheet of some material, and trapped by laying a light object upon it such as a small stick. This does not give any resistance if the bait is taken and gives you time to take up the rod and strike.

One of the important factors to consider when fishing for carp is the water temperature. Due to their requirement for plenty of oxygen, if the sun raises the water temperature above 70°F (21°C) they will lose interest in feeding, being too busy taking in a meagre supply of oxygen. The best water temperatures are between 61–64°F (16–18°C), a level when the inclination to feed is high and plenty of oxygen is available.

It is important to find where your fish are likely to be to save wasting time on unpopulated places. The location of carp is influenced by conditions existing at the time of visiting the water, although individual fish may have different movement patterns.

In the early morning, carp like sunshine, heading for the shallows to the west of a fishery where they will first enjoy a glimpse of the sun. As evening closes they tend to migrate to the opposite bank and deep water. Plants give out oxygen in daylight and cease to do so at night, when carbon dioxide is produced. (This is why when an invalid has flowers in the room they are removed at night as they give no aid to respiration.) Your observations based on the above facts will give you more hours of rewarding fishing than you will experience if you settle down at the first likely spot. Go for weedy places by day where plants are giving out oxygen.

There is much controversy as to which is the best fishing time, day or night. Some prefer the night, but it has been proved by a number of anglers that they have more sport by day. I suspect that if more people fish at night, and this may fit in for those working by day, more fish will be caught at night. The converse also applies and so we shall never really be able to form a concrete judgement. Make your own trial by fishing five days and five nights and then add up the results, even then conditions are likely to alter during your trial.

Should you prefer night fishing, the realm of electronic bite detectors, shaded lamps, bivouac tents and thermal underwear is entered. Even in mid-summer, nights can be cold especially when dawn breaks and fatigue has taken hold.

There is little I can advise on striking and hooking fish.

Carp fishermen enjoying the sunshine after a night in a bivouac tent.

Above: A 16-lb mirror carp on an unhooking mat to prevent damage.

Strike too hard and you may have a break; too soft and the fish is gone. Only experience brings the right touch. You will know all about it when you hook the fish, especially if it is heavy, so keep your fingers away from the reel and line until the fish is under control. I know of a friend fishing for salmon who hooked a very large fish which hightailed off at speed. His line looped, trapping his little finger and off came the tip!

When your fish is under control keep the rod well up in an endeavour to keep it off the bottom. If the fish runs for lilies or weeds tip the rod in the opposite direction, as this may throw the carp off balance. Above all do not rush things, play the fish carefully and gently. Too much strain tends to panic them, leading to a harder fight. They turn on one side when beaten, so draw them over the submerged net and gently drag the fish up the bank to be placed carefully on the carp or unhooking mat (an accessory laid on the bank to avoid damage to the fish). Then, take out the barbless hook. I slide them back gently into the water with wet hands, allowing the fish to recover before it swims away. It is a triumph to catch and safely release a carp to provide another angler with an exciting catch.

Below: A proud angler with a 16-pounder.

CHAPTER 9

ROACH

Roach

Description

The roach is one of the most common and sought after fresh-water fish. This member of the carp family is a fish whose colouring varies tremendously through the seasons, from a bright silver in the winter to an orange bronze in the summer.

This illustration shows the noticeable difference between roach and rudd. The dorsal fin on the rudd is further back than the roach and the lower lip of the rudd is undershot while that of the roach is slightly overshot.

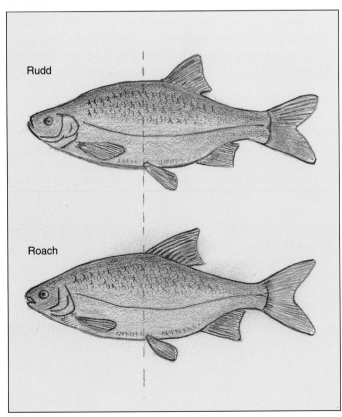

The shape of the roach also varies from one water to another.

The pectoral, ventral and anal fins are orangey-red, and the dorsal and caudal fins are a rich reddish-brown. The fish has a small neat head and small mouth. The top lip overhanging the bottom lip is one of the distinguishing features between roach and rudd, the rudd having an undershot lower lip. The dorsal fin in relation to the ventral is also different from the rudd: in the roach the ventral is only slightly behind the dorsal, whilst the rudd ventral is considerably further behind. Both dorsal and anal fins have a concave trailing edge, the tail being well forked and the same colour as the dorsal. This fish is a jewel of nature.

Distribution

In England the roach is the most common fish in our rivers and lakes. They are difficult to catch and, as I have already mentioned, much sought after, especially the magic two-pounder. They are not found in great numbers in Wales, Devon and Cornwall, but are fairly prolific in parts of Ireland, notably the rivers Shannon and Blackwater. Generally, the roach is to be found throughout Europe.

Habitat

Roach are gregarious fish and seem to swim about in shoals of the same-sized specimens. My personal opinion is that this suggests that when a batch of spawn hatches the fish stay in a group. Roach thrive in rivers, ponds, lakes, gravel pits and canals. They prefer slower water in rivers, and lies where currents meet and provide them with a constant supply of food. They like shade and can be seen in shoals under bridges, in slow eddies and in weir pools. They are a hardy fish that respond to being in water which has suitable characteristics; it is likely that they do not prosper in the streams of Devon and Cornwall because of the acidity and peaty character of some of the rivers.

Roach fishing on the Dorset Stour below White Mill Bridge, Sturminster Marshall, Dorset.

Spawning

Roach spawn from April to May, sometimes as late as June, depending on the water temperature. They gather together in large shoals and are prolific breeders. The pale yellowy eggs are shed on water weeds, submerged roots and gravelly river-beds, hatching in ten to twelve days, water temperature permitting.

Feeding habits

For its size the roach has large pharyngeal teeth capable of crushing shrimps and water snails, and responsible for a

squashed-up bunch of maggots on your hook. Early in the season roach show a preference to feeding in weir pools and similar places where their favourite silkweed grows on the walls. They eat the weed itself or the small snails, worms and other water creatures that live in those places. At dusk roach tend to retire under banks and into deeper water.

I have found that one or two hours before dusk is the prime feeding time to catch roach. In floods, the roach will follow the spreading water into fields to gather worms and other grubs in water a few inches deep, making sure to return with the 'tide' to the river.

Tackle

For float fishing use your Shakespeare 13ft match rod, Mitchell 240 fixed spool reel and a 4-lb line. The hook should be a size 12–14 connected to a $1\frac{1}{2}$-lb hook link for bread mixes and worms, or a size 16–20 hook for maggots and other small baits. Groundbait the swim with bread and bran, adding a little of the hook bait; throw in a little and often (e.g. half a dozen maggots every few casts).

One of the waggler floats should be used to sink the line if the weather is windy, or a stick float if you have heavier water and need more shot to cast a longer distance or get down quickly to the fish. If your fish are shy biters, use an insert waggler which is a super-sensitive indicator. Don't forget to take a plummet to check the depth.

Left: The pharyngeal teeth in the back of the roach's throat.

42

Techniques

LOCATING THE FISH

As you have gathered roach do not like fast water, so your swim will be in long quiet runs under shade, in slow eddies and the quiet parts of weir pools. Roach tend to lie near the bottom, so plumb the depth in several places. An underwater indentation in the bottom may be a place where food gathers, and that is where your fish will be. In cold weather all fish hug the bottom.

CHOOSING THE METHOD

If your fish are far off (be it in pond or river), and the swim is fairly free of weed and snags, ledgering is the answer. If the bottom of a pond is cluttered, you may fish a float whilst groundbaiting between the weeds. When river fishing in reasonable weed, in pools, eddies and weir pools, go for a float to trot a bait down the stream to explore eddies and cover a lot of water. Do not forget to check the depth.

LEDGERING

Using a Shakespeare Cosmos ledger rod, you will be able to cast the outfit a long distance accurately into your chosen spot. As bite indicators use a simple bobbin of dough on the line between the first ring and the reel, a butt indicator or, (if it is windy) a swing tip which will not be much affected by the wind. If it is calm, a quiver tip should be tried as described in the Chapter 'Ledgering'.

I favour a fairly heavy weight, as the fish or the current will not move it. Swim feeders can replace the weight and are an excellent method of depositing groundbait beside the hook bait, especially in a river where there is a strong current. There are three types of swim feeders (see page 34), all do a good job. The frame feeder needs care, as if the groundbait is not of the right consistency it will be lost when the feeder hits the water. Remember, the hook bait should be 12–18in from the weight.

FLOAT FISHING

The recommended tackle has already been described. The main difficulty is shotting the rig according to the swim you are fishing, whether in a lake or a river. For either water the straight waggler float is good, especially if you are fishing a lake and there is some wind, as you can then sink the line.

For a turbulent river you need a stick float, or even an Avon if the water is very heavy, or in a mill race where heavy shotting is needed to sink the bait quickly. In deep or heavy water the bulk of the shot should be positioned a few inches above the hook link and the rest equally spaced between the float and bait.

When trotting a stream I favour placing the bulk of the shot just below the float and the rest equally spaced down the line to the hook bait, ending above the hook link. I sometimes pinch on one small shot several inches from the hook. When fish are taking on the drop, space all the shot equally between the loop on the hook link and one small shot just above the hook.

Roach are very quick biters. It is best to hold back a little when trotting the stream so that the bait waves out attractively in front of the float, of which only the tip should be above the water. This practice enables a firm, quick strike.

Playing and netting a small fish is not a problem. Handle your roach carefully with wet hands and, preferably, put it straight back into the water. Remember, you should look after the Jewel in the Crown.

A fine roach on the bank.

Chapter 10

Tench

Tench swimming amongst reeds

Description

The common tench, known deceptively as 'the green tench', is an attractive fish. Like the chameleon, its colour varies with its environment and also to an extent with age, altering from a deep olive green to a golden bronze with tinges of brown and shimmering gold. It has a light belly and very small mucous-covered scales. The dorsal and anal fins are short and rounded, the tail fin being rounded and powerful. The tench has two barbules, one at each corner of the mouth, and its eyes have a distinguishing red iris.

Nature has given the tench colouring to match its life-style. A lethargic fish, it spends much time on the bottom of its haunts or among weed-beds, where its camouflage hides it from the main cause of worry – the pike! The stocky, powerful build of the tench enables it to forage among the weed-beds and muddy areas, seeking food with the help of its barbules. Such is its build, the tench is able to bury itself in the mud as a method of escape if hooked.

A fine tench.

The fact that tench have very small eyes suggests poor eyesight. This may be true as a tench may swim around a floating piece of bread, only eventually sucking it down, possibly due to poor vision or plain suspicion. As with carp its sense of vibration is acute; your approach to the water's edge must be stealthy to ensure success. The tench's sense of smell and taste are excellent. It has been written that the body also has taste buds, which has also been suspected of other species and is an interesting theory.

Distribution

Tench are to be found throughout England, Wales, Ireland and Scotland. East Anglia and the Fens have good numbers, and it is a native of the European mainland. The stocking of tench has proved to be successful, and areas where they were previously not present or were thin in the water now have good numbers of fish.

The eastern part of Britain holds the best head of fish, while Devon and Cornwall also have excellent fisheries. Tench are present in areas of France but are not as popular amongst anglers as elsewhere. The Netherlands are well populated with tench, as ideal conditions exist in the lakes, ponds and miles of drains and canals that criss-cross the country. Poland and Hungary are well stocked and in these two countries they are bred in farms and eaten, as also in former Czechoslovakia and Yugoslavia where they are also a favourite fish of anglers.

Habitat

Tench are lazy fish which prefer quiet waters like canals, slow-moving rivers, lakes and ponds. They ideally need a water shallow, which produces substantial crops of weed, plankton and nourishing invertebrates, some of the water supply coming from rich agricultural land. In addition to shallows it is important to have some areas where the tench can migrate in cold weather. Weeds are particularly popular with tench which spend a great deal of time in these watery retreats. Starwort and crowfoot (*Ranunculus*) are particular favourites and also water lilies. I dislike lily roots as I have lost too many fish in them. Tench have an appetite for snails, and the undersides of lilies are often places where snails lay their eggs which are vulnerable as food during certain periods.

A bag of tench, bream and roach.

Spawning

Females are usually courted by several males. Tench have been found fat with spawn as early as May and as late as August; the operation extending over quite a length of time. They mature at a very early age and are small in size, a 3-year-old may be only 8in or 9in in length. As with other freshwater fish, water temperatures are an important factor during spawning. When temperatures rise to around 66°F (19°C) tench have been observed swimming with their fins folded back, only propelling themselves with the actions of the tail; this is a typical warm water spawning show. When temperatures rise further, males and females become restless, chasing each other in a disturbed manner in warm reedy shallows, where there are usually two or three males in close attendance to each female.

A mature female will shed up to 400,000 small eggs, not all at once, whilst the males follow wherever the females choose to go. The eggs are shed in sticky batches on soft green weed, hatching in about six to seven days. The period depends on water temperature. After hatching, the very few which survive the numerous predators spend most of their time in the shelter of the weeds, and from about 1lb upwards venture out with the larger fish to feed.

Fish species which shed their spawn casually on weed suffer huge mortality from all spawn-consuming predators. They also suffer the destruction caused by river maintenance, cutting weed and raking the river-bed.

Feeding habits

Tench are primarily scavengers, sometimes feeding on dead and decaying matter in the mud and weed-beds. Their main diet consists of larvae, worms, snails, shrimps and caddis. They are timid and cautious feeders, tending to lie low until the shadows fall in the evening. They are not nocturnal feeders. This latter characteristic is strange as tench can be caught during the first hours of darkness but night brings a continuous blank to anglers.

When the water temperature drops below about 58°F (10°C) tench cease to take an interest in food; very hot weather above 70°F (21°C) also puts them off feeding. From October to early March they are in a state of hibernation. As most of their food is in the mud, they virtually stand on their heads when feeding and if in very shallow areas in warm weather, a tail can sometimes be seen waggling on the surface.

Tiny groups of bubbles coming to the surface give away their position as they feed. These bubbles are distinct from those of a feeding carp which are in greater numbers and larger in size. When tench share a water with carp they become a poor second in the quest for food; although avid feeders they are timid and easily bullied by the carp to the extent that when food is short they may be in danger of starvation. The only exception to this applies to tiny fish of a few ounces which have the ability to put on weight in a lake inhabited by carp, as their diet is different and made up of smaller particles of food.

In studying the locations of feeding fish, the tiny bubbles made by a tench must not be confused with frothy bubbles coming from rotting vegetation on the bed of the pool.

However, on those occasions when a tench is rooting for midge larvae rotting vegetation may be disturbed, releasing gases. Bubbles, on their own, are quite a study!

Daphnia reproduces in warm water in such numbers that when driven into the margins by weather conditions the population resembles a red dust. Tench feed on this water flea.

Tackle

There is such a tempting range of tackle that it is essential not to clutter yourself with too much and have to transport it all to the waterside. Travel light but do not leave any essential items behind.

RODS

Two methods of fishing for tench are float fishing and ledgering, described in Chapters 5 and 7. A carbon fibre float fishing rod is a sound investment, so a Shakespeare Zenith carbon match 13ft 3-piece at around £45 is a good choice. For ledgering an excellent arrangement is a rod with a threaded end ring to take a swing or quiver tip, such as the Shakespeare Cosmos ledger 9$\frac{1}{2}$ft 2-piece available at about £32.

REELS

A fixed spool is an ideal all-rounder, such as the Mitchell 240 which takes 656ft (200m) of 8-lb line and costs about £25. If you prefer to use a centre pin, they are excellent for trotting and casting short distances, but more expensive. The Shakespeare Eagle has a $\frac{9}{16}$in wide spool of 4$\frac{1}{2}$in diameter at £54. This model is delicate for trotting but difficult to cast any distance if there is little weight in the rig.

LINES

I have always used Maxima and Platil, a 6-lb line covering most situations.

FLOATS

For pond fishing a waggler suits most conditions, especially in a wind as the line can be sunk from the rod tip. If you prefer to have a floating line a stick float is the answer.

WEIGHTS

A box of assorted split shot and one or two Arlesley Bombs will be needed for float and ledger fishing.

BAIT

Baits for tench are both animal and vegetable. The worm is a favourite, as are bread and maggots. The detailed chapter on hook baits includes many forms of bread and flavours which can be purchased from the tackle dealer. Today, many tench are caught on boilies, probably because more anglers are devotees of carp fishing.

GROUNDBAIT

Some ponds are over-groundbaited thus tending to sour an area. This also fills fish with food to the extent that they are not interested in the hook bait. The maxim is always little and often. Long-term groundbaiting of a swim you intend to fish can give good results, that is, you pre-bait over a few days prior to fishing.

HOOKS

The size of hook to use varies with the size of bait. You need a No. 14 or No. 16 hook for a worm or sweetcorn; a small or very small No. 22 hook for maggots or a maggot on a $1\frac{1}{2}$-lb hook link. I always use barbless spade-end hooks with a wide gape (the gap between the hook point and the shank).

NYLON FOR HOOK LINKS

I make up a hook link of $1\frac{1}{2}$-lb or 2-lb nylon in 6–12in lengths.

ACCESSORIES

Disgorger and artery forceps, net, keepnet, a 3ft-square piece of polythene sheet is always useful, towel, scales and a weighing net.

Techniques

LOCATING THE FISH

We now know where tench feed, so we should spend some time walking stealthily around the water watching for those tell-tale

---

Lift method for tench
A stick float weighted with a pierced bullet stopped by a shot or a ledger weight and baited with a worm. The rig is set at the same depth as the water depth with the bait on the bottom, so that when the tench lifts the bait the float falls on its side. It then usually slides under when the fish swims off – that is the time to strike.

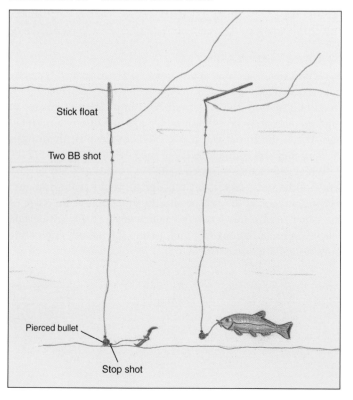

needle-size bubbles. If none can be located you have probably arrived at the water at the wrong time. To avoid disappointment seek out a typical area, put out groundbait and watch for the signs whilst assembling tackle. If it is a fine windless day and you enjoy float fishing put on one of the floats I have mentioned, plumb the depth (quietly) and you are ready to fish.

One of the favourite methods for tench is the lift system which entails having a heavy shot (perhaps a swan shot) 4in from the hook bait, with no other shotting, and a waggler float. If the tench takes and swims away your float goes under; if he lifts the bait and the shot, the float falls flat and then slides away as he runs. It is important that the depth of the 'float to bottom' is exact and the float fixed to the line by one end with an elastic band. Remember that the tench is a bottom-feeder therefore it is of little use suspending your bait above the bottom of the lake.

If bites are slow the method described is sometimes improved by gently moving the bait a few inches, as the movement may attract the attention of a fish sufficiently to encourage it to investigate. If the float tilts or wobbles it is worthwhile striking as almost certainly the tench has the bait in its mouth; if left, it will feel the hook with its delicate barbules and spit it out.

Ledgering is another successful method. I always slide a swivel on the rod line with an attachment clip and stop it about 12–18in from the hook. This can be utilised to clip on various weights such as the Arlesley Bomb or one of the swim feeders.

If you tire of ledgering there is the alternative of removing the weight or feeder, slipping two small elastic bands up the rig and attaching a stick float. Then tie a loop in the end of the rod line and attach the looped bottom or hook link. Check that the rig is such that your bait is about 12–18in from the source of weight. You now have the rod ready on the rod rests, but need a bite detector. The cheapest, and readily available, is a small ball

---

A tench coming to the net on a Hampshire lake.

A young angler patiently waiting for the float to slide away.

Will it come out of the lily pads?

At last a tench has taken the bait.

There are two further ledger rigs involving a swing tip or quiver tip which screw into the top joint of your rod. These are assembled at the time you put your rod together before the line is attached; both these methods are described in detail in Chapter 7, 'Ledgering'.

WEATHER CONDITIONS

The weather conditions are critical with tench, as previously stated. Water temperature is most important, the direction of the wind and position of the sun also affecting fishing. It is well documented that fishing for tench after October is not really worthwhile.

STRIKING AND PLAYING

Sometimes bites are very timid and a strike on chance may pay a dividend. Tench are not a walkover, they invariably head for a weed-bed or bore into the mud. You must keep them out of mud as there may be rubbish and snags to cause nylon breakage. When the initial run is over you should turn them from weed as they will continue to try to snag the line.

When your tench is landed handle it as little as possible. Use wet hands and place it on the net to avoid scale damage. Having unhooked the fish be sure to support it at the edge of the water until it has recovered sufficiently to swim away. The tench is a great fighting fish and, pound for pound, one of the most sought after quarries.

of dough made from your loaf. Others are a butt detector which clips on the rod between the bottom ring and the reel and hooks to the line. A Monkey Climber detector or one of the more expensive electronic types can also be used.

CHAPTER 11

BARBEL

Barbel

Description

The barbel has a shape which indicates power: narrow tapered head, long streamlined body and a powerful tail. The belly is flat and adapted to lie on the bottom of the river and stay there with ease in a steady current. Its name is probably derived from its four barbules, one pair at the end of its nose, and the other at the rear of the top lip. These are sensitive and used to find food on the river-bed and, no doubt, inspect your bait!

The tail is of a browny green shade and wide and strong. The pectoral and pelvic fins are coloured pinky-orange, the dorsal is a dark green, and the flanks and back a green-gold with a pale belly. When lying it is so well matched to the surrounding colours that it is difficult to locate other than by the waving tail or a glimpse of orange.

Barbel shoal, and it is said that, whatever the time of day, night or season they are there to be caught if you have the skill. Hard fighters, they are often called 'the poor man's salmon'.

Distribution

They are present almost throughout Europe, and are particularly prolific in Spain. Exceptions are Ireland and Iceland, and in mainland Britain they are not present north of Yorkshire. Barbel are a major quarry on the famous Royalty Fishery of the Hampshire Avon, and farther up that river they are taken from time to time on spinning baits when the angler is after salmon. The River Thames has a reputation for barbel as has the Wye in Wales.

Habitat

Barbel do not like turbulent water, preferring a steady flow without back eddies. In summer and autumn when rivers are low they are located in well oxygenated water but are difficult to find. During summer, avoid open water with little cover during the daytime. They prefer to lie on a hard bottom with adjacent undercut banks where they can take cover. They feed well at the start of a flood but do not appreciate coloured flood water until it has fined down; they are then likely to come again on the feed. Barbel, chub and carp all like the seclusion of cover, especially among roots, rushes and dense weed just out of the current where ample food is available.

Spawning

Barbel do not live where they spawn. They gather in large numbers in late spring in rippling weedy shallows for spawning, particularly shallow runs below sluices where there is plenty of oxygen. In April and May the female, attended by several males, sheds her eggs on stones and weeds where they are fertilised by the milt of the male fish. The ova hatch in about two weeks depending on water temperature, and the little fish are then subject to the usual predation by other fish, including the barbel.

The Parlour Pool, the Royalty Fishery, Hampshire Avon.

Feeding habits

Barbel have an overshot mouth which makes them well adapted for feeding off the river-bed. Their long, sensitive feelers explore sand and gravel for insect larvae, shrimp, crayfish and snails, and anything thrown in by the angler. Small fish dwelling on the bottom such as gudgeon, loach and bullheads form part of their diet.

The eyes of a barbel are not well situated; any food rooted up is hidden by the long pointed nose but is felt by the barbules and sucked in to the mouth. They gather small particles of food and snails by searching in weed, and can be heard making sucking noises like a carp.

Tackle

A 13ft coarse fishing rod will work admirably with either a fixed spool reel or centre pin, a 6-lb line being of sufficient strength. A short float such as a Chubber is ideal, or any similar float which you might use for grayling.

Bait may be bread (always available in the larder), worms from the garden, sweetcorn from a tin, or maggots and casters from the tackle shop. Groundbait should be frequent small doses of the hook bait, and although I have only specified four baits, barbel will take most of those used to attract roach and chub. The hook should be a No. 10–14 tied directly to your reel line.

Techniques

As much barbel fishing is done whilst wading, do not forget to carry a spare pair of socks in case you go over the top.

Ledgering is a good method for catching barbel. If a weir pool is studied, quiet lies close to the current can be covered, as can runs between flowing weed-beds, especially with a lump of luncheon meat. Few problems will be encountered if you cast upstream into the run and work the ledger back, thus causing fewer tangles with roots. I mention a rolling ledger in the 'Grayling' chapter, and this is an excellent system in open shallows or even deeper water if there is a good flow. The rolling system also keeps you on the move, casting then moving

A 10¹⁄₂lb barbel caught on the Royalty Fishery, Hampshire Avon.

one or two paces before casting again. A pierced bullet stopped about 12–18in from the bait can be cast across in the manner of wet-fly fishing to search the shallows in a semi-circle – takes are definite! A bait can also be freelined down a channel, a worm being excellent for both these methods as it stays on the hook which should be a No. 10 or No. 12 depending on the size of the worm.

Trotting with a short stubby float like the Chubber is a fascinating way of searching for barbel. The bulk of shot should be 12–18in from the bait, and the depth set to allow the bait to trip along 6in above the river-bed. If the water is very shallow the shot may need to be close to the bait, or it will be swept to the surface by the current.

The ideal angler's position for this method is in the water (in waders) directly above the area to be fished. The bait is then trotted directly downstream to the area you wish to fish. This system avoids the bellying of line experienced when casting down and across from the bank. The bait should be held back to allow the worm to flow out in front of the float, and then dropped again by a slight slackening. It is very important to place the shot the right distance from the bait according to depth and current; if placed incorrectly the bait will pass over the head of the barbel.

When fishing deeper runs where the flow is not so fast, your shot should still be in a bunch, with a few extra small shot pinched on between the main bulk and the hook bait, but not closer than 6in from the hook. The float should be large, perhaps a good swan's quill or an Avon type.

Barbel take a bait in various ways: the wrench of the rod out of your hand; the tap tap and pull away; the quick snatch and off; all need to be struck with care and regard to the strength of the line. They fight deep down in the water and not much is seen of them until they are ready for the net. If using a centre pin reel, keep your fingers away from the handles during the fight, or at least be ready to let the check run out, as the runs are quick and fierce, often resembling that of a salmon.

When the fish is ready submerge the net, draw the fish over, lift, then drag it up the bank with the net closed. Unhook with wet hands whilst holding the fish through the wet mesh and return the barbel carefully with the minimum of delay.

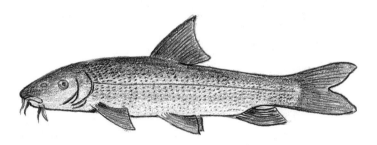

Barbel

CHAPTER 12

CHUB

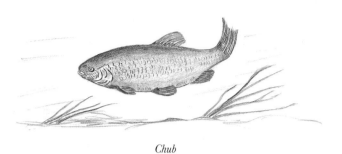

Chub

Description

The name chub means plump which is a good description of this thick-set, beautifully proportioned fish which has a cavernous mouth with thick white lips. Its dorsal and anal fins are convex, which marks small chub from dace which have concave fins.

The colouration of the large scales reflects the colour of the water the fish inhabits. The greyish black head and back merge into an off-white belly. The tail has a trace of black, whilst the pectoral, ventral and anal fins have an orange-red tinge. Like the carp family, chub have a pair of pharyngeal teeth in the throat for grinding up their food.

Distribution

Chub are well distributed in Europe and populate most of the English rivers with the exception of Devon and Cornwall. Some Scottish rivers have chub and there are a limited number in Wales, the Wye being well populated. One Wye chub of about 4lb took a salmon fly when my co-author, Charles, was after that fish. Some still-waters have recently been stocked with chub as a worthwhile sporting fish.

Habitat

Chub are primarily river fish. Their haunts differ with the seasons, for they can be found in shoals in both shallow and deep runs and in open places. They are a timid fish, preferring to lie where there is overhead cover of trees and bushes, which also provide them with a supply of food in the form of beetles and bugs falling from the branches. Favourite lies are near fallen trees, bridge buttresses, overhanging banks and weed-beds where they can seek cover if frightened or hooked by an angler.

After spawning chub can be seen in fast runs, probably for the purpose of freshening themselves, and also seeking food in an attempt to recover condition after their rigorous efforts to procreate. Summer and autumn are shoaling time, when they prefer slower currents and deep lies with cover. As you walk the river, sometimes carelessly, you may see a dark shadow dissolve into the deep, the chub having seen you first. They are very shy but do not dart off like other fish, preferring to fade away quietly.

Spawning

Coarse fish do not always spawn at the same time. Chub spawn at greatly varying times, usually after dace, pike and perch probably due to climatic conditions. The usual period is at the end of June just after the season opens, but fish have been noted to spawn in late spring and early summer.

Chub need clear, fast-running water to urge them to spawn, shoals appearing on weedy gravel shallows which provide their ideal site. The males are easily identified at this time by the fleshy rough growths on their heads which are used to nudge the females to encourage them to shed their spawn; this is fertilised as it falls by a cloud of milt released by the males.

The eggs adhere to weeds and stones and hatch in seven to ten days depending upon water temperature and flow. Should there be a flood or river work many eggs may perish by being swept away and damaged. The fry feed on minute organisms, turning to larger items as they grow. Their numbers are reduced at the egg stage and during growth by the usual predators.

Feeding habits

Chub, next to the carp, is commonly recognised as the greediest of fish with an endless list of food on the menu. In winter and summer it will accept most baits if the angler is well hidden and the baits appear to come from a natural source.

Chub will eat insect life in all its forms, and anything of acceptable size that swims and inhabits the river such as crayfish, frogs, all the shrimp family and small fish of all species including carp. Small fish are very popular, figuring largely in their diet from an early age when small chub feed on fry. I have caught them on occasions when fishing a wet fly or nymph for trout and grayling. Chub, to an extent, eat some types of weed.

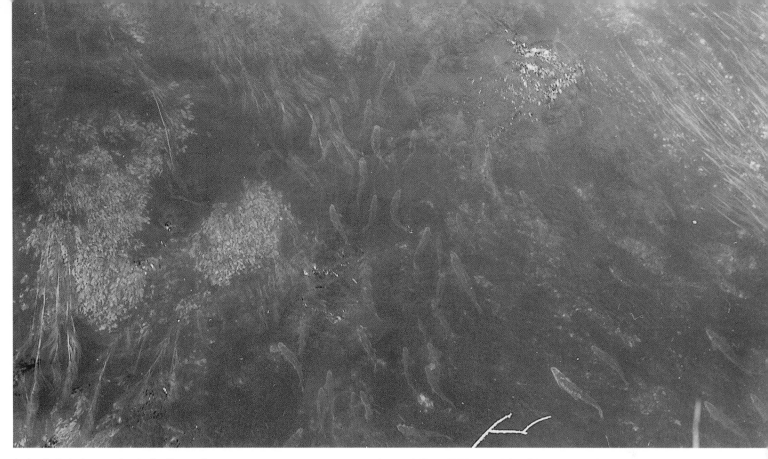

A shoal of chub spawning in the Dorset Stour.

Also, in the summer, when lying under overhanging elderberry bushes they eat not only the bugs which fall upon the water but also the fruit. The chub is not fussy about diet and can be caught on a multitude of baits.

Tackle

RODS

There are two methods of bait fishing for chub, float fishing and ledgering. There are two chapters on these methods, so I will only advise on my choice of rods and not how to use them.

A fine chub caught on bread flake when the river was rising.

A good float fishing rod by Shakespeare is the Zenith Match Cat. 1821/390 which is a 13ft 3-piece rod retailing at about £50. For ledgering choose a rod with a threaded end ring to take swing or quiver tips. I recommend the Shakespeare 1801/285 Cosmos, a $9^{1}/_{2}$ft 2-piece rod available at about £30.

REELS

A fixed spool reel is a good all-rounder and I recommend the Mitchell 240, which takes 656ft (200m) of 8-lb line, at a cost of around £30. A centre pin reel is excellent for trotting and casting short distances, but is more expensive. The Shakespeare 2900/400 Eagle centre pin has a $^{9}/_{16}$in wide $4^{1}/_{2}$in spool and costs about £54.

To play a fish on a centre pin is easier than on a fixed spool reel, but care must be taken when trotting as an overrun may tangle line. They are difficult to cast any considerable distance if there is little weight in the rig. I prefer Maxima and Platil lines at

about 4-lb breaking strain.

FLOATS

For slow currents the straight waggler is best. For trotting a bait searching the bottom, the rig should be overlong by several inches with most of the weighting by the float and a few equally spaced small shot between the float and the hook bait.

If you are fishing turbulent weir pools of fast water with a waggler, it should be a big float capable of carrying heavy shot. Try a size AA close to the base of the float with some smaller shot 18in from the hook bait, the float being attached with rubber bands. For faster water I like a stick float which is attached to the line with rubber bands at the top and bottom, making it easy to change to another float.

If the water is turbulent choose a wire-stemmed stick as suggested in the Chapter 'Float Fishing'. With a floating line the stick can be regulated for speed in the current by holding it back and allowing the bait to precede the float in an attractive manner.

WEIGHTS

All you need is the usual plastic container with a selection of split shot.

BAIT

The chub is greedy and not at all selective. The 'Hook Baits' Chapter gives a detailed choice. Easily accessible and needing no preparation are maggots, worms, bread, sweetcorn and luncheon meat, all avidly accepted by chub.

GROUNDBAIT

The best groundbait is a frequent small offering of the hook bait you are using. The placing of the groundbait must be such that the current does not carry it past the area in which you are fishing.

HOOKS

My choice is a spade-end hook tied to a looped hook link of 6–12in in length and of a lighter breaking strain than the rod line; if you break in a fish, or snag, all the fish goes away with is the hook. Hook size varies according to the bait, use a large hook for bread mixes, worms and sweetcorn, perhaps No. 12–16, and a small hook of No. 20 or No. 22 for a single maggot. I prefer wide gape hooks, the gape being the gap between the hook point and the shank. Spade-ends are a personal choice – they look neater. Nylon for hook links should be small spools of 1–4-lb breaking strain.

ACCESSORIES

Use a selection of floats, weights, a rod rest, net, keep net, artery forceps, hooks, disgorger, a needle for untying knots and a pair of scissors.

Techniques

Chub are very shy. A shadow on the water will send them to the bottom like a slowly descending lift, and then your chances of

catching them have been reduced.

In the section on habitat you will have noted places where chub lie at different periods of the year. In spring and summer search the likely lies for your fish which, if you have been stealthy, are not hard to find. You will either see chub alone or in a shoal. When winter comes it is almost certain chub will inhabit quiet eddies and deep pools when the river is high. The method used must suit the position of the fish, whether in shallow or deep water, slow or fast current. The weather must be considered in summer, autumn and winter.

Chub, as already mentioned, are exceptionally greedy and feed all the year round, albeit in winter they slow down somewhat. However, they can still be caught on a freezing day if you are able to locate their whereabouts. In winter, ledgering is an excellent way of finding fish if they are encouraged to look for your bait by the use of a swim feeder which takes the place of a ledger weight. This deposits groundbait, accompanied by some of the hook bait, in exactly the same spot as the hook bait, thus defying the action of eddies and currents.

When you can see a shoal in summer, freeline a worm. If necessary, to add distance, use a bullet as you would a ledger weight and allow it to roll freely over the shallow towards the shoal. Another summer freelining method to try when chub are basking on the surface is to throw in some pieces of crust to start them feeding. Then out goes your hook crust on a floating line with a little Mucilin on the nylon to assist floatation. Let the crust drift freely over the fish to provide a good chance of a take. This method may be tried with a freelined lob worm, a better bet than crust as a worm sinks slowly, but can then be twitched to the surface in an enticing manner. Chub can be caught by all the standard methods used for coarse fish and, in correct conditions, float fishing is exciting and efficient using a waggler or stick float.

Fly-fishing

Tackle

RODS

The 9ft Shakespeare 1640/270 Zenith 2-piece fly rod is competitive in price and has a good action with an AFTM No. 6 or No. 7 fly line. It is a good general purpose fly rod, well priced at about £30.

REEL

The 3½in diameter Shakespeare 2530 Zenith fly reel takes a double-tapered No. 6 or No. 7 floating fly line and backing at a cost of about £13. It has a quick-release lever for changing spools, with a spare spool supplied in the price. It is a good policy to have a sinking line on the spare spool in order to fish a sunk lure.

FLY LINE

I suggest a Shakespeare 3226 DTF (double-tapered floater) in green at AFTM No. 6 which is approximately £13. A double-tapered line may be taken off the reel and reversed annually to give it a longer life. The AFTM Scale of line weights is fully explained in the Game Fishing half of this book (page 80).

LEADER

This should be a 9ft 3X (5-lb) knotless taper of nylon to cater for large chub which always head for cover when hooked.

FLIES

A collection of flies and lures for chub need not be extensive. Chub have always been associated with huge bushy flies but these are not necessarily of the best size. I seldom fish a fly (dry, wet or nymph) on a hook larger than a No. 8, particularly for the buzzy patterns of Soldier Palmer, Red Tag and Zulu which are favourites of mine.

Floating patterns of grasshoppers, beetles and the like are killers under bushes on a hot day when chub are on the surface. When there is a natural hatch of flies, especially sedges, imitations are excellent in the dying light of evening.

Natural olive imitations in the spring are the Greenwell's Glory and Pheasant Tail on a size 16 hook. Later, the blue winged olive and sherry spinner naturals may be represented by a size 16 Pheasant Tail. The pale watery dun is covered by the Tupp's Indispensible size 16. A general year-round nymph is a size 14 Pheasant Tail. These patterns should be sufficient although you may add a Daddy-long-legs and, if there are hawthorn bushes in the vicinity, the Hawthorn Fly which is blown off the bushes on a warm windy day in spring.

ACCESSORIES

These include a tin of solid Mucilin to make the leader float, dry fly floatant (liquid or spray), scissors, polarised spectacles to see into the water and protect your eyes from a wind-blown cast, artery forceps, a suede fly reel case and a folding net to clip to your belt. Acquire a plastic fly box with partitions for the collection of flies which will grow in number, especially if you learn to tie your own.

A fly-fishing day

On a summer's day in a green landscape where birds sing you may find a few cows grazing. Look out for the one lacking an udder, easily recognised by size and physical appearance. It may, if jealous of his 'ladies', chase you up a tree or into the river. Apart from that risk you have no worries, so survey the river for a tell-tale rise or the dark form lazily swimming near the surface whilst looking for food.

Chub may be lying quietly in the shallows sipping flies, or on the bottom weaving from side to side whilst taking nymphs, or standing on their heads rooting shrimps out of the gravel. Having observed these activities and noted the area, move on to a tree-lined part to peer under the trees and bushes. Chub will be here, possibly with their backs out of the water, cruising about whilst waiting for a beetle or grub to drop on the water.

Certain movements tell you what food the observed fish is feeding on: tailing in shallow water indicates water snails and shrimps; a fish lying mid-water and weaving from side to side is taking nymphs as they rise from the bottom to hatch on the surface. The action of taking an underwater nymph often raises a bulge on the water surface. A circular ring radiating out with a bubble or two in the centre indicates the fish has taken a newly hatched dun which was floating along: this we call the 'sucking rise form'. When a large fish takes a midge you see the same form and hear a quiet sipping sound. When sedges hatch and are blown across the water by a wind you witness a slashing rise as a fish rushes at the fly and breaks the surface.

Having spotted your fish, decide what it is taking and knot on an imitation. Approach quietly and unobtrusively from downstream, creeping as close as possible. It is pointless to cast further than necessary as the further away your fly the more difficult it is to strike and make contact with the fish.

When in position, false cast to let out line and put your fly on the water well to the side of the fish (in between the bank and the fish if it is out in the middle) to judge correctly the casting distance. Then cast over the fish, covering it solely with the leader or you will 'line' the fish by placing the line above and in front of its position. Lining frightens fish which will then disappear. If you have floated the fly over the chub two or three times with no effect, try casting to the left and right, then just behind its head. If all fails go away and return later with the same tactics. Fishing a nymph is similar, but when cast over the fish bring it back with little twitches for that is how a nymph propels itself through the water.

A strike should be firm but not too vigorous. When the fish is hooked, strip in line but then recover it on to the reel as soon as possible or you may tread on it and lose the fish. A chub makes determined rushes for snags, so apply all the pressure the leader will stand whilst keeping the rod well up to let the spring of the flexible top take the strain. When the fish is tired bring it gently over the net, lift, then walk back closing the net, dragging the fish up the bank into the field. If possible keep it on the wet net. Handle with wet hands and gently return it to the water, making sure it is not too exhausted to swim away.

Fish rising to a fly.

CHAPTER 13

PIKE

A pike chasing a shoal of small fish

Description

The popular name for a pike is 'Freshwater Shark'. It is a predator which lives up to its reputation of astonishing cunning and speed when hunting its prey of mainly fish. In appearance the pike is built for speed with a long streamlined body and flat head, the anal and caudal fins and powerful tail are all built for rapid acceleration. The pike's camouflage is so good that one will often walk past its grey shadow by a weed-bed, with only the puff of mud as the fish darts off to tell you where it was lying. Coloured to blend in with the surroundings, it has a deep green back and white belly with flecks of white along the sides. A handsome fish, it gives marvellous sport on the right tackle.

The pike has gained a reputation of being a killer because it does not eat weed, nymphs and other small insects. Yet, even if the pike's diet consists largely of other fish it must be remembered that all our river fish eat spawn, baby fish and minnows. Trout take stone loach, bleak, gudgeon and other fishlets, whilst chub and even barbel are piscivores.

The term voracious has been applied to pike, but when an angler has fished all day without a run, as I did recently, this can hardly be true. It is often a matter of luck to come on a hungry pike as it is well known they feed until they are quite full and then rest until all has been digested. I have caught other fish which have been bloated with food and were just trying to force down one more bite!

A small pike is called a 'jack pike'. An article in *The Field* magazine in 1903 showed the estimated average weight of pike caught in England was between 3–4lb, but do not let this lead you to use fine tackle and small hooks. The article also showed that a number of the fish weighed over 20lb. Today, fish of over 30lb are caught every year.

The tendency in the past was to kill the large fish and throw back small ones, thus reducing the chance of catching a really big one. Ireland and Scotland record fish of over 50lb, and it has been said that 70lb has been reached. I read, long ago, of two anglers fishing a private pond and killing 25 pike weighing from 5–18lb. Killing is not the way today. Unless you are fishing a trout water, put your pike back unharmed to allow them to grow into real glass case specimens.

Distribution

Both ponds and rivers are home to pike in England, Ireland and Scotland.

Habitat

The pike is a fish which believes in reserving its energy for a sudden burst of speed to catch its prey. It prefers slow-running water, and quiet water with plenty of weed for cover. Rivers, lakes, ponds and canals provide ideal surroundings. Hungry pike will visit open water to feed and forage for their food. Generally, however, they prefer to find the cover of weed, some underwater obstruction or quiet eddy where they lie in ambush waiting for unsuspecting prey to swim past. There is then a sudden attack and a snap and it is all over for the unfortunate victim.

When river levels are down the pike will venture out from the weed-beds to feed, but in flood conditions the opposite applies for they will be found in slow-moving eddies and backwaters where they lie motionless until the floods subside. Other lies are in deep pockets downstream of waterfalls and sluices. Cattle drinks are favoured hunting places as small fish are to be found there feeding. Any obstruction under water providing an effort-free place out of the current will hold pike: rotting trees, boulders, weed-beds, islands in the river and so on.

Fishing a lake is more difficult and one has to move around trying different spots which may hold a fish. Areas where small fish congregate to feed are likely spots; the sluice which admits water is good as shoals of small fish like a current; at the side of sluices is always an eddy or dead spot where pike lie in ambush. Experience has shown that pike, like other fish, favour early morning and late evening to come out of hiding and search for food.

Above: A pike lying in the sun among lily pads.

Below: An evening pike fishing scene on a Hampshire Lake.

Spawning

During the months of January and February a hen fish is usually attended by two or more males, actually spawning during March and April in the close season. Pike tend to migrate to suitable spawning areas weeks before the actual laying of eggs takes place. It is said by some authorities that when the time comes the eggs may number several hundred thousand, depending on the size of the hen fish. The hen is often the larger of the species and if attended by a small cock fish it has been known for the hen to eat her spouse. (This is not uncommon as I believe spiders have the same tendency.)

The hen will only shed her ova if she feels the site is suitable. If the site becomes too shallow for her liking she will delay until June, or even reabsorb the ova. Shallow weed-beds next to ditches are good sites which you should visit when spinning at the end of the season. When laid, the eggs adhere to weeds and stony undulations in the river-bed. According to the water temperature, the incubation period varies over several weeks. Pike grow rapidly and are mature breeding fish at about 3lb. They continue to grow rapidly and I have mentioned outstanding sizes. There is one unsubstantiated claim of an Irish pike of 90lb but the effect of Guinness may have something to do with the claim.

Feeding habits

A quotation from a very old book reads 'a pike will hardly feed of anything except it stirre and be alive'. This is a true observation as if one opens a pike's stomach fish of all types will be found, some of them fresh, others part rotted. Sometimes present are the remains of ducklings, coots, moorhens and other waterfowl, together with frogs and crayfish.

I once caught a fish which had a livebait and snap tackle disintegrating in its stomach, doubtless causing much discomfort. Do not fish with light tackle and have the same happen to your bait. A fallacy exists among anglers that perch are not included in the pike's diet but examinations of stomach contents has proved this to be untrue. There is a record of an Irish pike weighing 53lb having a freshly swallowed 10lb salmon in its stomach. This I believe, and you will also if you catch a large pike and examine its opened mouth which distends (almost like a snake which dislocates its jaw) to swallow prey.

Pike feeding habits are mysterious, perhaps a better word is incalculable. Some days when you are spinning every cast seems to bring a fish up into sight, not always takers, but all are very interested. On other days a complete blank is experienced. My observation is the result of nearly seventy years of fishing. Do not go home discouraged after a blank day, for the next outing may provide many runs and perhaps a fish of glass case proportions which should, nevertheless, be returned after photography and weighing.

Tackle

RODS

The 2-piece 12ft Shakespeare Zenith pike rod of $2^{1}/_{2}$-lb test curve, with a fast tip action will cast all the baits you need and handle any fish. A carp rod is also suitable.

REELS

I favour a Mitchell fixed spool reel, having a 300 model which has served me for many years. There is also the Mitchell 200 series, of which the Mitchell 260 is an excellent choice on a fixed budget. A centre pin is not worth considering as it would only be useful for bait fishing.

LINE

My choice of line is Maxima or Platil of 16-lb breaking strain to cope not with the fish, but with weeds and snags.

FLOATS

I use a Fishing Gazette float for fishing dead bait.

HOOKS

Always use strong pike hooks: No. 2 or No. 4 trebles on plugs and spinners, and No. 4 and No. 6 on dead bait tackles.

SPINNERS AND SPINNING

A Mepp No. 5 in a silver or copper colour is an excellent bait. I advise always using large baits as they attract large fish. The Colorado spoon, on which I have caught many pike, is a pear-shaped spinner which revolves slowly around a centre pin; the kidney spoon is also useful.

I make a 3in long wobbly spoon by cutting a large serving

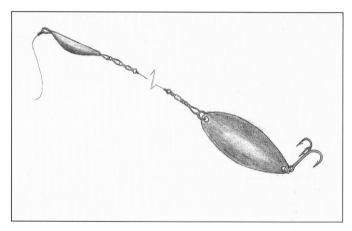

Above: Wobbling spoon rig with wire trace and Wye lead.

Below: Solid and jointed plug baits which float and dive when fished.

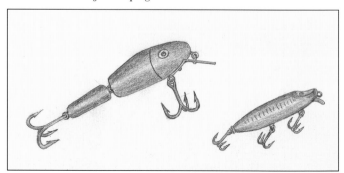

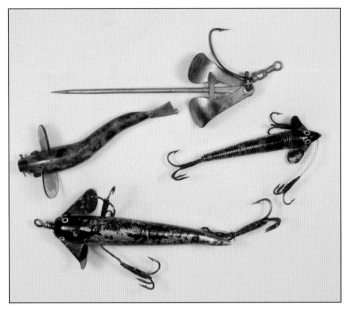

A mount for spinning a dead bait and three old-fashioned artificial baits.

spoon in half down the middle. A hole is then drilled at each end for a split ring to take a treble hook at the small end and a swivel for line attachment at the front, blunt, end. The belly is then painted red with yellow stripes. This bait wobbles like a sick wounded fish and is most successful. There is also the huge Jim Vincent Broads spoon of about 5in in length which feels as though you are playing a fish as it is reeled in. Do not forget one-piece and jointed plugs, available in many sizes and colours.

Illustrated overleaf is a dead bait spinning mount for use with a sprat or small herring on which I have caught fish. Herrings

Assorted baits. From the left, a Toby Spoon, a slim wobbling bait, a Hardy Extra Heavy Special Spoon, a kidney bar spoon, and home-made wobbling spoons.

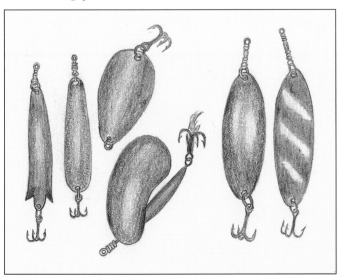

and sprats should be put in salt for 24 hours in the refrigerator to toughen them up or their life in the river will be short.

Spinning is a successful and exciting way of fishing for pike, especially on a frosty day when you would freeze if sitting. Keep walking and warm by making two or three casts and then moving on. In this way you will cover a lot of water and put your bait in many interesting and 'pikey' lies. It pays when almost at the end of retrieving a cast to stop and turn your rod sideways to bring the bait along parallel to the bank. Very often a pike which has followed just out of sight will appear to make a lunge at the bait.

Spinning can truthfully be said to be the most scientific and sporting way of fishing. Casting must be accurate, then the bait must be retrieved in spurts and rushes to make the spinner look alive. A delicate feel of the bait touching bottom means you must speed up a little to clear the river-bed. Pike usually hug the river-bed, the easiest place to lie prone looking like the extension of a weed, or a dark shadow, and fool the prey into a false sense of security.

A Toby Spoon, a wobbling spoon, a Hardy Spoon, and a kidney bar spinner.

Fishing the Toby lure, the action is to reel in and then stop for two or three seconds. This allows the spoon to flutter towards the river-bed. Then, when you start again, it rushes and wobbles towards the top, a tantalising action to all fish attracted by a spinning bait. Large pike lie deep. Where your venue is deep, sultry water you must feel the bottom when you cast and risk being snagged on retrieval.

DEAD BAITS

Sprats and herring can be used as dead bait, or any small dead fish such as dace, grayling and roach. Rather than have the bother of float fishing for bait and then having to kill the catch, I use sprats and herring. The bait can be hooked on a snap tackle and suspended from a float – the Jardine Snap is my

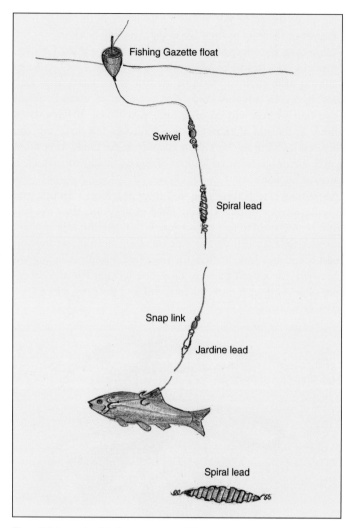

Float fishing a dead bait on a snap tackle.
Tackle for fishing a dead bait comprising a Jardine Snap tackle which provides for one hook of a treble in the base of the pectoral fin and the other in the base of the dorsal fin. The snap tackle is attached to an 18in wire trace by a snap link and the reel line to the barrel swivel at the end of the trace. A spiral lead completes the tackle which should be fished about 10in off the bottom depending on the character of the river-bed.

choice. This tackle has two trebles, one to hook in below the dorsal fin, whilst the other is of two hooks and a spike with a barb which is pushed into the muscle above the pectoral fin. A weight is needed on the wire trace and is usually the spiral type illustrated. The float is the Fishing Gazette.

A dead bait rig is usually two trebles mounted on a wire trace attached to the line via a Wye weight. It is cast out to your chosen spot and lies on the bottom with your rod on a rest and any bite detector you favour. If the bail arm on the fixed spool reel is left open, and you lay one or two coils of line on a plastic sheet, you will see them gradually drawn away if you get a run. When using this method, really a form of ledgering, some anglers bait the swim with 'rubby dubby' which usually consists

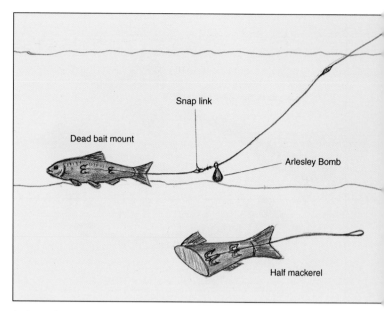

A dead fish or tail of a mackerel on a dead bait mount connected to an 18in wire trace with a snap swivel and an Arlesley Bomb.

of bits of chopped up sprats and herring. Both oily fish, they exude a scent which a pike is sure to investigate.

WIRE TRACES
Usually made of braided wire, I use 20-lb breaking strain to compete with the cutting teeth of a pike and any sharp snags. The trace should be about 18in long with a swivel at one end and a link swivel at the other to clip on to the mount.

WEIGHTS
The Wye weight is excellent for all rigs, especially spinning, as its shape promotes anti-kink if your bait is a true spinner.

SWIVELS
Use the standard barrel swivel of the correct size for the weight of the tackle.

Unhooking a pike with the help of artery forceps – no gloves so hands off!

ACCESSORIES

Carry a long pair of pointed-nose pliers or artery forceps to release trebles from the pike's mouth. I always carry a small screwdriver and a spare bail arm spring for the fixed spool reel, a spring balance weighing up to at least 25lb, a clean towel and, most important, a good-sized folding net, to carry on my belt as most fisheries ban the use of the gaff. Also needed are a box of assorted spinners, weights, swivels, traces and spare treble hooks.

Techniques

The pike is a lazy fish, so go to slack water and good hidey-holes behind piles, rotting wood and weed-beds. Having arrived at the river, viewed the colour of the water and whether the sun is shining, you have three choices:

- If the water is clear, spinning will give you more chances than any other method.
- If the water is coloured, a dead bait may be the answer, either ledgered, or you will cover a little more water if float fishing.
- A nice quiet back eddy which your float can slowly go round and explore is a pleasant way of spending the day. Try another spot if there is no activity.

HOOKING

When a pike takes a spinner an immediate hard strike is necessary. I always strike and hold tight for a split second as the pike has a very bony mouth. If you are dead baiting let the fish take your coils of line, then pick up the rod and strike as before. If you are float fishing a dead bait a pike usually takes a fish across the back and swims off. Then it pauses whilst it turns the fish prior to swallowing, and then runs off. Strike as follows: see the float disappear and run off, it will stop and after a few seconds

A nice pike on the bank, with the lure it fell for, and spinning rod.

run again – that is the time to strike. Remember, always strike sideways against the direction of the run.

PLAYING THE FISH

Pike make a very strong run when hooked, so be sure not to be taken unawares. After the initial run a dogged fight will go on and I always reckon that it takes one minute to the pound to land the fish. Play the pike gently as the jaw is bony and the hook may be only hanging on to bone. When played out, like any other fish, submerge the net and draw the fish over. Lift, then walk back closing the net to drag the fish well away from the river. Treat the pike with care and wet hands so that it can be returned undamaged to fight another day – on this care your future sport depends. Pike fishing is a great autumn and winter sport.

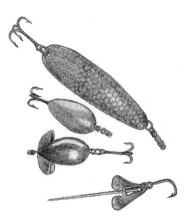

A Jim Vincent Broads Spoon, a vibro bar spoon, a Colorado spinner and a dead bait spinning mount.

CHAPTER 14

PERCH

A perch chasing small fish

Description

The perch is one of the most strikingly colourful coarse fish. It has bronze flanks with vertical green bars, bright red ventral and pectoral fins, and a dark humped back with sharp-spined dorsal fins which bristle if the fish is alarmed or attacked. The main dorsal is spiked, whilst the other is a normal, soft fin. The scales are rough to the touch, tending to stand up and feel abrasive when handled.

The perch has the adaptability of a chameleon to assume the hues of its surroundings. In clear water the colours are less brilliant. The gill cover extensions are part of its armour, being sharp enough to give you a bad cut when unhooking, a time when great care should be taken. The perch has a large mouth capable of taking fairly big fish, the bony jaws being expandable. It has a bristly tongue and mouth, but no teeth. Nevertheless, it can take a fish nearly half its own size and pass it into a large stomach cavity. It is a true predator.

Distribution

The perch is found in many areas and counties in the British Isles, in Europe, parts of South Africa, Asia and Australia. Eire is an angler's dream for big perch.

Habitat

Perch thrive in rivers, lakes, ponds, reservoirs and canals, and

---

The dangerous spines on the dorsal fin of a perch.

Perch

can always be located where fry and small fish (their main source of food) are to be found. They favour backwaters and eddies away from the current and are usually found in shoals. In the early summer months large shoals of tiny perch about 1½–2in in length can be seen in shallow water. They will suddenly disappear in a dark cloud as several bigger perch appear; these are anticipating taking some of their small relations as a meal.

Perch can be found where the best use of their camouflage comes into being by sunken rotten trees, baulks of bridges, tangles of roots, flood remains and beds of weeds. If you catch a perch in the deep water of a reservoir return it quickly to the water. Its physical make-up responds to being raised in the same manner as the human deep-sea diver suffers the 'bends', caused by hydrogen bubbles in the blood. This can be fatal if the fish is not able to return quickly to the depths from which it came.

In the *Compleat Angler* of 1653 Izaak Walton aptly describes the fish and its ability to feed on large portions of whatever it fancies:

'A very bold biting fish; he is one of the fishes of prey that, like the Pike and the Trout, carries his teeth in his mouth; which is very large, and he dare venture to kill and devour several other kinds of fish.'

This confirms the perch as an avid feeder which needs a big bait to entice his interest.

Perch are wanderers, but one factor I have noticed is that they follow a set route. Sometimes, when fishing for perch I have had a bite and landed a fish. Nothing stirs for several minutes or longer, then another bite and another fish. This continues with a fish every several minutes as the shoal follows a fixed route. If you locate a shoal, stay put and you will have similar success.

Spawning

Perch, being gregarious, do not depart from their normal shoaling pattern when they group up to spawn. All the shoal has to do is find a stretch of gravelly, weedy water which suits their requirements.

Spawning takes place in the close season between 15 March and 15 June (inclusive) or earlier in some cases. The female casts her glutinous mass of eggs on weed, roots or the gravel bottom, and the males shed their milt over the eggs to fertilise them. The number of eggs is said to be in the region of 200,000 but, as with all other spawn, much is consumed by predators or killed by river maintenance or cold weather.

If suitable conditions prevail, alevins hatch in 7–21 days and sink to the river-bed where they remain, absorbing the yolk sac for three or four weeks. After this they feed on minute organisms, growing gradually to about 6in over three years, when they become sexually mature.

Feeding habits

Their greedy feeding habits are often mentioned in angling books, even as far back as 1496 in the *Treatyse of Fysshynge with an Angle*. The perch has a main diet of live fish, including members of the perch family, insects, worms and grubs. Haunts favoured by perch are rotting trees, woodwork, rubbish and weeds which are inhabited by minnows and fry feeding on the minute organisms living in this environment. The roots of lilies and weeds, and rotting vegetation, are the homes of caddis and fly larvae, also food for perch.

Perch will take a large bait. This fish took a 2in pike spinner.

Tackle

RODS

Float rod – Shakespeare 1821/390 Equaliser Carbon Match 13ft 3-piece (£45)

Ledger rod – Shakespeare 1802/270 Firebird Ledger. 9ft 2-piece (£25)

Light spinning rod – Shakespeare 1503/180 6ft 2-piece (£15)

REELS

Shakespeare Centre Pin Eagle 2900/400 $9/16$in wide, $4^{1}/_{2}$in spool (£45)

Mitchell 240 fixed spool (£30)

The above prices prevailed at the time of writing.

LINES

Maxima and Platil 6-lb BS

FLOATS

Straight waggler or stick float.

WEIGHTS

A box of assorted split shot and an Arlesley Bomb for ledgering.

BAIT

Freshly caught dead minnows, maggots, worms (lob and red). Perch may take other baits, but fish and worms are the best.

GROUNDBAIT

Use mainly cloud bait to attract small fry into the swim, and perhaps chopped worms if you are using worms as the hook bait.

HOOKS

It is pointless using small hooks where the favourite bait is a worm. Size 6 or 8 wide bend spade-ends are my choice.

NYLON FOR HOOK LINKS

Use 12–18in of Maxima or Platil with a loop at one end. This link should be of a lesser breaking strain than the reel line. Perch are not shy of nylon and have rough mouths which will cause a break if the nylon is too fine.

ACCESSORIES

Artery forceps, scissors, disgorger, net, split shot, ledger weights.

Techniques

LOCATING THE FISH

Attention should be paid when walking the bank of the water to be fished to the areas previously described. As mentioned, these include the baulks of bridges, sunken trees and roots, lilies and weed-beds, in fact where I have described as inhabited by minnows and small fry. Also watch the water closely for that tell-tale disturbance which may be caused by small fish breaking the surface in fear of a pursuer – this is more likely to be a perch than a pike.

Having found a site well away from the main current, probably in a quiet backwater or eddy in a river, or by weeds or lily pads in a pond, it makes sense to use a method which is not going to lose tackle. If the place is cluttered with roots and rotting matter a ledger would be lost in no time, so the choice is either a float or spinning between obstacles. This can be exciting and rewarding, making you cast your spinning bait with care.

Assuming there is a clear swim cut in a pond or lake, or the river has a clear swim or back eddy, try ledgering. Taking the ledger rod, attach a quiver tip to the screwed socket in the top ring. There is little difference in using swing or quiver tips as may be studied in the 'Ledgering' Chapter. With rod and line prepared, take the line and slide a link swivel up it first, then a small plastic ledger stop, a ring into which a little plug is pushed to lock it into place. Fix this 18–24in from your hook bait. Now tie a loop in the end of the reel line to which you attach the looped hook link. Take a $^{1}/_{2}$oz or heavier Arlesley Bomb and attach it to the link swivel. This rig is very easy to change weights for a swim feeder. You can even remove the Stop and Arlesley Bomb to revert to a float which, in an emergency, can be satisfactory on a ledger rod with the quiver tip removed.

Throw out some cloud bait to attract any fry in the area, in the hope that a perch will have a look. Now add a small ball of groundbait into which is mixed a worm or worm pieces. Put a juicy worm on to the No. 6 hook, with the hook through the middle and the tail. Set the rod on the rest with the quiver tip just bent to the bait. If the tip is slowly drawn down this indicates a bite which should be struck. If the tip draws down and flips back, it is either a small fish playing about or a fish swimming by and knocking the line, so sit on your hands and do not be tempted to strike. If the tip swings round suddenly – strike.

As the favourite food of perch is fish I will describe how to use a dead bait. (I do not approve of live baits.) The dead bait can be a freshly caught gudgeon, dace, roach or even a perch – they like eating their own relations! Unscrew the quiver tip from the rod and use it as a ledger rod with no additions. The fixed spool reel and 6-lb line are standard. Slide a swivel up the line and attach another to the loop in the line. Tie a 5in length of heavier nylon to the first sliding swivel and attach a 1oz Arlesley Bomb to the other end. A 2ft length of 10-lb Alasticum mono wire should be attached to the first swivel and then to a No. 4 eyed hook which is passed through the chin membrane of the dead bait.

Dead bait may also be attached with a made-up two-treble tackle which may be bought from your dealer. Hook one treble in the tail of the bait and one in the back just below the dorsal fin. In this manner the bait is presented head first. Again, put out some cloud bait and cast your bait into the swim. The rod should be on a rest with the bail arm off and a coil of reel line on the ground, weighted by a small stick or stone. When the line starts to draw-off, you have a run. Now, pick up the rod and firmly strike straight up and the perch should be hooked.

FLOAT FISHING

Consider fishing a pond or river with a float rig and a worm. The pond should have a swim cut between the lily pads to give a stretch of open water, but there may be some obstacles under the water. A stick float or waggler are possible. If it is windy use a waggler because you can sink the line and not be bothered with the effect of the wind. On a calm day choose the float you prefer to watch, the stick being fished off a floating line. Shotting in both cases should have the bulk just below the float, and the rest evenly spaced down the rig between float and bait, as perch will take a lively worm on the drop. Perch can be present at almost any level in the water as they are not bottom-feeders. Put cloud bait out and place a lob worm on a No. 6 hook. Use a 6-lb hook link attached to the 6-lb reel line as the perch has a rough bony mouth unsuited to fine nylon. The rod goes on a rest whilst you await activity. Perch are deliberate in their feeding pattern. If the float disappears after one or two bobs strike firmly away from the movement of the float.

SPINNING

The 6ft light spinning rod now comes in to its own. Using your fixed spool reel and fine Alasticum 6lb wire trace you are ready to select a natural bait on a spinning mount. Also available are Mepps and similar spoon baits, plugs (jointed or solid), metal minnows and even a tiny Reflex Devon minnow. (A selection of spinning baits is illustrated on page 59.) Having assembled rod, reel and line, put a loop in the reel line for attaching to the Alasticum trace which has a swivel on one end and a small link swivel at the other for ease of changing baits. The trace should be about 12in in length. If your bait is light in weight, a small

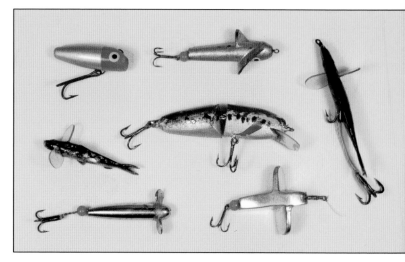

A selection of plugs and minnows for perch fishing.

fold-over weight can be fixed around the trace at the reel end. The fold-over has an anti-kink action.

Whether you are fishing a pond or river, cast out and let your bait drop to about mid-water depth before starting to retrieve. Then wind and stop, allowing the spoon bait to flutter down before continuing to wind. If using a minnow or plug, just wind intermittently to impart life to the bait. On a take, strike firmly and keep your rod tip up.

Playing fish of this size is not a problem, just draw the fish over the net. If possible avoid hand contact, and beware the sharp dorsal fin and those gill flaps. Unhook carefully and return to the water. Keep nets should not be used.

CHAPTER 15

DACE

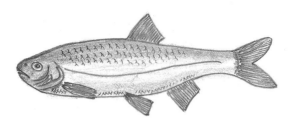

The dace

Description

The dace has a dark olive-coloured back, silver sides, a white belly and a neat slim body. The forked tail and dorsal fin are pale yellow, the other fins having a yellowish tone with a touch of pink. For true identification the dorsal and anal fins have a concave edge and this is the only way to distinguish a large dace from a small chub, whose fins are convex. A dace of 1lb is the ambition of all coarse fishermen as the record is only a few ounces above that weight. It feeds avidly to bait and in summer is a free riser to the dry fly.

There are times when a small chub is mistaken for a big dace. The distinguishing difference is in the dorsal and anal fins; on the chub (bottom) they are convex on the edge and with the dace (top) they are concave.

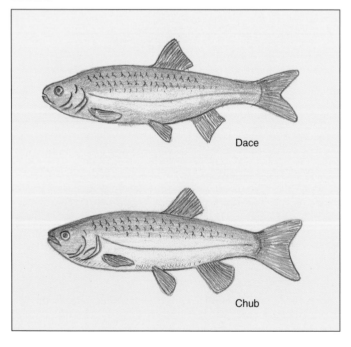

Dace

Chub

Distribution

The dace exists throughout Europe and England, but is not found in western Wales or Scotland. It is absent in Ireland with the exception of the Blackwater in County Cork. Dace arrived in that river some years ago, and it is said they were transferred there in a pike fisherman's bait can; after a bad day he tipped the remainder of his dace into the river. Since then they have bred so well that, because of the game fishing interests, there have been requests to have them thinned out by netting.

Dace waters exist in some Hertfordshire streams, in Northamptonshire, the Dorset Stour, the Hampshire Avon and rivers in Surrey and Warwickshire. It is also reported that dace swim in the tidal waters of the Thames. As dace favour fast clear streams, many trout rivers such as the Test and Itchen hold these fish, as do small trout streams throughout England.

Habitat

Dace are shoal fish which favour fast, clear waters running over clean gravel beds. Shoals move restlessly, darting about,

Dorset Stour at White Mill Bridge, Sturminster Marshall.

justifying their old English name of the 'dart'. They can be found in fast, gravelly runs between weed-beds below sluices and weir pools, only seeking deeper runs when the weather grows cold in autumn and winter.

Spawning

Dace spawn in April, earlier than some other coarse fish, and unfortunately at the beginning of the trout fishing season. Many are caught accidentally by trout fishermen, especially if their methods are not strictly 'fly only'. Like the chub, the males grow tiny rough lumps on their heads, making it easy to identify male and female.

The females migrate to deeper, less turbulent water and when ready to spawn return to gravelly shallows, depositing the ova which are then fertilised by the males. The eggs mature in two to three weeks, the period being influenced by water temperature.

Feeding habits

Dace are not predators. They live on surface flies and anything unfortunate enough to fall on the water such as caterpillars, insects and grubs. Underwater, they feed on the mass of hatching nymphs, together with the shrimp population and some types of weed. Thus there are many baits they will take, in fact they have been caught on a bare golden hook decorated with a strip of something shiny. Feeding times are not set and I have found them fairly eager to feed at almost any time.

Tackle

NYLON LINES

I recommend Maxima and Platil nylon lines. Whether you are fishing fast shallows or deep runs, a light line of 3–4-lb BS (breaking-strength) is ample to tackle these little fighting fish, unless a marauding pike comes along and takes the fish you are playing. Then it is a different story. You may be lucky enough to land them both, but a $1^1/2$-lb bottom is almost certain to be cut by the sharp teeth of a pike.

FLOATS

For fishing over fast, gravelly runs a tiny bubble float is my choice as shotting is minimal. In deeper water use either one of the wagglers or a light stick float, depending on your preference.

WEIGHTS

Carry a box of assorted split shot.

BAIT

These little fish will accept almost anything presented on a very small hook: worms, any of the bread mixes, crust, maggots, grubs, barley, hemp, elderberries, even cubes of banana and tiny boiled shrimps. Remember, bread mixes come readily off the hook. In fast water you may be re-baiting frequently. You may even lose your hook bait halfway down the swim and be left fishing with an empty hook!

GROUNDBAIT

Use very small amounts of bread and bran mixes, or whatever hook bait you are using. Maggots come into their own, several at a time should be thrown out.

HOOKS

Hook sizes should be very small. My favourite wide-gape spades are from sizes 14–20, tied to a 12–18in hook link of $1^1/2$-lb BS with a loop for easy replacement.

ACCESSORIES

Travel light if you are fishing the shallows: bait, artery forceps, Mucilin to keep the line above water, and a small folding net – a one-pounder dace would be memorable. Polarised spectacles are useful and, if sitting, a rod rest.

Techniques

LOCATING THE FISH

Locating your fish is important as there is not much future in fishing a blank stretch of water. In clear water conditions this is comparatively easy, especially as dace are shoal fish, sparkly in appearance and always on the move. Dace will be present where water runs over sand or gravel beds and in runs through flowing weeds. Any fast, clear water is 'home' to the dace, for you will find them at the tail of runs from sluices, where a side stream joins the main river and in very shallow water. In floods they will retreat into slack water with their fellow roach, chub and other fish until conditions improve. Weir pools have a special attraction, especially in the areas where the water bubbles and becomes oxygenated at the tail of the run. If you are searching for dace in deeper water, always try where the run speeds up through a narrower part of the river.

METHODS

The method to adopt is really your choice, although weather and water conditions have some bearing on your effort. One of the beauties of dace fishing is that you can enjoy a wonderful day's sport, wandering from swim to swim or shallow to shallow. Be sure to travel light, whether carrying a ledger rod, float rod, or a fly rod as this is a relaxing way of spending a day by the water.

LEDGERING

All the various methods of ledgering apply to dace although I recommend a float or fly unless you prefer to sit and watch a quiver or swing tip. If you settle for ledgering, a quiver tip is my choice as bites are quick and slight. The hook link should be fine, 1-lb or at the most $1^1/2$-lb. If fishing bread mix or a worm, use a No. 14 spade hook, or No. 16 or No. 20 for a single or double maggot. The weight can be an Arlesley Bomb or a swim feeder. The choice of venue should be the deeper, fast runs or parts of a mill pool.

One method to try is a rolling ledger in the shallows. This uses a pierced bullet stopped with a single shot just above the 18in hook link, and a No. 14 hook baited with a succulent worm. Wade carefully to the side of a shallow where you have seen a shoal with the aid of polarised spectacles – these I hang around my neck to be sure they are there when needed. Having taken up your station, cast your bait straight across and let it trip its way over the river-bed in an arc. Then retrieve slowly to your feet – a fish may follow to the end before taking.

The rolling ledger is an exciting way of pursuing dace as anything may take the worm, even a trout. The shallow has to be fairly weedless or, if there are beds of weeds, cast your bait between them and work it back. This is not so successful as you invariably bump into your fish and frighten them off. Remember to take your Environment Agency licence with you, fortunately 'Coarse' also covers 'Non-Migratory Trout'.

FLOAT FISHING

As I favour fishing the fast, ripply shallows, a tiny bubble float supporting a worm or maggot is my way of searching for a specimen dace. I must write that having tried all the methods I have only managed to achieve 15oz, and not the magic 1lb dace. To fish a bubble with only two feet or less below the float, I weight the rig with some tiny shot, just enough to keep the bait trundling over the gravel without becoming snagged.

When casting into runs between weeds and trotting as far as you can see, takes are felt immediately as the current has kept you in touch with the hook and there is no 'line belly'. In deeper water you have the choice of a waggler or stick float as you are fishing in some current, but not necessarily very turbulent or excessively deep. The method is to trot with the bulk of weight near the float, and have the float cock evenly spaced between the float and the hook bait. One very small shot should be on the hook line about 6in from the bait. As the flow is less vigorous than over shallows you can choose any of

A 12oz dace caught on a maggot.

the hook baits, although the head of a small red worm tends to be readily accepted.

Changes in bait and fishing at different levels will often prove profitable, as dace sometimes feed well off the bottom. The hook size for the bigger baits should be No. 14 which is suitable for any bait size unless you are down to a single maggot. You can profit in this situation with balls of bread and bran groundbait mixed with some of the hook bait. Remember to use small quantities frequently, especially hook bait alone.

Dace are very quick biters. If your float starts to go – strike. Do not wait for it to go right under or you will be too late. Most of the techniques applying to roach can also be used for dace.

FLY-FISHING

I have had many happy sessions with a fly rod, my favourite way of fishing for dace. Whether fishing by dry fly or wet fly use the same tackle as for chub but with a 4X or 5X leader, preferably the latter unless there is a bit of colour in the water.

You must consider the weather and choose a fine sunny day, or even a fine overcast one. Forsake your first day's tench fishing for a day with the fly rod pursuing the sparkling dace. Early morning fishing will probably be rewarded by a wet fly or tiny nymph, as hatches of fly in early June may be sparse if the weather is not warm. Dace are not as fussy as trout or chub. When conditions are right they will have a look at any small fly floated over them or passing them under water.

If there is a hatch of natural flies you should take an imitation from your fly box. A fancy fly such as a Red Tag on a No. 16 or No. 18 hook will be taken whatever is on the water, as will a Coch-y-bondhu. The natural fly will be imitated by designs such as Wickham's Fancy, Pheasant Tail, Greenwell's Glory, Gold Ribbed Hare's Ear and Iron Blue, all on No. 16 or No. 18 hooks. With a 5X leader, a fly knotted on and anointed with floatant, you will be ready. Approach the fish from a downstream position to present your dry fly upstream. Watch

for a rise on the surface which may tell you a dace is taking a dun. The dun is the floating natural fly which has just emerged from the underwater nymph stage, sailing downstream on the current like a ship. Make two or three false casts to check your distance by letting the fly fall to one side of the fish. Having ascertained your cast length is correct, throw so that only a foot or two of your 5X leader lands over the fish. If you cast too far the line will be in the fish's window and line it, scaring it away. The dry fly is now floating downstream towards the fish, so gather in line with your free hand to keep in touch with the fly. Do not recover line too quickly or the fly will drag on the water surface in an unnatural manner.

Some fish show no interest as the fly passes, in which case lift off when the fly is well below the fish and try again, making several false casts in the air to dry the fly. If the fish continues to rise to drifting naturals, continue to offer your artificial until it either stops rising or takes.

On a take, strike quickly but gently as your fish is small. If it is hooked keep your rod tip up and the line tight, reeling in any slack line to avoid it tangling with your feet and any bankside growth.

Just before sunset on a warm summer evening dace will be rising everywhere. Small groups will be in the shallows close to the bank with their backs out of the water – all are likely takers. On a day which is windy and inclement, when nothing is rising, you should fish the river instead of addressing individual fish. Having had the luck of seeing a shoal flashing as they move about in the shallows, try a wet fly or a nymph. Your flies can be some of the patterns I have mentioned for dry-fly fishing, but tied as wet flies with hen hackles and laid-back wings, or even just hackle without wings. Wickham's

Fancy, Greenwell's Glory and Hare's Ear are all acceptable, as are the fancy flies such as Butcher, Invicta, Red Spinner and the Red Tag.

Fishing the wet fly, your approach is different in that you present the fly downstream and sunk under the water surface. As dace are mainly in shallows you can use the floating fly line, but rub the 9ft leader with mud to make it sink and suck the fly for a second or two. These treatments will encourage the fly to fish under the water and not skate across the surface. To fish an assorted team of flies to the shoal you can add one or two droppers, joining short 6in lengths of fine 5X nylon to your leader with a dropper knot.

When tackled up and ready to go you must be careful in your approach as you are fishing downstream and in full view of the shoal. Having taken up position, cast diagonally across at about 30° downstream, giving the line a gentle twitch to aid your leader and flies to sink. Let the flies sweep in a semi-circle across the river from the far bank towards the near bank. When the cast is fished out and directly downstream, retrieve the line to casting length and repeat the process after taking one step down the river to cover fresh water. A take will be a gentle pluck, the fish usually hooking itself.

Playing the fish is simple and the fish are so small that a net is not used but should still be carried as you may hook a chub, grayling or trout. All these fish should be unhooked with a wet hand and held facing upstream in the water to recover. Grayling, especially, become exhausted and will float off upside-down to drown if not held in this manner.

Your accessories are a fly box, artery forceps, Mucilin for the leader, fly floatant, a pair of scissors and the all-important polarised spectacles.

Dace swimming

CHAPTER 16

GRAYLING

Grayling

Description

The grayling is a beautiful fish which aptly takes the title 'Lady of the Stream'. Its Latin name is *Thymallus Thymallus* for it has a strong scent of thyme. On its back is a huge dorsal fin which is violet-coloured and spotted purple. Behind this, but in front of the tail, is the adipose fin present in all game fish. The tail is deeply forked and pointed, and grey like the adipose. The head and back are a purple-black changing in shade to a steely blue; golden streaks and grey lines are on the black spotted flanks. The mouth is small with an overshot upper lip, and the eyes are pear-shaped with indigo pupils.

A fine grayling.

Distribution

The grayling is not present in Ireland but is well represented in Northern Europe and North America. It is prolific in Scotland and especially in some English rivers such as the Test and Itchen where large grayling are caught on bait and on fly, as in almost all the chalk-streams of the south. The rivers Dever in Hampshire, and the Kennet in Berkshire are noted grayling rivers.

Habitat

Grayling can be found in the silvery shallows of chalk-streams and at the tails of sluices and weir pools. Generally, where grayling haunt trout rivers, they prefer quieter water than the trout, the larger fish tending to lie under the rough water pouring into the pool. They only seem to lie close to the surface when a hatch of fly is evident. Then they dart up freely to take.

Spawning

Grayling spawn in the close season between April and May in their usual habitat, fast, clear gravelly shallows. When fertilised, the ova take about three weeks to hatch.

Feeding habits

Feeding takes place during the morning and afternoon in the summer, and midday in the winter when the water has warmed up a little. Their natural food is snails, shrimps, all aquatic insect life and floating fly life.

Tackle

Take your coarse fishing rod, Mitchell reel and 4-lb line, a $^1/_2$-lb hook link connected to a No. 12 or No. 14 hook, and a box of worms or maggots. Bullets and split shot, a grayling float and the usual accessories are needed, including polarised spectacles. Then you are ready to locate your fish. Groundbait should be frequent doses of half a dozen maggots.

Techniques

FLOAT FISHING

Start by using a float with one or two shot to sink your bait and cock the float when fishing fast shallows which are only one or two feet deep. Bait-up and cast, letting the float trundle down the run whilst holding it back slightly to avoid the line bellying out and losing touch with the bait. Fish as far as you can while remaining able to control the float, then let it sweep around to

Above: Trotting a maggot for grayling on the River Test.

Below: Netting a grayling from the shallow end of a weir pool on the River Test.

your bank at the end of the run before retrieving. A bite will be seen by the float suddenly disappearing, and I have no doubt you will feel a tug as the fish takes and (usually) hooks itself.

To recover line where the water is fast, lift your rod up with the line being drawn towards you, then wind the reel as you let the rod tip drop down to water level. Then stop winding and lift again, repeating the process which is known as 'pumping'. Finally, you will have the fish sufficiently close to be drawn over the net and landed. Grayling become very exhausted in the playing, so free the barbless hook with wet hands, then hold the fish in the water, head to current, until it has recovered enough to swim away.

Ledgering

Now to a form of ledgering. To prepare for this unloop your hook link from the line, remove the shot and float. Slide a pierced bullet up the line, then a ledger stop. You can pinch a shot on in place of this if you wish, but I feel this may be a weak link in the line. Re-attach your hook link loop-to-loop to the line. The worm should be attached by passing the hook once through the head.

If you are still in the shallows, cast across towards the opposite bank at about 30° downstream and let the bullet roll across in the current in a semi-circle like a wet fly. Retrieve slowly when the bait is directly downstream, pausing briefly towards the finish as a fish may follow and take in the final few yards. The fish will probably self-hook, all you have to do is smartly lift the rod. Play, land and return carefully as you did when float fishing.

The grayling is fond of lying over clean gravel at the tail of sluices and, as mentioned already, where the water pours into a weir pool – these places may be float fished with the same rig used in the shallows. Extra weight may be needed, a 9in swan quill weighted with three AAA shot. Bait with three maggots, throwing in half a dozen occasionally to go round in the eddying part of the flow. An Arlesley Bomb can be substituted for the bullet if you wish to ledger in the sluice pool with a ledger rod and quiver tip. Grayling do not fish well in flood conditions, and will go off the feed if an east wind blows.

These fish fight with a peculiar rolling action, and because a barbless hook is being used a tight line must be kept whilst they are played. Their bites are quick and definite and your reflexes must be good to hook them. They are a wonderful sporting fish which fight all the way to the net.

CHAPTER 17
FLY-FISHING FOR COARSE FISH

Assorted natural and artificial flies

A coarse fisherman arrives on the bank with a substantial collection of tackle. He carries a rod carrier and rod rests, net, bait and a tackle box, the latter usually containing a full picnic. The fly-fisherman carries just a folding net attached to his belt, a small box of flies and leaders and a fly rod. In his pocket is, perhaps, a flask and a sandwich – he travels light. You too can walk the river unencumbered and enjoy the wildlife and scenery over many yards, or even miles, of lovely river.

Water has always had a great attraction for me, especially the bright shallows where the river tumbles and burbles over silver gravel with waving throngs of weed hiding fish of all sizes. Chub, dace, grayling, roach and even perch and pike fall for a well presented fly. Although perch are unlikely to be fished for with intent, they sometimes cannot resist the attraction of a brightly coloured wet fly.

Patrick R. Chalmers in *At the Tail of the Weir* (Philip Allen 1932) states, 'The chub has a hundred good qualities to recommend him to the Thames angler, but he has one outstanding merit. He is the only important fish in the river who will take a fly'. This wonderful quotation confirms that the chub is an outstanding coarse fish which may grow to considerable size (I have had one of 5lb $10^{1}/_{2}$oz on fly) fights every ounce of his weight on the way to the net, and is full of cunning.

Tackle
The outfit I use is the same as that taken to the river to fish for trout: a 9ft carbon rod, $3^{1}/_{4}$in Hardy reel and a No. 6 floating fly line. The leader is usually a 9ft knotless continuous tapered nylon of 3X strength, 5-lb breaking strain. A strong leader is needed as chub always lie within close reach of cover such as lilies, old rotting tree trunks and Cooper's reeds – if the fish

Casting a fly for coarse fish on the Dorset Stour.

reaches any of those it is usually curtains for the angler. The first dogged rush complete, he has to be kept on the top of the water. Beware his last rush to freedom which will leave you with a broken leader if you are unprepared.

Stalking a rising fish with a fly rod and making use of bankside cover.

Chub flies

When these are mentioned, great bushy bumbles are usually produced on No. 6 hooks. These may, at times, do the job but I prefer smaller hooks such as No. 10 or even No. 16. On the No. 10 hooks I tie my own fly of a conventional Zulu-type black body ribbed with tinsel and a black hackle. For a Red Tag I use red cock hackle, a peacock herl body and a red tag. In the evening try a sedge pattern on a No. 10 hook or any imitation of a natural fly which is on the water.

Techniques

LOCATING THE FISH

You must learn your river if you are to succeed with chub. They are shoal fish which change their locations from season to season if the river is altered by winter floods or maintenance work. You must rove the river bank to locate shoals. Do not allow your shadow to be cast across the water, nor silhouette your body against the sky or you will see the dark shadows of chub fading out of sight. When you have them located mark the spot and return with rod and line. I find the best time to find chub is in May when they tend to throw caution to the wind and lie on the fin, lazily sipping mayfly. Many a chub rise has been taken for a trout, much to the disgust of the game fisher. Large chub especially show at this time whilst keeping hidden during their open season.

If a fly is presented well, a chub will swim up in such a manner that you are sure he will take. However, after a close inspection he turns and goes on his rounds looking elsewhere for a genuine fly. In such cases try him again, he will inspect and, if about to swim off, you should twitch your fly. Nine times out of ten, he will then turn and take. Then the fun begins.

A balmy hot summer's day is ideal, the fish will be cruising on the surface or lying under the shade of bankside bushes close to 'home' which will be amongst the roots. In this position they expect a grub or beetle to fall upon the water.

THE TONY ALLEN BEETLE

One day in August on the Dorset Stour I was confronted with the 'beetle and bush' situation. I had spotted a solitary fish under overhanging bushes quietly swimming up and down, inspecting an insect or two, and being very selective. I made some beetles from small pieces of cork cut to shape and a hook glued on with Araldite. I added some short nylon legs, painted the beetle brown and put on a coat of varnish. At the river I crept into a casting position and watched. Along came the chub which then turned to swim away. I cast the beetle about 12in in front of his nose, at which his speed increased, causing a ripple. The beetle rocked up and down on lively legs. The beetle looked as a beetle should: brown, plump and helpless. The chub was almost there, then on went his brakes and he dropped out of sight. The tension was unbearable but I did not give up. There was no current under this tree, only a slight back eddy, and there was my beetle swimming in a little circle. The chub was absent, but could not have seen me. Perhaps the leader, or something else had driven him away.

I waited in a very cramped state for what seemed ages. Then, there it was again, coming back and facing me with, I hoped, intent. The beetle bobbed up and down. The fish turned, had another close look and again swam away only to reappear right under my nose. Then, its great white mouth opened and the beetle disappeared. I could not believe it. Stunned, I struck and the battle started. Straight for the roots the fish went – I turned it. It headed straight for the lilies, I brought him to the top. After a few splashes it was in the net, a bronze beauty of 4lb 7oz. Wetting my hands I unhooked him and slid him towards the roots, but I will never know which of us was more exhausted.

AN UNUSUAL METHOD

Long ago I read an article in the *Angler's News* which is no longer in print. An Army captain described a technique he evolved using a small float to which he tied a greased leader and fly. He then floated the assembly down to where chub were feeding and had great success. The operation was conducted from a punt anchored some way upstream from the fish.

Chub may also be caught by dapping a bushy fly from a concealed corner and I am sure, although I have never tried it, that blowline dapping would catch the most wary fish on a windy day with a ripple on the water.

ROACH AND DACE ON THE FLY

Roach are to be found in the same vicinity as chub, often in deep quiet pools where they can be seen taking flies from the surface. I have caught small roach when fishing for trout with a natural imitation tied to a No. 16 or No. 18 hook. Dace can provide excellent sport on the dry fly, when a 4X or 5X leader is required. These fish are small, and so should be the flies you use. Summer and autumn are the best times. Then, fishing a dry fly is the most exciting and rewarding way of taking them as, ounce for ounce, they are great fighters.

Dace are best taken by imitating the natural fly on the water. Those hatching in summer and autumn are the iron blue which can be imitated by a No. 18 Iron Blue; the olive dun, represented by a Greenwell's Glory and, for a nymph, the Pheasant Tail.

The blue winged olive is an exciting fly which, when there is a fall of spent fly, is represented by the Sherry Spinner. When

Dace and chub flies. Left to right: Pheasant Tail Nymph, Shrimp, Gold Head, Green Shrimp, Grayling Bug, Sedge, Little Sedge, Pheasant Tail, Caperer, Iron Blue, Wickham's Fancy, Tupp's, Greenwell's Glory, Lunn's Particular, Sherry Spinner, Grey Wulff, BWO, Daddy-Long-Legs.

this egg-depositing fall occurs the air is filled with little orange sparks as the flies dance in mating flight and fall spent upon the water. Tupp's Indispensible, Kite's Imperial, and my favourite fancy fly the Red Tag on a No. 16 hook are all successful. If a rise is not taking place, fish the water with the Red Tag and you will not be disappointed.

PIKE ON THE FLY

Pike will take a wet fly below the surface when it is worked to represent a small fish. The flies should be tied on very large double or treble hooks and be a gaudy mixture of bright features, often the whole being the same size as some Devon minnows. I have two flies which are at least one hundred years old and have avoided the ravages of the moth which was, perhaps, frightened away!

I have never tried the method, the thought of a large fly whistling over my head is no encouragement, and I wish to retain my hat and ears. A friend of my co-author, Charles, regularly catches pike on the fly in Devon on a salmon rod.

Fly reel and fly

PART TWO

GAME FISHING

INTRODUCTION

Trout fishing is more readily available than salmon and sea trout fishing, particularly if you live in East Anglia or the Home Counties. I therefore suggest that a game fishing beginner starts by learning to fish for trout, not because they are easy to catch, but because trout waters are widely spread, often inexpensive and ability may be acquired and experience gained on them.

I teach game fishing and am a founder member of The Register of Experienced Fly Fishing Instructors, Schools and Guides (REFFIS). My suggestion to the beginner is to take two consecutive days of trout fly-fishing instruction from one of our instructor members, the address of The Hon. Secretary is on page 141.

The first day of instruction should be spent on a lake stocked with rainbow trout and the second on a river fishing for wild brown trout. During these two days you would be taught to cast, which cannot be learned from a book without wasting time and acquiring faults. You would learn: basic tackle needs; how to tie fishermen's knots; the difference between fishing with wet flies and lures, and imitative dry flies and nymphs. Entomology would also be touched upon. Hopefully, and usually, trout will be caught, played and netted.

You would come to accept that there is a fascinating world opening before you which the instructor has made accessible. There is so much to learn and so many experiences to analyse that the opportunity to fish regularly is essential. Only then will different conditions of water, stages in the life-cycles of insects, weather and fish behaviour be met and provide food for thought. With thought will come correct decisions on the methods to be employed to catch fish under varied conditions.

There is a brigade of anglers who know only one style of fishing – casting a lure out as far as possible on a lake and pulling it back again, and again! Sometimes they catch a trout, perhaps many trout, but sometimes nothing at all when other anglers are catching fish. This is because, unknowingly, they are waiting for conditions to suit their one method. They need to learn to fish a dry fly, a wet fly and a nymph. The decision about which method to use should be based on observation and an understanding of the behaviour of the trout which may, or may not, be visible.

Salmon fishing, and casting with a double-handed rod, is an easily acquired skill. Catching salmon depends upon this ability and, particularly, knowing the lies in a river and being there in the right water and weather conditions at the right period of the season. Salmon fishing skills are more readily gained than trout skills; knowledge of where to place the fly and when is the study of a lifetime for each water.

Sea trout fishing at night is a simple and fascinating sport which depends upon good casting to avoid tangles in the fly and leader. Do not go sea trout fishing in the dark until you are able to handle your tackle competently by day when fishing for trout.

Many pupils remark that there is much more to learn than they had imagined. I have done my best to describe and illustrate only the essentials.

Charles Bingham

CHAPTER 18

TROUT FISHING IN STILL-WATERS

The fish, lakes and reservoirs

Anglers are mainly concerned with two types of trout in the British Isles: the native brown trout and the rainbow trout which was originally imported from America. The brown trout spawns naturally in rivers and up the feeder streams of lochs.

The rivers to the west of the British Isles commonly fall steeply from high ground to the sea, the fast flow keeping the gravel bed of the feeder tributaries free of silt. Such beds are suitable for the cutting of redds in which hen fish deposit their eggs, resulting in numerous small trout. The rivers are often acidic, producing a poor supply of trout food. Thus, there prevails the situation of numerous small trout which rarely exceed $^1/_2$lb in weight because there is little food for so many to eat.

The slower-flowing alkaline chalk-streams of the south of England, and some limestone rivers elsewhere, produce more food which results in larger trout. These rivers tend to deposit

Rainbow trout

silt on the spawning redds due to the ploughing of agricultural land close to the water's edge, and rain then washing mud into the river. Trout grow larger in these waters but attention has to be paid to cleaning the spawning areas to prevent silt from covering trout eggs which will then rot. This cleaning can be carried out by river keepers forking-over the river-bed, or by applying high-pressure water jets from a pump to loosen the bed in autumn prior to spawning in the winter.

Rainbow trout are mainly produced in fish farms fed by river water, or from springs in the chalk valleys. They breed in the wild in very few rivers, notable amongst these is the Derbyshire Wye. Brown trout are also raised in hatcheries to stock rivers and still-waters. This is because the natural production of trout and trout food may not create sufficient numbers of fish of suitable weight to match the fishing pressure of anglers.

The stocking of large hatchery trout takes place mainly in the slower-flowing chalk rivers and still-waters. It is unwise to stock 1lb and 2lb trout into a West Country or Scottish acid spate river. In such cases trout will lose weight due to lack of food, and in high water following heavy rainfall may travel out of the stretch in which they were intended to be caught.

The life history of the trout

In autumn the ovaries of hen brown trout enlarge until they fill the major part of the body cavity. Similarly, the testes of male brown trout fill with white sperm containing milt. If caught such fish should be returned to the river to spawn. In any case, they would not be worth eating, the flesh being soft and pale at that time of year.

Spawning takes place between November and January. With her tail the hen digs a redd, which is a trough in the gravel of the river-bed. The redd is 3–4in in depth and about 1ft long for a trout of roughly 1lb in weight. It is usually cut where a fast water flow clears the river-bed of silt, often in the shallow tail of a pool where the flow is compressed.

Hen and cock lie alongside each other in the redd, depress their vents into the trough and release eggs and milt through the urino-genital pore which is behind the anus. One sperm nucleus enters the egg through the micropyle, a tiny pore in the egg membrane. Fertilisation then takes place and the pore closes.

Trout ova are heavier than water and thus sink to the bottom of the redd where the movement of the current and, perhaps, the cutting of upstream redds covers them with gravel and small stones. If the gravel is clean, water will percolate down through the redd, supplying the ova with oxygen. If the redd becomes silted, the flow will cease and the eggs will rot.

Brown trout

If the river water is at a temperature in mid-winter of 40–42°F (4.4–5.6°C) the eggs will hatch after about 80 days, soon after becoming 'eyed'. An alevin then emerges with a sac of yolk beneath its chin, which is absorbed over a period of about three weeks. The alevin then swims up through the gravel to open water, faces head to the current, and becomes known as a fry.

Both brown and rainbow trout are also produced in hatcheries. The ripe hen is held, tail down, over a bucket or bowl. The operator's thumb is then run down the belly of the fish to strip the eggs from the naturally ruptured ovaries in the hen's body. The cock is treated similarly. Ova and milt are then stirred by hand or with a feather, and fertilisation takes place.

The fertilised eggs are then placed on trays over which water flows. Any eggs which are diseased become white in colour and are sucked out with a pipette and discarded. If the water rises from a chalk spring it will do so at a temperature of 50°F (10°C). Due to a higher temperature than winter river water, brown trout eggs will hatch in approximately 40 days, and rainbow trout after a slightly shorter period.

Growth then depends upon the availability of food which in turn is dependent upon the environment. A moorland brown trout may take two years to reach 4$\frac{1}{2}$in in length; a pellet-fed hatchery brown may reach 12in in two years, whilst a rainbow trout will grow more rapidly.

Rainbow trout are more likely to be stocked into a commercial fishery than brown trout because they cost less. This is due to the fact that, not only do they put on weight faster than brown trout, but are more efficient converters of food into flesh. Rainbows do not live as long as brown trout but, in a commercial fishery, this is of little concern as they may be caught within days or weeks of being stocked into the water.

Still-water fisheries

In the last 40 years the demand for trout fishing has increased. This is due to a number of reasons, amongst which are the higher disposable incomes of anglers, and increased holidays and leisure hours. Over the same period the mileage of fishable trout rivers has decreased due to water abstraction and increased acidity following afforestation of land adjoining many spawning streams. The water table in some areas of excessive borehole abstraction has sunk to the extent that streams and river headwaters have sunk into the earth to leave dry, barren watercourses. This loss of river, and certainly there has been no increase, has channelled the new fly-fishermen to be accommodated on still-waters, some recently created. Others, previously fishless, have been stocked with trout.

The stocked lake

These are often privately owned, run as commercial enterprises, and regularly stocked with trout. The fish are usually rainbows upwards of 1lb in weight, an average of 2lb being common. Trout may be introduced into the lake three or four times a season, monthly, weekly, or even daily, depending upon the fishing pressure. However frequently the owner may replenish the stock I wish this could be arranged to take place unseen in the early morning. Anglers know the fishing is artificial, but seeing a dustbin full of trout tipped into a lake does not add a natural flavour to the scene. Those trout, used to a diet of fish pellets, soon educate themselves to the natural food available:

insects in various stages of their life-cycles, shrimp and so on. The small, heavily-stocked lake is the place for the beginner. Success is not assured but is likely. With success comes confidence and the knowledge·that the angler is applying a correct method.

Some commercial lakes are fished solely by season rods, but this is unusual. The owner of a fishery wishes to sell (i.e. have caught) as many trout as possible, provided the angler is correctly charged. This leads to satisfied fishermen, greater ticket sales and income.

Tickets are usually available for a day, half-day, evening, or a set number of hours. Catches will be limited to a brace, or two or three brace, within the cost of the ticket purchased. Some fisheries charge a small fee to cover entrance and then the angler pays a price per pound in weight of trout caught. Where stocked with non-breeding rainbow trout, small commercial fisheries are often open throughout the year. It is unusual for there to be a close season for rainbows although there may be a close season in rivers to coincide with that for wild brown trout.

These fisheries are rarely scenes of solitude, but they are confidence boosters for those making a start. Husbands can also take home trout to their wives to prove where they have spent the day!

Rainbow trout for stocking into a lake.

Reservoirs and lochs

Water supply reservoirs, the natural lakes of Wales and the lochs of Scotland may vary in size from a few acres to over 3000 acres. Some rely solely on the wild brown trout therein, others may be stocked with brown trout fingerlings in the hope that they will grow. Some are regularly stocked with substantial fish. Many are acidic, populated with large numbers of thin, small trout and a few large cannibals, and will never be generous to anglers; others are alkaline and yield wild brown trout of 1lb and above in weight.

In general, the majority of reservoirs are not the place for the beginner because there are fewer fish per acre and long distance casting may be required. Failure to catch fish will cause an inexperienced angler to conclude that he is fishing incorrectly, which may not be the case. Reasons for failure are many, but include natural factors: the air may be colder than the water, the water too warm, the sky too bright and dominated by white puffy clouds. You cannot compel trout to take your fly.

It takes many visits to 'learn' a large reservoir. Knowledge of hot spots must be acquired such as underwater banks and old walls defining fields now flooded, where feeder streams enter, and the corner of a dam into which the prevailing wind blows insects and pushes warm surface water. There is much to learn, and whilst 1000 acres may stretch dauntingly before your eyes, many such waters are in beautiful surroundings and offer

solitude to the angler and wildlife.

Tickets to fish are usually available on a cash basis from self-service kiosks. The angler is required to return to them at the end of the day to fill in a catch return card. Boats are often available if booked in advance, but the novice would be well advised to fish from the bank without the extra worry of handling a boat.

Fly-fishing tackle

When fishing a lake or reservoir from the bank it is an advantage to be able to cast a reasonable distance, perhaps 25yd. This is because trout, with instincts of self preservation, seldom rise close to the bank on which a prominent active angler is stationed. The angler cannot enjoy a close relationship with the trout because he cannot walk out upon the water.

Trout in still-waters have to move about whilst seeking food. There may be many trout, and the farther you can cast the greater the area covered by the fly. In so doing the fly may be placed close to a trout. River fishing presents a different situation – you do not need to cast a long way as most trout are caught at a range of not more 15yd. This is because you can creep along the bank towards the fish you have seen rising, which is unlikely to move because the river is bringing food to it.

Rods and fly lines

Unlike spinning, where the weight of the spinning bait pulls a lightweight monofilament line off the reel, in fly-fishing it is the weight of the fly line which carries out an almost weightless fly. The fly line must therefore have an appreciable weight which, coupled with the speed with which it moves through the air, produces a momentum sufficient to transport itself, the nylon leader and the fly to the target. The fly rod must be capable of propelling the fly line which if too heavy for the rod will overload and possibly damage it. If it is too light it will not utilise the power of the rod.

Fly line weights are therefore categorised by manufacturers who classify according to the AFTM Scale (Association of Fishing Tackle Manufacturers). Scale categories are based upon the weight of the first 30ft of the fly line, excluding the level expendable tip which is usually about 6in in length. Watch an angler false casting a fly line, if he is an average performer he will have about 30ft of the fly line outside the rod tip and then, possibly, shoot extra line on the final presentation throw. The rod must therefore be capable of lifting the weight of the 30ft of line and be neither over nor under loaded. The Scale in practical terms for trout fishing is in the range AFTM No. 4 (light) to AFTM No. 8 (heavy). An 8ft rod for use in a small stream might be rated No. 5/6, whilst a 9ft 3in rod for a reservoir is likely to be rated AFTM No. 7/8.

Manufacturers design rods to fulfil certain purposes. For example a 9ft delicate *all-through* action river rod, intended to handle a 3-lb nylon leader point without snapping the nylon when a fish takes, may be rated AFTM No. 6. A 9ft stiff *tip* action rod used for distance casting may be classified AFTM

No. 7/8 but would be too powerful to handle 3-lb nylon and a finely hooked dry fly, as it may cause the nylon to snap or the hook to bend open. Such a stiff No. 7/8 rod would have been designed for use with wet flies and lures on stronger hooks attached to leaders of a greater breaking strain. Let us now choose suitable equipment for trout fishing on still-waters.

RODS

Fly rods are made from split cane, fibreglass, carbon fibre and boron. A split cane rod is heavy when compared with modern materials. An 8ft or 8ft 6in split cane rod could be chosen for river dry fly work, but above this length the rod will be tiring to use in comparison with the other materials available. Do not start your fishing career with grandfather's warped soft, heavy split cane all-purpose trout rod which has been stored in a cupboard since the 1930s. It will be soft in action and ineffective.

Fibreglass is inexpensive, light and maintenance-free. It is ideal other than in one respect, the tube is fatter than carbon fibre and thus has greater wind resistance. It is therefore more tiring to cast against the wind.

Carbon fibre is the best choice and almost all fly rods are made of this material. It is light, thin in the tube, maintenance-free and is no longer available only to those without an overdraft. Boron is unnecessarily light in weight and costly for the beginner. Let your choice be carbon fibre.

When I write that carbon fibre rods are maintenance-free, there are two matters which repay attention. Inspect the silk wrappings to the line guides annually and varnish these if necessary; rub the spigot(s) with a candle from time to time, the wax prevents wear in the joint and stops it coming undone. If two sections of a rod cannot be pulled apart, immerse the joint in cold water for a couple of minutes – this usually loosens it.

Ideally, two rods are needed on still-water, and both could be 9ft in length. One could be a stiff *tip* action rod, rated at AFTM No. 7/8 and used for wet flies and lures on leaders tapered to about 6-lb; the other could be a more bendy rod with an *all-through* action, rated at AFTM No. 6 for lightly hooked dry flies on a 3-lb or 4-lb knotless tapered leader. The all-through action rod will bend and accommodate the stress of a sudden strong pull when the fly is taken by a heavy trout.

If you can only afford one rod, choose the No. 6 which will deal with all situations, including river fishing, other than casting readily into the wind or as far as the tip action rod.

It is almost impossible to cast far against the wind with an 8ft 6in AFTM No. 5/6 all-through action rod. This is because the rod (being bendy) throws a lightweight, wide, wind resistant loop of line slowly, and thus with little momentum, into the wind which blows it back. On the other hand the 9ft tip action AFTM No. 7/8 rod throws a narrow looped, fast-moving heavier line which cuts into the wind to achieve the required distance.

If fishing from a boat the angler should be sitting down whilst using a longer rod than would be used for casting from the bank. The rod should be between 10–11ft in length and rated AFTM No. 6. The all-through action is suited to this situation, as the majority of casts will be made downwind. The length also allows a dropper and a bob fly to be trickled across the surface as the line/leader is retrieved towards the boat.

FLY LINES

To achieve momentum a fly line must have a diameter which, coupled with its density, will provide weight. A line may have a thickness roughly the same as the lead in a pencil. If such a thickness were uniform throughout its length, and then the end was attached to a 4-lb length of nylon 0.007in in diameter (the leader), which you hope the trout will be unable to discern, the step down in diameter at the line/leader junction will be great. Such a disparity in diameters will cause the nylon to fall back upon the line when cast, instead of unrolling ahead of the end of the line. To overcome this problem the fly line is tapered to a thin point where it joins the leader; the leader is also tapered from about 0.020in at the looped butt to the point of 0.006in (3-lb nylon) or 0.009in (6-lb nylon) or other diameter/strength.

Only the final 8–12ft of the line is tapered, at the extremity of which is a thin level tip of about 6in which is slowly shortened over the months as knots are tied or braided loops fitted. The remainder, known as the body, may be of varying thicknesses. These taperings are known as the profile of the line. There are three profiles which concern us: double taper, weight forward and shooting head.

DOUBLE TAPER

Fly lines for trout fishing are usually 30yd in length. The profile may be as follows: 6in level point, 8ft taper, 73ft body, 8ft taper and 6in level tip – a total of 30yd. When one end is worn the line may be reversed and the other end brought into use, doubling the life of the fly line. This is the most common line in use on rivers where long distance casting is not required. It is suited to overhead and roll casts but is not the best line for casting a long way on a lake.

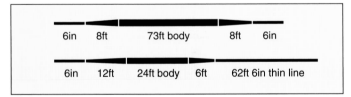

Fly line profiles
Top: Double taper line. Total length 30yd. Bottom: Weight forward line. Total length 35yd.

WEIGHT FORWARD

This is the best line for the reservoir angler who requires a long cast. The profile may be: 6in level point, 12ft taper, 24ft body, 6ft reverse taper and $62\frac{1}{2}$ft of thin running line to be shot forward through the rod line guides.

If the angler is false casting 10yd of line outside the rod tip he may need extra distance to reach the trout – this is achieved by *shooting* line forward through the line guides. The line being shot is pulled out at the final moment of the casting delivery throw, by the forward momentum of the line outside the rod tip. It follows that the lighter and thinner the line to be shot, the greater the length which will be drawn forward to extend the cast. This kind of line cannot be reversed.

SHOOTING HEAD

To achieve the greatest distance, cut 10yd from either end of a double-tapered line and join this by a needle knot to 25-lb monofilament backing. The dressed 10yd of the double taper is false cast at speed outside the rod tip. When released and projected, it pulls out several yards of monofilament which have been placed close to the angler's feet in coils on the ground. Many yards of monofilament, being thin, smooth and almost weightless, will follow the dressed line out over the water. I am not keen on shooting heads, finding that the coils of nylon tangle and catch under my boots or on twigs or brambles.

In my view the best lines for still-water are: double taper for the dry fly and weight forward for the distance casting of wet flies and lures.

When purchasing these lines make sure that the surfaces are smooth by running them through your fingers; a rough surfaced line will not shoot readily through the line guides. Lines are available in many colours: white, red, green, orange and blue. A white line flashes in the sky. My choice is green, but I have seen fish caught on all of these colours.

BACKING

The spool of a fly reel should be almost filled with line, thus enabling each turn of the handle to recover as much line as possible. To fill the spool, 25-lb monofilament or braided backing is attached to the rear end of the fly line. Monofilament is joined by a needle knot; braided backing by the Albright knot or a whipping. To ascertain the length of backing required (usually about 75yd for trout reels), wind the fly line on to the spool followed by the backing to the required capacity. Then reverse the whole.

FLY LINE DENSITIES

If a fly line has a density that is less than water it will float. It will not float better if it is greased, and such a dressing may cause the coating of the line to crack, let in water and cause the line to sink. The line has a braided core, often of Dacron, covered by a plastic coating containing microscopic air bubbles which make it lighter than water. The line should be kept clean – if dirty it will not be buoyant. Fly lines can be cleaned by drawing them through a cloth soaked in warm water.

If a fly line is heavier than water it will sink. Whether it sinks quickly or slowly depends upon the extent to which its density is greater than water. We thus have fast and slow-sinking lines to fulfil certain requirements yet to be explained. In addition there are lines of the same density as water which fish in the surface film and are termed *neutral*.

Sink-tip lines have a body which floats whilst the tapered end sinks. As the sections of such a line are of different colours, it is easy to know how much line is beneath the surface when retrieving the line and about to lift into the back cast. If the line is retrieved until the colour change enters the rod tip, the angler knows the sunk part is not too long to be lifted out by the rod. In contrast it is hard for a beginner to judge how much of a fully sinking line remains submerged on the retrieve. I suggest that a beginner to still-water fishing purchase a floating line and a sink-tip – the sink-tip line bought to go on the No. 7/8 and the floater on the No. 6 rod.

Lines are identified in the shop as follows:

- DT8S – Double-tapered AFTM No. 8 sinking line, with sinking rate described
- DT8F/S – Double-tapered AFTM No. 8 sink-tip line
- DT6F – Double-tapered AFTM No. 6 floating line
- WF7F – Weight forward AFTM No. 7 floating line

Reels

At the time of writing reliable trout fly reels may be purchased in the price range £17.50 to £200. The cheaper price will buy you the LEEDA Rimfly which has been on the market for so many years that its trustworthiness is beyond doubt. It is sold with only one spool, but spare spools are available.

The next step up in quality and price are the LEEDA Dragonfly Concept Disc which comes with two spools and the LEEDA LC range which is supplied with one spare spool. Both of these reels are made of carbon fibre and are light in weight. All three, and other models, are manufactured by British Fly Reels Ltd of Falmouth in Cornwall, and in sizes of different capacity to accept lines throughout the AFTM Scale. The House of Hardy make a range of reels of superb quality in the price range £77 to just over £200.

The beginner must decide how much he wishes to spend, but if a reel is purchased which has been made by either of the above manufacturers he will obtain a reliable product. My own trout reels are:

- LEEDA Dragonfly 100 – for AFTM No. 7 and No. 8 lines
- Hardy Marquis No. 7 – for AFTM No. 6 lines

You may notice that I use a Hardy No. 7 reel for No. 6 lines. When purchasing a reel choose one that is one rating higher in the spool than the line for which it is intended, i.e. a No. 8 reel for a No. 7 line. (This is particularly important where a floating line is concerned, as it is more bulky than a sinker.) This will enable extra backing to be fitted and the spool, being of greater diameter, will recover more line for each turn of the handle.

It is not advisable for your first reel to be a multiplier which, if splashed by grit when placed on the ground in a rainstorm, may become jammed. In this situation there may be difficulty in taking it apart to wash out the grit – a simple operation with a straightforward centre pin reel.

The chosen reel should have an adjustable drag, and an exposed rim to which a finger may be applied to put additional pressure on a running fish. The drag should be set to be light when fishing a fine leader and dry fly, but a little more severe for wet flies on stronger nylon.

Spare spools are always available for reels. It is thus possible to have one reel and two spools to take floating and sink-tip lines. Don't fall for this economy. If you drop and damage the reel you have to cease fishing – buy two identical reels between which spools may be moved.

Leaders

The length of a leader, which joins the fly line to the fly, is at the discretion of the angler, but 9ft is a common length. If a longer leader is chosen it will be more difficult to cast, particularly against the wind. Manufactured knotless tapered leaders are best for dry-fly fishing. Inexpensive home-made leaders may be constructed and tapered by knotting together lengths of nylon of different breaking strains, and thus diameters.

My choice for sunk line wet-fly fishing is:

- 2ft of 20-lb BS (breaking strain) nylon
- 2ft of 15-lb BS nylon
- 2ft of 10-lb BS nylon
- 3ft of 6-lb BS nylon

For the floating line and clear water a finer point of 4-lb nylon is advisable, particularly for small flies such as those on size 14 hooks:

- 2ft of 20-lb BS nylon
- 2ft of 15-lb BS nylon
- 2ft of 8-lb BS nylon
- 3ft of 4-lb BS nylon

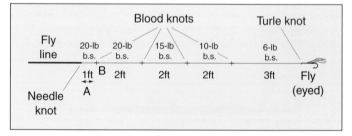

Home-made leader for still-water wet fly and lure trout fishing. Section A is permanently inserted into the fly line by a needle knot, but will have to be replaced from time to time when it becomes short due to leader replacement. The leader is replaced by cutting at point B. If the fly line terminates in a braided loop connector, a blood bight loop should be tied at the end of the leader at point B.

At the butt of the leader should be a blood bight loop. The sections are knotted together by water knots or blood knots, provided the nylons are not too dissimilar in diameters. Thus, 15-lb nylon may be joined to 8-lb nylon, but it would be unwise to join 15-lb to 4-lb, or 20-lb to 8-lb. The eyed fly should be tied to the point by a Turle knot. The leader is then joined loop-to-loop to the braided loop on the end of the fly line.

I advise the beginner to have only one fly on his leader. As casting expertise develops he may wish to fish an additional fly, which is called a *dropper*. With experience two additional flies can be used in which case the fly closest to the fly line is known as the *bob* fly, the fly on the leader extremity is called the *point* fly, and the one between is known as the *first dropper*. Droppers can be constructed at the junctions of two sections of the leader by tying a water or blood knot, and leaving one of the joined ends in a 6in overlength to which the fly is tied, the other end being cut close to the knot.

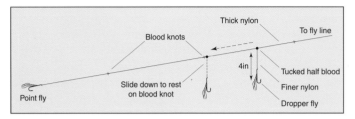

Dropper attachment.

Nylon near the butt of a sectional tapered trout leader is usually too thick for a blood knot, joining two sections, to make a dropper by leaving one end of the knot long whilst clipping off the other. Instead, take a length of finer nylon, usually of about 8lb, tie a tucked half blood against the leader just above the chosen position and slide it down against the blood knot.

In recent years 5ft tapered braided leaders have become fashionable. To the thin end the angler ties a 4ft tippet or point of thin monofilament of the chosen breaking strain. Braided leaders can be made to float, sink slowly or quickly, and some are of neutral density. The sinking types are useful when fished off a floating fly line as they keep the fly below the surface to the required depth, but the depth will not be great.

Braided leaders usually have a loop at both ends, one for attachment to the braided loop at the end of the fly line, and the other looped to the blood bight loop which you have tied at the end of the tippet. Alternatively, the tippet may be joined to the braided leader by a water knot if neither have loops at their ends, but this will gradually shorten the braid if repeated as tippets are replaced.

DRY FLY LEADERS

A leader used for dry-fly fishing rests on the surface of the water where it is particularly visible to fish. For this reason it is sensible to purchase knotless tapered leaders, because blood or water knots joining nylon sections of a home-made leader are clearly visible to trout. I use LEEDA Profil knotless tapered 9ft leaders in the following classifications:

Number	Tip diameter (in)	Breaking strain	Loop colour
6X	0.005	2lb	Natural
5X	0.006	3lb	Green
4X	0.007	4lb	Yellow
3X	0.008	5lb	Blue
2X	0.009	6lb	Lilac

The 'X' is an old-fashioned method of classifying the strength of gut casts (the noun *cast* being an out-of-date name for a leader). It is better to consider your requirement in pounds breaking strain.

When fishing in summer it is exciting to see trout taking midges as they hatch at the surface of a lake. These fish may be caught on a No. 18 Black Gnat on a 3-lb leader; sedge imitations on a No. 14 hook matched by a 4-lb point, and a No. 10 mayfly on a 5-lb point. Always take into consideration the size of fish and the presence of weed when deciding on leader strength. The chosen leader is always a compromise. If you tie a 3-lb point to a No. 16 hooked fly, a heavy trout may be deceived but is then lost through breakage in a weed-bed. So, you may choose a 4-lb point, but the trout takes a look and says to itself 'Not on your life' and swims away. When removed from their individual packages LEEDA Profil leaders may be identified, as listed in the table, by the colour of the butt loop.

Trout net on Hang-All Belt Loop. The priest is in a pocket of the trousers, secured by a cord around the neck.

Nets

The net should have a rigid metal bowframe. If it has two 'Y'-shaped arms joined by a cord, the cord may sag and a fish balanced halfway into the net may slide back into the water. A 20in wide net hinged where it joins a telescopic handle is a good choice for still-water. If the net has a 30in handle with a 20in or 22in bowframe it will also be suitable for night sea trout river fishing, the handle acting as a short wading probe. If the hinge is grasped as you venture out in the dark into the river, and the water reaches to your hand, you will know the river is about to flow into the tops of your thigh boots!

For river fishing a smaller net with a shorter handle is convenient. My choice is the Hardy Favourite Trout Fisher's net. The bowframe is $13^{1}/_{2}$in by 19in wide and the telescopic handle is 20in or 34in when extended.

Nets can be suspended from the trouser belt by a 'Hang-All Belt Loop' obtainable from The Orvis Co.

Fly boxes

Wet flies and lures can be carried in boxes equipped with clips, or lined with dense foam into which the hooks are pressed. These boxes should not be used for dry flies as the hackles will be squashed flat on one side. Dry flies should be placed in compartment boxes such as those manufactured by Richard Wheatley Ltd. My Wheatley box has ten compartments with spring-loaded flip-up lids. It was given to me in 1947!

Floatants

To make dry flies float dress them with Supafloat or Gink. To make the 6ft of leader closest to the fly line float, dress with solid Mucilin. To make a leader sink wipe it with Mucilin Quick Sink.

To make my wet fly leaders sink I wipe them with a damp 6in square of cloth sprinkled with Fuller's Earth (from the chemist) and a few drops of dish-wash liquid. The cloth is stored in a 35mm film cassette.

Tippet spools

My home-made leaders are made from Maxima Chameleon. To replace tippets, carry 50m spools of 4, 6 and 8-lb nylon.

Additional equipment

My priest is a 6in length of $^{1}/_{2}$in metal pipe carried in my trouser pocket. This has a split ring at one end to which is attached a cord which is placed around my neck. Expensive priests are available from tackle shops – my daughter uses an 8in metal gate latch.

Also thus suspended on cords are a Swiss Army knife for leader repairs and a pair of artery forceps to remove hooks from the mouths of trout. These cords or ribbons prevent the items falling into the river.

Still-water flies

There are two distinct branches of still-water trout fishing: imitating natural insects at some stages of their life-cycles; and

Artery forceps are useful for unhooking trout, particularly if the hook is deep inside the throat. This should be done underwater if the fish is to be returned.

attracting fish to non-imitative wet flies and lures through hunger, curiosity or aggression. Rainbow trout fishing takes place throughout the year in many still-waters. In the cold months of November to March insect activity is at a minimum, angling methods being largely confined to fishing sub-surface wet flies and lures. This sub-surface approach also continues throughout the warm months of April to October, and is then supplemented by dry-fly fishing and the use of imitative nymphs when natural flies are seen to hatch. These hatches may be of water-bred insects and take place at the water surface, or of land-bred insects which are then, by chance, blown or fall upon the water.

A stiff bent grass thrust down the throat of a dead trout, twisted and withdrawn, will bring out items of the trout's diet for identification.

Fly dressing materials and hooks

Dry fly hooks must be of fine wire and light, or the hook will sink the fly. They must also be of sizes to match the natural insect being imitated. The smallest hook I use is No. 18 on the Redditch Scale for dry flies representing midges and the smallest olives. No. 14 is suitable for medium-sized olives, No. 12 for large sedges and No. 10 for mayflies. Wet flies are commonly available on slightly larger hooks of heavier gauge wire in size No. 14, increasing to the large No. 8 for some lures and for the longest attractors if they are long-shanked hooks.

Dry fly hooks usually have upturned eyes, whilst wet flies and lures are downturned. As far as I am aware there is no reason for this arrangement, which can be reversed without disadvantage or gain. The hook wire may be round in cross-section, or flattened (forged) for increased resistance to bending open.

Hooks may be made without barbs (barbless) for use when fish are to be returned to the water. If flies with such hooks are obligatory on a water, and are unavailable, the barb can be flattened by squeezing with a pair of snipe-nose pliers.

Dry flies must float. The hackles are thus tyed from the non-fluffy neck feathers (cape) of a cockerel which are not water absorbent; they are also dressed of deer hair. The flies may be tied with wings and hackles (winged) or without wings (hackled). Wet flies are dressed from the soft water-absorbent hackles of a hen and may have wings sloping back along the body (winged), or without wings (hackled).

Imitating insects (dry fly and nymph)

There are four orders of insects of importance to river and still-water anglers: Ephemeroptera, Trichoptera, Plecoptera and Diptera. Trichoptera and Diptera are of marked importance to the lake angler, and all four to the river fly-fisher. In this section I shall describe Diptera and Trichoptera.

Diptera

These insects have two flat wings and no tails. Easily recognised members are the house flies and bluebottles which buzz in the windows of a greenhouse.

THE MIDGE

The midge life-cycle commences with an egg which hatches into a tiny red or green bloodworm on the lake bed. The worm pupates and the pupa swims to the water surface where it hangs, breathing through tiny white tubes which pierce the water skin. If you go to the leeward side of a lake on a warm day the tiny white heads, not much larger than the head of a pin, may be seen, together with the grey outline of the pupa body. This stage may be imitated by a black, green or amber nymph on a No. 18 hook commonly known as a *buzzer*.

The pupa hatches, dries its wings and, almost instantaneously, takes flight, leaving behind the grey pupal case. The aerial stage can be represented by a No. 18 Black Gnat. Midges hatch from April onwards throughout the season.

THE BLACK GNAT

These tiny, black land-bred species may be blown upon the water and consumed by trout. When this takes place, fish a dry No. 18 Black Gnat. They are present throughout the summer.

THE HAWTHORN

This is a land-based fly of late spring and early summer, the hatching weeks depending upon the altitude and the warmth of the season. The hawthorn is a substantial black fly with two long back legs which hang down as it rises and falls in flight on warm days.

If blown upon the water they sink into the surface film under the weight of the shiny black thorax. They are usually taken with appetite by trout, but if fish are apprehensive of the insect I have found that a hackled No. 18 Black Gnat is preferred to a No. 12 Hawthorn.

THE CRANE FLY

The land-based daddy-long-legs may be blown upon the water in August or September. The artificial, dressed with legs made from the fibres of a cock pheasant tail with knots for knee joints, is readily eaten by trout. Two natural flies impaled on a hook may be dapped upon the water if fished from a boat with a 17ft rod and a blow line.

Trichoptera

Commonly known as sedge or caddis flies, members of the order have two pairs of roof-shaped wings folded back over their bodies, the wings being covered with tiny hairs. They have two antennae and no tails.

The life-cycle follows the sequence of the butterfly and moth, except that it takes place mainly underwater: larvae in a caddis case constructed of tiny pieces of grit and vegetable matter. Inside the case the larva pupates into a fly which crawls, with its head just outside the case, or swims to the water surface. There, the fly hatches, mates, lays eggs and dies. About once a week, in summer, I kill a wild brown trout to examine the contents of its stomach. It is rare not to find a complete larva in its case amongst the contents. Sometimes, the trout has eaten so many cases that its belly feels crunchy when squeezed.

Three stages in the life-cycle may be imitated: the larva in its case, the emerger at the water surface and the fly.

THE CADDIS CASE

This may be imitated by a green body and brown head on a No. 8 or No. 10 long-shanked hook.

THE EMERGING FLY

At eclosion, when a caddis has swum up to the water surface and is struggling through the water skin, the fly and its wings are wet. At that stage it can be represented with success by a No. 12 Invicta wet fly. Some years ago in one season my pupils and I took about 320 trout of over 1lb. Of these fish about 160 fell to the Invicta fished wet off a floating fly line an inch or two below the water surface.

THE EMERGED FLY

It is possible to fill one's fly box with far too many artificial patterns. I now carry only one sedge pattern, a No. 14 winged Red Sedge. In imitating the four insect orders I rarely use winged artificials which can land upside-down. However, sedge wings bulk the silhouette of the fly when seen from below by a trout – I thus enlarge the outline of the Red Sedge with wings. The most prolific sedge hatches takes place in the late afternoon and until dusk from June until September.

DAMSELFLY NYMPHS (*ODONATA*)

Damselflies are commonly present on still-waters in the summer months. Imitations are usually confined to the nymphal stage on No. 8 or No. 10 long-shanked hooks. If a little weight is added to the nymph and it is fished slowly off a floating or slow-sinking fly line it will account for many trout.

PHEASANT TAIL NYMPH

This is an imitation of the nymphal stage of the insect order Ephemeroptera which will be fully described later in this chapter. It is a successful catcher of trout in summer when fished off a floating fly line on still-water. The retrieve should be slow and the hook size No. 12 or No. 14.

COCH-Y-BONDHU BEETLE (*PHYLLOPERTHA HORTICOLA*)

This tiny brown-winged, black-bodied beetle, common on the heather moors of Wales and the West Country, may be blown upon the water. Fish a dry pattern of the same name on a No. 16 hook. The beetle is also known as a June Bug and is blown off the north bank of Fernworthy reservoir on Dartmoor on to the water by a north wind.

There are, of course, a host of naturals which could be imitated. The beginner should concentrate on carrying a small selection of dry flies, each being of a different size. Size, quality of hackle, and delicate presentations are much more important than pattern.

FISH FRY

Trout eat their own fry and those of other fish. When chasing fry, large trout slash at speed through the shallows, breaking up the shoals of fishlets. Two artificials stand me in good stead. The white Baby Doll on a No. 10 hook stripped-in fast across the surface triggers trout to take at speed. An alternative which has brought me many fish is the No. 8 Appetizer fished slowly close to the lake bed. This lure is mainly white in colour, but the dark natural squirrel hair along the top of the fly resembles the dark-coloured back of a minnow or troutlet.

Non-imitative fishing (wet flies and lures)

Trout see in colour, as do sea trout and salmon. Most noticeable to them are the colours red, orange and yellow; the striped bodies of wet flies and lures also attract attention, the striping being provided by silver or gold tinsel ribbing. Black is seen in stark outline against the sky when viewed from below by a fish,

even at night. If I had to rely on two colours for all my game fly-fishing, orange and black would be selected.

The colour sensitivity of trout was ascertained in about 1960. This led to the dressing of lures which incorporated the newly acquired knowledge. Prior to this, the popularity of various wet fly patterns was based on their fish-catching qualities, but without the knowledge of why some were successful in attracting trout, whilst others failed. There is no difference between the terms *wet fly* and *lure*, other than the fact that the former term is of long-standing over many generations. The description *lure* mainly refers to flies, often large and gaudy, designed since the colour-discerning capacity of trout became known.

Traditional wet flies

PETER ROSS

A study of this fly, invented at the end of the 19th Century by Peter Ross of Killin, Perthshire, reveals the reasons for its success which extends back over many decades. The fly incorporates silver stripes of ribbing tinsel over the red body, black throat hackle and a wing of the clearly striped flank feathers of a teal. The fly is also a great sea trout pattern.

BLACK PENNELL

The Black Pennell was produced by trial, but without scientific knowledge, by H. Cholmondly Pennell. The fly has a black body ribbed with fine silver tinsel and long black cock hackles.

MALLARD & CLARET

This is an excellent trout and sea trout fly on both river and still-water. The body is claret in colour ribbed with gold tinsel, the hackle is red cock and the wing is of bronze mallard flank feathers.

DUNKELD

The noticeable feature of this salmon and trout fly is the jungle cock cheeks. This feather is striped black, white and yellow along its length.

THE INVICTA

A superb wet fly which both imitates a hatching sedge and takes account of the colour-discerning capacity of trout in the inclusion of a yellow seal's fur body ribbed with gold tinsel.

All the above should be selected in hook sizes No. 10 to No. 14. It will be noticed that all incorporate scientific colours, ribbing stripes, or both.

Lures

As stated previously, lures are large wet flies, mainly of recent creation; hook sizes tending to be long-shanked No. 8s and No. 10s. Their main use is in the cold months of November to March in still-waters when insect activity is at a minimum.

Fished close to the bottom off sinking fly lines they account for many rainbow trout in the months when brown trout are out of season. As with successful wet fly patterns, the colours at the red end of the spectrum are effective. In addition, silver or gold ribbing to the lure body adds attraction.

THE SWEENEY TODD

This lure, the invention of master angler Richard Walker, was one of the first to hit water after the colour-discerning abilities of trout became known. It incorporates a black wing, a black body ribbed with silver tinsel and a red throat hackle. Hook sizes are usually long-shanked No. 8 or No. 10.

BLACK LURE

The wing of this lure is black, as is the body which is ribbed with oval silver tinsel. Fished off a sinking fly line, and on a No. 8 long-shanked hook, it takes trout close to the river-bed. It is also an excellent sea trout fly.

BLACK MUDDLER MINNOW

The bulky pea-sized spun natural bucktail head causes the lure to float if it is greased. Allowed to rest upon the water surface it will take trout in a flat calm. The body is of black floss silk ribbed with fine silver tinsel, and the wing is of squirrel tail dyed black. This lure also takes trout when fished just under the water surface in rough weather, and at varying depths.

WORM FLY

This lure is not an imitation of a worm. It consists of two flies dressed in tandem (one behind the other). Dressings of the two are identical (bronze peacock herl bodies and red cock or hen hackle), but the rear fly has a red tag of wool. I fish this lure slowly, close to the bottom of the lake or reservoir.

MONTANA NYMPH

This lure is not a nymph in the correct sense of the word. It is a gaudy lure striped in the manner of a green and black, orange and black, or yellow and black football jersey. It is usually weighted on a No. 10 hook. The Montana has a great reputation as a taker of rainbow trout.

The methods of fishing wet flies and lures will be considered on pages 90–93 of this chapter.

Dry-fly fishing on still-waters

Some anglers rely upon one method to catch stocked rainbow trout in lakes. Fishing a sinking line they cast out a lure, allow it to sink, then retrieve slowly or at speed. Although they may not appreciate the fact, they are waiting for a single set of weather and water conditions to materialise to match their single method. If this does not happen they are likely to remain fishless.

Yet, on some days the water surface is dimpled by the rises of trout taking midges as they hatch. If only they knew the supreme joy of seeing a trout rise to take their No. 18 Black Gnat on a knotless tapered 3-lb leader. If they had the knowledge to fish

dry fly, when trout are rising, they would not have to suffer giving a negative answer to their wives' question 'Any luck?' on returning home.

Correct tackle

The rod may be of any length between 8ft 6in and 10ft, rated AFTM No. 6 and thus of easy, all-through action. The line should be a double-tapered No. 6 floater, and the leader knotless tapered.

Before the leader strength, fly size and pattern may be chosen, it is necessary to observe the insect on which trout are feeding. It is not essential to identify the insect as a lesser-knobbly-kneed-greenfly; it is essential that the size of the insect is observed. Size is important. Thus, fish a No. 18 if fish are taking midges, a No. 12 or No. 14 for a sedge and a No. 10 or No. 12 for a daddy-long-legs or a mayfly.

An almost insoluble problem now arises, which point strength should be selected for the knotless tapered leader? In theory, a No. 18 fly should be knotted to a 3-lb point, a No. 14 to a 4-lb point and a No. 10 to a 5-lb point, or thereabouts. Thus, if midges are seen to be hatching and eaten, knot a No. 18 Black Gnat to a 5X (3-lb) leader. But then, you observe that three and four-pounders are present, weed-beds too, and a 5X leader will be broken. You therefore select a 4X (4-lb) leader. But, the water being clear, unruffled, and the sky bright, the trout cocks an eye at this thicker attachment, shakes its head, and swims away. You can only do your best in matching nylon strength to hook and fly size whilst bearing in mind the size of fish and the presence of obstructions.

If a fat mayfly is fished off a 3-lb point the leader will not 'turn over' and extend, or the fly may be 'cracked-off' in casting. If a No. 18 fly is fished off a 2X (6-lb) leader the fly will be static and lifeless at the end of this rope.

Attach the leader, loop-to-loop, to the 6in braided loop on the end of the fly line. The nylon point should then be passed through the eye of the fly from front to back and then the loop settled around the neck of the hook in a two-turn Turle – the meaning of this statement will be clear if the drawing of this knot is studied (see page 147). In this manner the fly always stays in line with the leader. The tucked half-blood should not be used, being free to move around the perimeter of the hook eye, it allows the fly to alight on the water on its head or at right-angles to the leader.

Now dip the fly in the Supafloat bottle, blow off any excess liquid to free the hackles, and allow to dry before use. Drying may be hastened by false casting the fly in the air. Then rub forefinger and thumb in solid Mucilin and grease a thin film on to the 2yd of leader closest to the fly line. The 1yd of nylon closest to the fly should be de-greased with Ledasink or another sink-mix preparation. This greasing and de-greasing will allow the nylon closest to the fly line to float and thus, on each back cast lift-off, the fly will not be dragged beneath the water and become sodden. The de-greasing will sink the nylon closest to the fly beneath the water surface where it will become almost invisible. All is now prepared.

Nymph fishing

If trout are rising, but the dry fly fails to tempt, try a nymph fished in the water surface film. Nymphing trout usually swim slowly, backs just breaching the water skin as they take midge nymphs hanging below the surface. A No. 16 Black Buzzer on a 5X leader is likely to bring success or, in rippled water, a No. 14 Pheasant Tail nymph on a 4X point. If changing from dry to nymph, the 1yd closest to the fly will already be de-greased, allowing the nymph to sink into the surface water film.

If fishing to rising trout from the lee bank with a dry fly, the angler may experience difficulty in casting out the wind-resistant, almost weightless, fly. In such a situation the nymph, being thin and a trifle heavier than a dry fly, may provide a solution.

Time of day and month of the year

This June, four rods fished a lake by wet flies and lures from 9.30 am to 11.00 am without success. Between 11.00 am and 1.30 pm trout fed on hatching midge and my pupil and I caught four fish on dry No. 18 hackled Black Gnats. The rise then ceased, but started again less intensely at 4.00 pm. The rods fishing wet flies were not successful.

Trout do not feed at the surface, and flies do not hatch, throughout the hours of daylight in each month of the year. In April, on a warm afternoon, there may be a midge hatch for an hour after midday. In May, again on a warm day, this hatch may extend from 11.00 am to 4.00 pm, taking place as warm air warms the water surface and before evening breezes cool the water. June may follow the pattern of May in the first half of the month, and then merge into the more difficult hours of hot July. In this mid-summer period the middle of the day is usually a fruitless time to fish – early to rise and late to bed is the way to success. The second half of August shows an improvement. September is an excellent month. The morning and late afternoon fly hatches merging to provide good fishing, often throughout the day until the chill of evening closes down activity. Brown trout become out of season at the end of September or in the early days of October. Rainbow trout may still be caught in the middle of the day on dry fly in October until cold weather brings this method to a standstill.

Weather

'When the wind is in the east, you'll catch the least'. The reasoning behind this line is twofold: the air is likely to be colder than the water and, being dry, it will cool the water surface by evaporation.

Good fishing is usually experienced on warm, damp, cloudy, drizzly days when the air is warmer than the water. Poor results are likely when the air is colder than the surface water, when the sky is clear and the sun bright, and when there are bright white puffy cumulus clouds in the sky in summer.

Warm southerly, south-westerly and westerly winds are usually beneficial. A gentle breeze ruffling the water surface disguises the nylon leader, moves the fly across the lake in the surface water drift and is helpful. Even rough warm winds are welcome if one fishes a fat buoyant deer hair sedge.

A heat-wave is unwelcome to the dry fly angler as trout will descend to the cool depths. Thunderstorms should cause you to cease fishing – there is danger in carrying your own personal lightning conductor, your carbon rod. When the storm ceases, trout sometimes feed voraciously.

Where to fish from the bank

The angler has to decide whether to fish with the wind at his back, in his face, or blowing along the bank. If imitating land-bred insects, such as the June bug and hawthorn, fish with the wind at your back, for the flies will be blown off the windward bank onto the water. The wind, being directly from your rear will make casting easy and, when the fly alights, keep it extended at the end of the leader.

For hatching sedges, midges and olives, all arriving from beneath the water, I look for a position where the wind blows parallel to the bank. The drifting surface water will sweep the fly in a curve at the leader extremity, covering an arc of the lake.

It is not necessary to cast a long distance with a dry fly. Casts are made infrequently, the water is thus less disturbed than when constantly casting and retrieving a wet fly, the angler remains still and trout approach close to the bank. The necessary use of an easy-action rod with fine hooks and nylon is thus not a disadvantage in its inability to cast a great distance.

Hooking trout on dry fly and nymph

To react to and hook a trout taking a floating fly requires concentration, good eyesight and good luck. I write 'react' in preference to 'strike'. Many substantial trout are lost to a violent strike on an unsuitable tip-action rod, due to the nylon snapping or the hook bending open. The first requirement is that the angler is able to see the fly at 15yd and watch it constantly. Secondly, with substantial trout, he must raise the rod tip after a pause of about one second to allow the trout to turn down. Thirdly, he must be lucky in that the trout is not facing in his direction and thus has the fly pulled out of its mouth. Even in this situation, a pause will find the fish pointing down and thus at an angle to the floating leader.

It is more difficult to hook a trout taking a floating fly on a still-water than on a river. In the latter situation the fish takes and turns upstream. The angler is downstream of the fish and is thus likely to pull the hook into the corner (scissors) of the fish's mouth.

If the eyesight of the angler is poor he may not see a rise at 15yd, or may react to a rise to a natural fly close to his artificial. Such an angler is well advised to fish a nymph on a leader of which the 2yd closest to the fly line are greased and thus visible on the water surface. If a fish takes the nymph the greased leader will turn down and curves in the floating fly line will straighten, prompting the angler to tighten by raising his rod. Even if he fails to notice these signs he will recognise the pull on the line which materialises in many cases, then raise his rod tip to hook the fish.

The rod should be kept high to act as a spring when playing a fish.

Playing and netting

Immediately after a trout is hooked the rod, having been raised, will be at an angle of about 45° to the water. Keep the rod point high, at or above this angle, to act as a spring to absorb the shocks of violent movement by the fish. Never lower the rod to point at the fish – nylon breakage is likely to result as there is no rod flexibility in this position. The rod tip should be kept high throughout the battle.

The next act is to deal with any loose coils of line resting on the ground, or floating on the water if the angler is wading. The coils will have accumulated during the gentle recovery of the line before the fish took the fly. If the fish swims away, the line may be allowed to slide out over the forefinger of the hand on the butt of the rod; if the fish approaches the angler the line may be stripped in. When movement of the fish stabilises, recover all loose line onto the reel. The fish is now played 'off the reel', the adjustable

When netting a trout the netsman should not be in front of the angler as the action may be obscured.

The angler should be to one side of the man with the net.

drag having been set according to the strength of the leader.

During the playing, line is recovered by turning the handle of the reel when the fish ceases to pull. However, the fingers are then removed from the reel to allow line to be released if the fish suddenly rushes away. If the fish attempts a sudden run whilst the reel is grasped, breakage may result as the reel cannot revolve to release line.

Some anglers, on hooking a fish, do not recover line onto the reel, but play the fish from the loose coils on the ground or floating on the water. This is a slack system. The angler may tread on and cut the line, or it may tangle in a twig or reed. It will certainly catch on something if the angler has to run along the bank to keep close to his quarry. As the fish tires, select a clear bank area from which to extend the net beneath the water surface. The net bag should be sunk by a small stone placed therein, or a sliver of lead or copper attached permanently to the bottom meshes. It is difficult to extend a floating net beneath a fish swimming under the surface.

Now, extend the net in one hand and trap the fly line under the forefinger of the hand on the rod, the tip of which should be moved to a position behind the angler's head. The trout may be drawn over the net which is then lifted, trapping the fish. The length of line outside the rod tip must not be too short or it will not be possible to draw the trout to the net. In practice, with a 9ft rod and 9ft leader, this means keeping about 1ft of fly line and the line/leader junction outside the top ring of the rod.

It is unwise at any stage to allow the line/leader braided loop to enter the rod tip, as a jam may result and the short leader does not allow any flexibility if the fish is violent. If netting a fish for someone else, do not stand behind the man playing the fish – you cannot see what is happening and raise the net at the right moment. Sit down to the right or left at a rod's length distance. You will then be able to see the state of play, and the angler is able to swing the rod over your head and draw the fish to your net.

With the fish on the bank, dispatch it at once with a blow by the priest to the back of the head. If the fish is to be released, grip it gently with wet hands through the meshes of the net and remove the hook with artery forceps. Return it to the water in the net which may be turned inside-out to effect release.

Wet fly and lure fishing on still-waters

By which method should a beginner commence his fly-fishing career? The answer must be by wet fly and lure on a still-water. The water is static, which is a simpler situation than casting a dry fly upstream. (Often, before the beginner takes in the situation, the line has been washed downstream by the current and is looped about his thigh boots, whilst the fly has departed in the direction of the sea.) Secondly, the hook is stronger, nylon tippets of 6-lb or 4-lb are used instead of the 3-lb point required for a No. 18 Black Gnat. The first two or three trout hooked are unlikely to be played with skill, but the stronger wet fly outfit copes with mistakes and rough handling and the shocked angler who grabs the revolving reel to prevent the trout

escaping. Thirdly, the wet fly may be fished throughout the year, there being no close season on many rainbow trout waters.

Tackle

A 9ft 3in tip-action AFTM No. 7 rod is ideal – it is the most efficient length for distance casting. Three weight-forward lines will be needed: a floater, sink-tip and a fast sinker. I use a green AirCel floater, a light green/dark green AirCel Supreme wet-tip and a dark green WetCel 2 fast sinker.

To learn how to cast, go to a qualified instructor – there is a list at the back of the book. I start a beginner with a floating fly line to which is attached 9ft of untapered 15-lb monofilament for use on grass. With this outfit he is taught the principles of overhead casting and how to extend (shoot) line. Then, a home-made leader tapered to 6-lb or 4-lb nylon is attached together with a fly, and a start is made on the lake. The floater is used whether or not this is the correct choice of line for the prevailing conditions. This is because the person being taught can see how much line he is casting and, on retrieving, judge correctly that the length of line remaining on the water is not too long to be lifted-off into the back cast.

When the floater has been mastered, try the sink-tip. Again, cast out and retrieve until the dark-coloured tip reaches the rod tip – this indicates that about 10ft of line is under the water. This 10ft is within the ability of rod and angler to lift out and up into the back cast. The WetCel 2 fast-sinking line should be left until last, the reason being that only experience gives the angler the ability to judge during retrieval the length of line remaining under the water. If too much is still submerged when the lift-off is started, the angler's rod will be in too high a position to continue into the back cast, a situation which may only be remedied by a prompt roll cast.

Depth of fishing and choice of line

Study the surface of the water on your arrival at the lake. If fish are rising, use the floating line to place the leader, after treating it with Ledasink, and the unweighted fly 2–3in beneath the water surface. If there is no evidence of surface activity, then trout are either not feeding, or feeding at a depth yet to be discovered. Try the sink-tip line and retrieve the wet fly in a slow recovery.

If this does not succeed, cast out a lure on the WetCel 2 line, allowing it to sink whilst counting to five, then retrieve at speed. Repeat this with counts of ten, fifteen and twenty. Sooner or later the lure will catch in sunken weed or the bottom. Now reduce the count by five and continue fishing. This suggestion assumes that a trout has not taken the lure at the five or ten count levels. If that happens, continue to fish allowing the line to sink to the successful level. It is, of course, necessary to retrieve at the same speed during these trials. If speed is reduced the line will sink to a lower level; if increased, the lure will fish closer to the surface.

The floating line is mainly used in late spring, summer and early autumn. These are the months of surface insect activity. This is also a period of weed growth in which a sinking line would take the fly to a depth where it may become entangled in vegetation rising from the lake bed.

Sink-tip and other slow and fast-sinking fly lines are the correct choice in the cold water (below 50°F or 10°C) of the period November to March/April. In this period insects rarely hatch and trout do not rise to take them off the surface.

There is an exception to this general advice – a heatwave. When the water surface reaches a temperature of about 70°F (21°C) trout descend to the cooler depths, only coming up in the early morning or late evening. They may be reached close to the bottom by sinking lines unless weed clogs the hook of the fly. If this happens, use the floating fly line, a 12ft leader and a weighted nymph of the Montana or Gold-head type. Cast out, allow the nymph to sink, and then recover. This floating line method will lift the nymph on each retrieve, allowing the return passage to take place over weed. It may be necessary to cast with the wind if an even longer leader is used, as it is difficult to cast a lure on a long leader against a stiff breeze.

Size of wet fly or lure

On many still-waters the management stipulate a maximum hook size. This does not limit the size of the fly, for the dressing can overlap the bend of the hook, but the rule should be discovered and obeyed.

The body temperature of trout is almost exactly the same as that of the water they inhabit. In cold winter water fish tend to be lethargic. This leads me to fish a large lure, perhaps a No. 10, to stir them up. This is also my choice if the water is cloudy after rain, and in a gale which creates great waves. In such rough conditions a little fly may not be noticed. When the water is warm, but not hot, trout are more active at the water surface – this is the time for a No. 14 wet fly such as an Invicta or Black and Peacock Spider.

Droppers and bob flies

It is unwise for a beginner to fish more than one fly until he is competent at handling his tackle and casting, or tangles will result. The fly on the end of the leader is known as the 'point' fly; one yard above this may be placed the 'first dropper'; and 2ft below the line/leader junction is the place for the top dropper which is also known as the 'bob' fly. This team of flies is cast out in the usual manner, preferably by a rod of about 10ft in length. On retrieval, when sufficiently close to the angler, the rod tip is raised to scuttle the bob across the surface of the water, followed by the first dropper as the bob lifts into the air. Each of these, in turn, creates a 'V' wake which is attractive to trout. A fish, interest aroused, may follow. If it rejects the wake flies it may then take the point fly as it passes by. The bob fly is usually of a bushy, palmered style of dressing, and may even be waterproofed with Supafloat if fished off a floating fly line.

Fish do not like to follow wet flies into the insecurity of shallow water. Thus, try this style of fishing where deep water comes close to the angler's bank. Rough waves are an advantage to dropper fishing, as trout come in close to the bank when the angler's outline is broken by the waves.

Droppers allow the angler to present two sizes of wet fly. Using a sink-tip line I often put a No. 10 lure on the point, and a No. 12 Black and Peacock Spider on the single dropper, but do not add a bob fly. The heavier fly should be on the point to extend the leader.

Droppers should be about 4in in length. If longer than this they tend to tangle on the leader. If using a home-made leader of:

- 2ft 20-lb BS (breaking strength) nylon
- 2ft 15-lb BS nylon
- 2ft 10-lb BS nylon
- 3ft 6-lb BS nylon

I would make my first dropper with a water knot at the 6-lb/10-lb junction by leaving the 6-lb end 4–5in long, cutting close the 10-lb end. To add the bob fly, tie a length of 6-lb nylon against the 20-lb section with a tucked half-blood, then slide this down to rest against the 20-lb/15-lb blood knot.

The point fly can be tied on by a two-turn Turle. The additional flies can only be attached by a tucked half blood, as there is insufficient nylon for the Turle to be constructed.

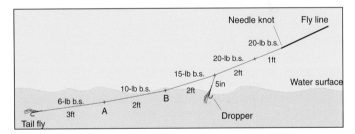

Fishing a dropper.
Before lifting off into the back cast, raise the rod top and scuttle the dropper (if at the top of a leader, it may be called a 'bob') across the water surface. A third fly could be added at points A or B.

Where to fish from the bank

For the beginner, correct site choice is limited by casting ability. When I arrive at a lake with someone who has yet to learn to cast, he is naturally taken to an area where the wind will be at his back. That is fine if land-bred insects are falling or being blown upon the water. However, it is not profitable if water-bred nymphs, duns, spinners and other morsels are being blown into the leeward shore. In such a situation the sport would be rewarding if the pupil could cast against the wind.

Where to make a start? Choose a bank where the wind is at his back or, if right-handed, blowing from left to right. If the angler is left-handed, place him on a bank where the wind blows from right to left. Such right/left situations will keep the fly permanently downwind of his head, minimising the risk of an accident. These suggestions are more to do with the early hours of learning to cast than the best position from which to catch fish.

For myself, I study the wind and the water depth. If trout

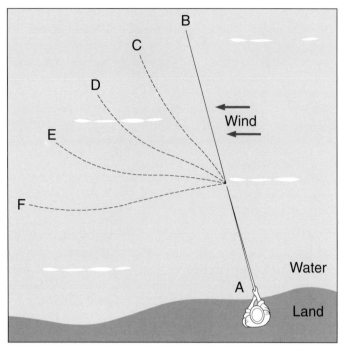

Drifting a dry fly.
Searching an area of water in a lake by dry fly with the help of a wind blowing parallel to the bank. The angler at point A casts a dry fly on a floating line to point B. He does not retrieve the line or move his feet. The wind pushes the surface layer of water and the floating line into a curve, moving the fly to points C, D, E and F. The angler may repeat this in the same place or move two or three steps downwind and cast again.

are rising, fish where there is this activity. In summer wet-fly fishing, go to the area into which the wind is blowing warm surface water and insect life. If competent, cast out against the wind from the leeward bank. For this a stiff-tip action rod is

needed, casting a No. 7 line in a fast-moving narrow loop to cut into the wind.

An area of rough water is always to be preferred when fishing a floating fly line and wet flies. The disturbed surface breaks up the flyline's silhouette, disguises the disturbance of casting and hides the angler. It also holds drowned insects! The dry fly outfit is unsuitable in this position as the softer rod throws a wide loop of line, slowly and without much momentum, and the weightless fly is blown back. If you wish to imitate naturals in this position use a nymph. This has a heavier hook and is streamlined in shape.

Now to address the depth. Most still-waters stocked with rainbow trout are man-made reservoirs or lakes. These generally have a dam at one end (the deep end), whilst the feeder stream will enter at the shallow end. In heatwave conditions, fish deep at the dam end, or else in the washed-out bed of a feeder stream where it enters the lake. In hot weather trout congregate where feeder streams run into a lake or reservoir.

If fishing droppers as wake flies, choose a rough deep area as trout do not like to follow at speed into shallow water. If fishing tiny nymphs very slowly, a shallow area at the end opposite to the dam may be rewarding – the infrequent casting allows trout to approach without being frightened.

It is difficult to generalise about where to fish from the bank. My advice, as with learning salmon lies in a river, is to visit one water many times until its secrets are revealed, rather than try a variety of still-waters. There are so many fruitful locations to be discovered: stream-beds, shallow underwater banks, submerged old stone walls, weed-beds and the directions of water drift according to the wind.

Catching trout on a reservoir . . .

. . . and cleaning the catch at once in hot weather.

Speed of fly retrieve and hooking trout

The smaller the wet fly, the slower the pace of retrieve should be when fished off a floating line. Thus, a No. 14 Invicta or Black Pennell of the same size ought to be drawn in by short pulls of 4–5in. The line should be trapped beneath the fore-finger of the hand on the rod butt as the retrieving hand moves forward to take the next grip on the line. In this 'grip-release-grip-release' of the butt hand forefinger, and 'pull-move forward-pull' of the retrieving hand, a taking trout will always meet the necessary resistance to set the hook. If you do not recover line in this manner, use a figure-of-eight recovery by palming the line in the hand.

If fishing a lure on a No. 10 hook, such as a Sweeney Todd, or Black Muddler, I increase the speed of retrieve if using a floating line. I am forced to recover at speed when using the fast-sinking WetCel 2 line, or the lure would become stuck on the bottom of the lake. In using such a line there is little one can do to increase success in hooking trout, they usually just attach themselves. Nevertheless, if the rod points straight down the line, rod tip at water level, tentative tweaks are sometimes felt. Continue without altering the rate of recovery; the trout may make up its mind, have another go, and take!

There is a tactic I use which has brought me many trout. This concerns the trout which follows almost to the bank and then flashes away. As the fly approaches the bank, swing the rod to one side to sweep the fly into a short path parallel to the shore. If, at the same time, the angler crouches low, a following fish may remain unsuspecting and take the fly.

When fishing a floating line, a boiling lift of the water by a trout does not indicate that the fly has been taken, only that a trout may have engulfed the fly or rejected the opportunity. The former will at once be apparent. In the latter case continue to draw in the line for the trout may try again. This is particularly true when fishing two or three flies – a boil at a dropper may result in the point fly being taken if the team continues to move at a steady speed.

Boat fishing

I advise the beginner not to fish from a boat until he has mastered bank fishing. The boat confers mobility and responsibility as safety has to be taken into account. More equipment is needed: a drogue to slow the drift, a buoy to mark a snagged anchor, life-jackets (which should be worn), cushions, a baler and so on.

If I use a boat on a Devon reservoir it is usually as a means of transport to a suitable shore from which to fish. There is an excep-tion: in a heatwave a boat may be placed over deep water where trout are sheltering in the cool depths, from which they may be plucked by a lure on a sinking line.

If you wish to fish from a boat, be sure to do so sitting down, for safety reasons as well as being less visible to trout. Being low down you will need a longer rod of 10ft or 11ft. This can be of all-through action, taking a No. 5 or No. 6 line, as casting will be mainly downwind. The extra length enables a dropper and then a bob fly to be scuttled across the water surface as they near the boat.

CHAPTER 19

TROUT FISHING IN RIVERS

Types of rivers

It is possible to provide trout fishing in many types of river if the water is stocked with fish, yet not all streams are suited to the production of trout by natural wild spawning. In all types of streams, the water flowing down a valley is derived from rain, but the manner in which the rain reaches the stream differs from river to river. This is because the rain flows rapidly into and down some waterways where the underlying rock is impervious to water (spate streams); and others where the rain is absorbed by the underlying rock, such as chalk and limestone. In this latter case the water rises up into the stream through springs. Spring-fed rivers tend to have stable flows, whilst spate rivers are unstable.

Spate and other rain-fed streams
The underlying rock of the western side of England, Wales and Scotland is usually granite, slate or other rocks which do not absorb water. Typically the land is hilly, of moorland or even mountainous characteristics which causes rain to run rapidly into a valley where many hill streams unite to form a river. The amalgamation of these streams, now constricted in a single channel, causes a bulge of water known as a 'spate' to run down the valley. The rise may be of a few inches or several feet. These considerable rises and falls in water levels create an unstable environment unsuited to the growth of weed, trout food and thus large trout.

Food is in short supply because the river-bed is washed clean of mud and silt, and the water is often acidic. These conditions inhibit weed growth, the production of algae and other food for troutlets. At the same time clean gravel on the river-bed provides ideal spawning conditions for trout. The presence of many troutlets reliant on a poor food supply produces wild brown trout averaging 4oz in weight, a half-pounder being the best to be expected in a day's fishing.

If these streams are narrow and rocky, the angler should

Healthy bands of weed in the River Bourne in Hampshire provide good invertebrate habitat, and cover for trout.

search the small deep holes, known as pockets, with his fly. If the bed is wide, sandy and featureless, covered with one or two feet of crystal-clear water, trout will notice all unusual activity (such as a line upon the water), to the detriment of the angler. Further, sandy rivers are a poor spawning environment, trout redds being stifled by the sand which deprives the ova of oxygenated water.

Some wide western rivers flow through agricultural land, gently dropping in level to the sea. The water in these rivers may be alkaline, leading to generous plant growth and the production of algae. All would thus be set to provide a good environment for trout but for one fact – the spawning beds become clogged with mud.

Spring-fed streams

In chalk and limestone areas rain falling on the hills and downs soaks into the underlying limestone or chalk rock. This chalk soaks up the water in the manner of a sponge and is known as the aquifer. If there is substantial winter rainfall (up to the end of April), the sponge fills, the water table rises, the springs 'break' and water flows steadily down the valley. After April the aquifer is not recharged as vegetation and trees take up the rain which is also lost through evaporation. Chalk and limestone produce alkaline water, perhaps with a pH of 7.5, which stimulates the growth of weed and trout food.

The characteristics of stable flow and plenty of food should produce fat trout in generous numbers. Sadly, in recent years, this has not been the case. Several factors have contributed to a

reduction in the population of wild brown trout including increased water abstraction for human consumption and reduced rainfall which have decreased water flow down the valleys. This reduced flow has allowed silt to be deposited on the spawning areas, covering and rotting trout ova. Silt deposition has increased in recent years due to the ploughing of land close to the river, allowing silt-laden rainwater to flow into the adjacent waterway. Many years ago water meadows lining the river banks prevented this by their filtering action. Water abstraction, pollution by agricultural fertilisers, low rainfall leading to low flow rates and the clogging of river-beds have left many streams mere shadows of their former, sparkling selves.

Stocking trout

A chalk-stream in Hampshire, Wiltshire, Dorset and other southern counties is an asset of great monetary value to the estate through which it passes. The estate needs a financial return on the investment, and probably has to maintain and house a river keeper, thus the river must provide an income. Rods are let at figures which may vary from £40 to £200 or more a day, or one to four thousand pounds a season. At this level of expenditure rods expect to catch trout of a weight and number beyond the natural productive capacity of the river, which may itself be limited by the adverse factors mentioned previously. The estate is thus forced to stock trout (brown or rainbow, or both) at weights between 1–3lb and above.

Many estates have their own hatchery. They strip the hen and cock fish of eggs and milt in the autumn, hatch the ova, feed the troutlets and enter fish of various weights at intervals into the river. Stocking may take place in April if the season opens in May, followed by an addition after the mayfly period and another when the June weed cut has been completed. There may be four weed cuts during the season and several stockings.

Chalk-streams are controlled by hatches which, in addition to their primary purpose of controlling water levels, act as a barrier to trout leaving the river section into which they were stocked. It is unwise and a waste of money to stock a spate river. Not only will trout fail to stay in the stretch to which they were entered, for a spate will wash them out, they will also lose weight due to lack of food. Years ago I stocked ³/₄ mile of a stream flowing off Dartmoor with 1lb brown trout. Of the 100 entered I caught about 10, the herons had several and the rest were mopped-up by the guests of a fishing hotel five miles downstream!

Open seasons
The statutory open season for brown trout in rivers is usually from 15 March to the end of September or early October. Regional dates vary and should be ascertained. Within the statutory season a riparian owner may set his own dates, 1 May

being common on the chalk-streams to coincide with the arrival of fly hatches and the recovery of trout after the winter. The rainbow trout season in rivers is usually the same as for brown trout. There may be no close season for rainbows in reservoirs, lakes and ponds. Grayling fishing may continue throughout the winter until 15 March, as this fish spawns in the spring. It is usually within the authority of a river keeper to allow friends and those who have helped him with his duties during the season to fish for grayling in the winter, the trout rods having departed.

Fly-fishing tackle

General descriptions of rod materials and actions, fly line ratings, reels and leaders have been given in Chapter 18. Below, suggestions are given for fishing rivers by dry fly, wet fly and nymph.

Rods
On 10 July 1997 I spent the day on the River Kennet, Hungerford with my co-author, Tony Allen, as guests of my father-in-law, Bill Waldron. My fishing diary reads as follows:

'2 brown trout, 4 rainbows. Total weight in the region of 15lb. No. 12 Pheasant Tail Nymph. I took the two superb browns of over 2¹/₂lb each. Had to use 5X leader, water too low and clear, and sky too bright, for 4X. Hot and sunny. Saw many voles as Bob (river keeper) had trapped all the mink. Tony took the rainbows, including one of 5¹/₂lb.'

A grayling

Small wild brown trout do not mean a short brook rod of 7ft. A 9ft rod reaches over obstacles to keep the fly line from dragging in fast channels.

Tony's rod was an 8ft 6in AFTM No. 6/7 Bruce & Walker Multitrout on which he has also killed an 8lb salmon on the River Test; mine was a 9ft 3in AFTM No. 6/7 Multitrout rod. Both of these rods are suited to river trout fly-fishing, possessing actions of authority and power without being stiff. They have served us well over many years but are now out of production. I am now the satisfied owner of one of the Bruce & Walker trout Powerlite range. This is the 8ft 6in AFTM No. 6 model which is ideal for river trout fishing and superbly finished with a matt, non-reflective, tube. In fact, I would gladly settle accounts with a 5lb sea trout when using this rod which has both power and delicacy.

Distance casting is not a necessity, as you can stalk up the river bank towards a rising trout. Essential is the all-through action needed (this does not mean softness) to hook and play a large trout without snapping a 3-lb tippet. Although carbon fibre is the most suitable material for a trout rod, split cane is still in use where the length of the rod does not exceed about 9ft (above this length the rod would be heavy). My daughter, Lara, has an 8ft Sharpe's resin-impregnated split cane rod rated AFTM No. 5. The rod is a pleasure to use, but the short length is a handicap in playing trout and keeping them out of weeds in a wide river.

Reels and lines

On the 8ft 6in Powerlite rod I use a Hardy Marquis No. 7 reel and an AirCel DT6F fly line, following my practice of using a reel one size larger than the rating of the fly line it is to accommodate. This allows me to recover line at a greater rate than a smaller reel, provided the spool is filled to capacity with line and backing. Another suitable reel for this rod is the LEEDA LC 80. This is less than half the price of the Marquis, comes with a spare spool and is light in weight.

Only one line is needed, a double-tapered floater. I like mine to be green in colour for use during the day, although white is preferred at night for sea trout. Do not buy a cheap line of which the coils have a 'memory', or one with a rough surface which will be difficult to shoot through the rod rings.

Leaders

On the end of my fly line is a 6in braided loop to which is attached, loop-to-loop, a LEEDA Profil knotless tapered leader. Breaking strains at the tip are 3-lb and 4-lb on the chalk-streams for artificial flies below mayfly size (i.e. for hook sizes No. 18 up to No. 12). For a mayfly a 5-lb point is a better choice to ensure a good turnover of the leader tip in presenting the fly. A 2-lb point (6X) is sufficient for small moorland brown trout.

I am not keen on 5ft braided leaders to which an untapered monofilament tippet of 4ft in the chosen strength is knotted. Braided leaders are more visible than monofilament and tend to splash down on the water surface when presenting a fly.

Fish senses

Vibration and hearing

I do not believe that fish hear sound which originates above the surface of the water. There is no physical basis to the suggestion that anglers should keep quiet so far as the fish are concerned; they need only keep quiet in order not to disturb other anglers and wildlife. Thus, if you observe a large trout taking mayfly with rash abandon and obvious appetite, and you wish your companion 100yd distant to come and catch it, shout at him to join you. Do not run along the bank with clumping boots to whisper in his ear, for the vibrations will scare many trout. The other alternative is to catch the fish yourself! Neither should you jump down from the bank onto the river-bed, or clump on stones or gravel with heavily-studded boots; shock waves and vibration will warn trout of your approach. So also will a fly line splashing down on the water without delicacy, even if out of the trout's circle of vision.

If a trout is examined, a line will be seen running centrally along the flank from the gill cover to the tail. This lateral line is furnished with sense organs able to pick up changes in water pressure. These enable the fish to remain with its head to the current by the pressure increasing on the upstream flank if the fish turns sideways to the water flow. It is essential that the fish stays head-to-current in order that it may open its mouth allowing water to enter, pass through the gill filaments where oxygen is extracted, and flow out through the gills. If a fish is held with its tail to the current it will slowly drown.

I think it unlikely that the senses of taste and smell need worry the dry fly angler, his fly being upon, not beneath, the water surface. I take care to fish fresh worms and prawns for salmon, for these baits may be mouthed by the fish and ejected if found unpalatable.

Sight

The eyes of a trout are placed slightly forward of the widest part of the head. This equips them with binocular vision to the fore, enabling them to judge distance when taking a fly. Monocular vision to the side warns of danger, and to the rear is a narrow arc into which they cannot see due to the thickness of the body behind the eyes. It follows that an angler casting upstream from behind a trout is likely to remain unseen. An angler casting a wet fly downstream is likely to be seen unless he crouches at a very low level.

Water, as we know, runs downhill. An angler standing on the river-bed whilst wading in thigh boots and casting to a trout 15yd upstream of his position, will be standing where the bed is vertically lower than the bed beneath the trout. Conversely, the angler casting downstream is placed on a bed vertically higher than that beneath the trout.

The angler should always keep as low as possible or light emanating from his head, shoulders and rod may be refracted down to the trout through the fish's window of vision. The diameter of this window increases as the fish descends towards the river-bed. A fish at a depth of 6in has a window 1ft 2in in diameter; at 1ft the window is 2ft 3in; whilst a salmon at 5ft has a window over 11ft wide. The angler should be more careful when salmon fishing whilst casting downstream than when casting upstream for trout. This is particularly so as he is unlikely to know the exact position of the salmon and thus the area covered by its circle of vision.

Any light coming from the angler or his rod and travelling to the water surface (which it penetrates inside the window), will be refracted down to the trout, provided the light beam is at an angle greater than about 10° above the water surface. If directly above the trout, light coming from an object such as a bird would travel directly down at 90°. If from below 10° it will be reflected up off the water surface of the window and the object from which it arrived will not be seen. In practical terms, as will be realised from the drawing, an angler who looks into the river whilst kneeling on the bank will have more success than the angler who walks upright to the water's edge whilst looking for a rising trout.

The cone of fish vision. A-B River 30 ft wide. B-D River bed is reflected down to salmon, at E, from the surface mirror. C-D 9ft window of vision of salmon at E, at 4ft depth. F-G 2¼ ft window of vision of salmon. J 2¼ ft window of vision of trout. K a fly on the water surface is invisible to trout at H.

An angler kneeling at A would have his head visible to trout at H, if his cap is 3ft above the ground. His head and shoulders would be visible to salmon at E.

What a fish sees: with binocular vision (L), it can judge distance to seeing a fly; with monocular vision (M) it can see approaching enemies; in the blind area of approach (N), the angler casting upstream is not visible.

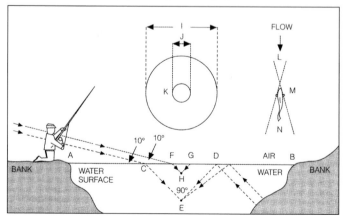

A subject which interests me is how close to a feeding trout a dry fly must be placed in order to be seen. Practical experience leads me to the opinion that the nearer the fish is to the surface the closer the fly must be placed to its circle of vision, if not inside the circle itself. It is true that the fish cannot see out of the water through an area larger than the window already calculated, but it might be able to see from below the depressions created by the insect on the water surface outside the window if it focused on them. In fact I do not think a trout takes flies outside its circle, for I have noticed that a trout feeding close to the surface does not move far to one side to sip down a drifting fly. It is thus essential to cast very accurately to a fish which is at a depth of three or four inches.

I was once told that a previous owner of fishing at Longparish on the River Test would not allow guests onto the river until they had passed a casting accuracy test. The test consisted of casting a fly onto a handkerchief placed on the lawn. My informant, who was talking of his grandfather, did not state the distance at which the handkerchief was placed – a matter relevant to the anglers' pride and the trout's preservation!

To sum up trout senses: cast upstream, keep low, don't stumble and cast accurately to fish positioned close to the water surface.

Natural insects, imitative dry flies and nymphs

If you are sitting by the river at 9.00 am on a late May morning and the keeper advises you 'You're a bit early. There will be a hatch of mayfly duns at 11.00 am' it adds to your status if you know what he means. He might continue, 'A fall of spent gnat usually takes place in the early evening'. Knowledge of the life-cycles of insects adds to enjoyment and satisfaction, and confers the ability to predict the hours of the day when trout will feed. It is also useful to know which flies are likely to be present in the months of the season.

We have already studied the life-cycles of the Orders Diptera and Trichoptera, and are left with those of major importance to the river angler: Ephemeroptera and Plecoptera, with further reference to Diptera and Trichoptera.

Ephemeroptera

These are known as 'upwinged flies'. They have a segmented body, six legs, two or three long tails and, usually, two pairs of upright wings of which the forewings are the largest. The duns (first aerial stage) may be identified by their upright wings as they drift upon the water. In flight their tails hang down below their spread wings imparting a parachute-like appearance, except that they are usually rising in the air instead of descending.

Flies of the Order include: mayfly, large dark olive, iron blue, blue winged olive and others. It is unnecessary to be able to identify a considerable number of the members of the Order, but the four mentioned are common and recognition gives satisfaction. It is much more important to note the size of the fly

and the stage in its life-cycle, and then present a dry fly of the same size. If a nymph, two sizes of one pattern are sufficient.

Egg

The Ephemeroptera egg is laid by the female on or under the water surface. The eggs sink to the river-bed and hatch after days or even months.

Nymph

The egg hatches and a nymph emerges to pass through a series of skin moults. This stage takes place under water and in the case of the mayfly may take two years.

Dun

The nymph propels itself to the water surface, breaks through, and the nymphal case splits. The insect struggles free of the case, treads it down, and then sits upon the water drying its wings as they unfold. When the wings are dry the fly becomes airborne. On a wet, warm day drying takes an appreciable time, and the dun drifts for several yards upon the surface affording trout a good chance of taking the passing morsel. On a dry day take-off is rapid after a short drift.

Spinner

The dull-looking dun moults, shedding its skin to become known as a spinner which is of shiny appearance. Male and female spinners mate over land. The male dies and the female returns to the river to lay her eggs and die. Dead spinners are known as 'spent'; they drift downstream, wings outspread and flat in the water surface film. To imitate a spinner which has died I take a winged dry fly and press the wings down flat if the fly was originally designed as a dun pattern.

When and where present

The Ephemeroptera Order is important to the angler, as it is common on many waters whether slow-moving chalk-streams or fast, rocky rivers. In late June and through July and August the blue winged olive can be observed on the fast acid rocky rivers of Dartmoor; the same fly in the same months and until October is to be seen on the alkaline River Test. The large dark olive hatches after lunch and until about 4.00 pm on warm afternoons in March and April, whilst the blue winged olive hatch in summer continues into the evening. The iron blue is present in April and the autumn, usually appearing in the afternoon. Knowledge of times of the day and months of the year when hatches take place may be acquired by reading and, much better, by being on the river.

Plecoptera

These are the hard-winged stoneflies and needle flies. They have two antennae, two pairs of wings and two very short tails. In flight they have a chunky appearance, lacking the delicacy of the olives. Their life-cycle comprises the egg which hatches under water into a nymph. The nymph is known as a 'creeper' and in that manner it crawls up the side of a boulder or reed to hatch.

I often pick their empty yellow/white nymphal cases off the sides of rocks above the water line on the River Dart. The emerged fly mates and the eggs are laid upon the water.

I do not carry imitations of common stoneflies such as the yellow sally, small yellow sally, early brown, medium and other stoneflies. My method is to fish almost any artificial of the correct size as will be seen from the following entry in my diary:

'5th April 1995. Cherrybrook. Caught 3 brown trout, total nearly 1lb, all returned. Fly – Partridge & Red. A hatch of early brown stonefly. Warm N wind. Fished from 1.30 pm to 4.30 pm'

The entry continues with a list of the wildlife I observed and recorded with a pen on the back of my cheque book:

'salmon fry, dippers, ravens, jackdaws, a rabbit, caddis cases, one iron blue, skylark, badger earth, fifteen golden plover, needle flies, wren, many spiders in the heather, heard a curlew, blackbird.'

Trichoptera

The life-cycle has already been described in Chapter 18. The earliest sedge to appear is the grannom which hatches in April. This is a small brown fly of which the female has a green egg sac beneath its tail. Do not trouble to carry an artificial grannom, as trout rarely attend to the fly.

Naturals are large and small red sedges, caperers, cinnamons, silver, grey, black, brown, marbled and others. If left to my own devices I would successfully imitate all of these with a Red Sedge in sizes No. 12 and No. 14. June, July and August are the sedge fly months. By September the fullness of the hatch has passed, evidenced by groups of empty caddis cases just above water level on the sides of boulders, wooden hatches and rushes.

Evening is the time of this fly, the hours of warm still twilight are described by John Waller Hills in *A Summer on the Test* (1924):

'On still summer nights . . . when the great red sedge is flopping about in his feeble aimless flight, and clouds of smaller sedges are flickering up and down over the unbroken surface, perchance some dim memory begins to stir in the slow mind of the old trout. All the season through he has fed at the bottom, grubbing on shrimps and caddis and water-snails and minnows and even on his own relatives. But he recalls seasons such as this, far back in former years, when all was quiet and warm and peaceful, when fat sedges would tumble clumsily on to the water, and in their efforts to escape would make a ripple and commotion spreading far over the placid pool, and he remembers how fresh and fair they were to eat. Then he forsakes his lair under the arched willow roots and rises to the top and takes up his old station in the shadow of the tussock, where he used to lie long ago in his active middle age, when he weighed a bare two pounds. Aye, he weighs more than twice two pounds now, perhaps three times or more, he is the prize of a lifetime – and perhaps as your sedge comes over him you will see a break like that of a big raindrop, a little circle like the

palm of a man's hand, and when you strike you will think you have hooked the trunk of a tree.'

Diptera

The life-cycle has already been described in the Chapter 'Trout Fishing in Still-waters'. Of particular interest to the river fly-fisher are the hawthorn in April and early May, and the daddy-long-legs in late summer and the autumn. Artificials to imitate these are listed on page 101.

Midges and reed smuts are very small, hard to imitate, but eaten by trout. It is possible to dress flies on No. 20 and No. 22 hooks, but hooking and landing trout on such tiny imitations is a risky business. If the naturals are being eaten try a No. 18 Black Gnat.

Natural flies and the equivalent artificial

We have now arrived at the heart of this section – the selection of artificials to match the hatching natural. At once, if you study those two excellent books on entomology by John Goddard, his *Waterside Guide* and *Trout Fly Recognition*, you will realise that a fly box the size of a suitcase is required, and this divided into matchbox-sized compartments to carry artificials. What to do? I ask you to read the reproduced article of mine which was published in 1986 by a field sports magazine, then I will supply an up-dated solution.

THE FIVE COMPARTMENT DRY FLY BOX

'A friend who lives and fishes the dry fly one mile upstream of our house is fed up with entomology. As he said, "What is the point in being able to distinguish a caperer from a large cinnamon sedge?" I had to admit that, in my experience, little practical advantage in fish catching would be gained by the knowledgeable over the ignorant. His question had been put after catching a six ounce brown trout in our little stream on a No. 12 Red Sedge. Noticing that the trout had a bulge in the flank he decided to clean the fish on the spot. His autopsy revealed a small, partly digested shrew which seemed, from the inside rawness of the bulge, to have used its best endeavours to regain the outside world before being suffocated! My friend was so overcome with rebellious thoughts on imitative fly-fishing that he never told me whether the six ounces did or did not include the shrew. Anyway, he was very put out. I think he may become a convert to the "Order of the Grey Wulff" which can be dressed with a rabbit's fur body!

'Acid rivers, which include most waters running down from the upland moors of western Britain, do not produce much fish food. A trout has to take what is going – and quickly too before the morsel is swept away downstream. No time to think, to assess the pedigree of the fly – just time to rush, to rise and to grab. In consequence a trout's stomach will be found, in season, to contain crane flies, wasps, bees, caddis larvae in their cases, nymphs, caterpillars and beetles. Little comes amiss, and this makes fly choice simple for the angler – four or five general patterns in one or two sizes, a nymph, and off you go. If this seems an ill-considered suggestion I would ask you to bear in mind the success of the late Oliver Kite fishing with a bare hook nymph and, in the dry fly, his general olive: The Imperial.

'Who can argue against the efficacy of the Grayling Bug and the Pheasant Tail Nymph – Frank Sawyer's killing nymphs work under almost all conditions in almost any place: civilised Kennet, Hampshire Avon, Test as well as wild Dart, Teign and Tavy. My two largest rainbows of 7lb 3oz from the Kennet and 7lb 10oz from Fernworthy Reservoir on Dartmoor, came to a No. 12 Pheasant Tail Nymph inexpertly tied by myself with far too many tail whisks.

'I have a compartment dry fly box with little "spring up" transparent lids. It was given to me over forty years ago. It has ten sections in which I have about twenty varieties of fly. The choice is unnecessary, seldom exercised and five or six compartments are rarely opened. The flies used are a No. 18 Black Gnat, a Kite's Imperial No. 14, which shares with a Wickham's Fancy of the same size, hackled Red Sedge No. 12, Grey Wulff No. 10 and a Sawyer's Pheasant Tail Nymph No. 12.'

The fly box mentioned in the article is still in use, finger-polished but battered, and some of the compartments have broken lids. The stock in the box is comprised of nine artificial dry flies, and one nymph in two sizes. The choice reflects my view that trout may be caught on a few general patterns provided they are the right size which must be close to the size of the natural on which the trout is feeding.

Month	Natural fly	Artificial	Hook size
April	large dark olive	Kite's Imperial	14
	iron blue	Iron Blue	18
	early brown stonefly	Wickham's Fancy	16
May	mayfly	Grey Wulff	10
	iron blue	Iron Blue	18
	hawthorn	Hawthorn	12
	medium olive	Kite's Imperial	16
	yellow Sally	Wickham's Fancy	16
June	mayfly	Grey Wulff	10
	medium olive	Kite's Imperial	16
	sedges	Red Sedge	12 & 14
	yellow Sally	Wickham's Fancy	16
July	blue winged olive	Kite's Imperial	14
	sedges	Red Sedge	12 & 14
	yellow Sally	Wickham's Fancy	16
August	crane fly	Daddy-long-legs	10
	blue winged olive	Kite's Imperial	14
	sedges	Red Sedge	12 & 14
	yellow Sally	Wickham's Fancy	16
September	crane fly	Daddy-long-legs	10
	blue winged olive	Kite's Imperial	14
	iron blue	Iron Blue	18
	sedges	Red Sedge	12 & 14

Midges all through the season may be represented by a No. 18 Black Gnat which will also imitate the natural iron blue, being of the same size. Almost all my patterns are hackled, meaning they are dressed without wings. The exceptions in the table are Wickham's Fancy, Grey Wulff (which has tufts of hair for wings) and Red Sedge. If I wish to imitate a spent fly on the water film I press the wings of a Wickham's Fancy flat.

In the table are nine patterns to go in the ten-compartment box. They are in sizes ranging from No. 10 to No. 18 in even increments. Add to this two Pheasant Tail Nymphs for the tenth place:

- No. 14 Pheasant Tail – the dressing material of a few fibres of the tail of a cock pheasant and fine copper wire
- No. 16 Pheasant Tail – dressed with silk instead of wire, this will fish in the surface film.

This simple selection cannot fail to bring success if fished off the correct leader diameter and well presented.

Note: on some rivers the nymph is prohibited at all times; on others it may be allowed after 1 July, a month when fishing becomes difficult in the hot, bright weather.

Fishing dry flies and nymphs

On arrival at the river the angler should walk downstream to the lower end of the water he intends to fish. In this way a view of the river over which to cast upstream will be obtained. An assessment can then be made of fish and insect activity, of weed-beds, boulders, undercut banks, water clarity, trees and thus the physical make-up of that section of the river.

Preparations may be made at the lower end of the beat. Thread the line through the rod rings, attach a leader loop-to-loop to the braided loop at the end of the fly line and knot on a fly. The choice of leader strength and fly size depends upon the observations made on the downstream walk.

If naturals are hatching and trout are feeding, a fly of the correct size may be attached. More difficult is selecting a leader of suitable breaking strain and thus visibility to the trout, for this is usually a compromise. If an iron blue or midge is hatching, indicating a No. 18 artificial, the fly would fish best off a 3-lb point. Then, you note that the trout are large and weed-beds abound – you will be broken if weeded. So, a 4-lb point is selected, but the trout cocks its eye at this nylon and says to itself 'I've seen such things before'. A risk must be accepted at times.

For myself, I fish on the fine side on a stocked chalk-stream of clear water, preferring a 3-lb point for No. 16 and No. 18 hooks, 4-lb for sedges on No. 12 or No. 14 hooks, and 5-lb to extend a mayfly on a No. 10 hook. On the moorland streams I fish a 2-lb point with all my artificials, as there are small trout, little weed and no mayfly.

The choice of nylon diameter is crucial to fly acceptance by trout. Consider this illustration of fishing the River Bourne near Andover in Hampshire. The fish are wild brown trout averaging just over 1lb on this rarely fished section of the river where the water is as clear as any I have seen. My diary reads:

'4 August 1996. Four brown trout, total 4lb, best 1lb 4oz. No. 18 Iron Blue. A shared basket with Lara. Fish rejected a 3-lb leader but took a No. 18 fly on a 2-lb point. There was a hatch of pale wateries, it seemed to me that the majority were female as the bodies were pale yellow with yellow eyes, and the wings pale grey. Michael joined us for lunch in the stable where we had a bottle of estate Grosse Pierre, Beaujolais.'

On that morning trout rose steadily, but refused anything offered on a 3-lb point; Lara and I were fishless until we changed to 2-lb.

Having made decisions on fly size and nylon strength, knot on the fly and dip it in the bottle of waterproofing Supafloat and blow off any excess liquid. Make sure the fly has fully dried before use or the Supafloat will be washed off the fly. Next, grease the leader very slightly with solid Mucilin for the 6ft closest to the fly line, leaving the 3ft closest to the fly ungreased in case it becomes necessary to fish a nymph beneath the surface. Hook the landing net to the hang-all belt loop, and take up other ancillary equipment such as priest, polarised spectacles, artery forceps, scissors and a plastic bag to hold caught trout. The small items may be placed in the pockets of a fisherman's waistcoat. If convenient to carry, it would keep caught fish cooler if they are placed in a wicker creel or fish bass.

Choice of bank

The right and left banks of all rivers are defined whilst facing downstream. If it is possible to fish from either bank, the right bank should be chosen by a right-handed angler, and the left bank by a left-hander. Such arrangements place the rod hand over the river bank and closest to the river. If allowed to wade, the right-handed angler will be tucked beneath the right bank, and the left-hander will fish whilst creeping up the river beneath the left bank. Wading aids concealment, but many caddis cases will be destroyed and other insect life disturbed.

Avoiding drag

When fishing imitative dry flies the cast will be made upstream so that the fly drifts downstream in the manner of a natural fly at the same speed as the current. There must be no interference by line and leader to slow or increase the drift of the fly relative to the flow of the water. Any such interference will cause the fly to create a wake upon the water surface, a 'V' pattern known as 'drag'. The unnatural wake-creating movement of a fly frightens fish and is to be avoided.

Do not by choice cast across a fast current mid-river to a trout rising in a slow flow under the far bank; the fast flow will drag the line, leader and fly, and the trout will take fright and depart. If it is necessary to cast across a fast flow, ensure that the line falls in wiggly curves upon the water. By the time the line has

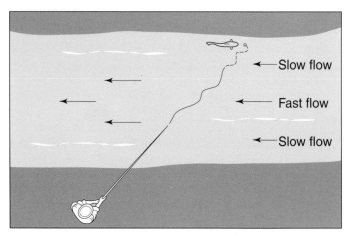

Counteracting drag – dry fly.
Elimination of drag when casting to a trout in slack water on the far side of a current. To create a wiggly line, aim high in the air. As the line straightens, pull back the rod and then push forward. In the time taken by the current to straighten the wiggles the fly will have drifted over the trout.

been straightened by the current and starts to drag, the fly will have drifted over the trout. To cast a crooked line aim high in the air, then as the line straightens, pull back the rod and then push forward. Drag is most readily avoided by casting to trout close to the bank from which the angler is fishing (i.e. upstream of his position).

I refer again to John Waller Hills' *A Summer on the Test* in which he describes an experience when a wiggly line brought him a trout in slack water on the far side of a fast current:

'. . . the cast was made, and by the mercy of fate the fly for once landed just right. There it was, floating gaily in the slack water, cocked, and the line being as it was beautifully crooked to absorb the drag. And there too was the trout., slowly turning himself out to look at it. He came out, raised his nose to it, and for what seemed an eternity backed down behind it as the stream carried it along; then he broke water and took it. Once more I had the fortitude to wait until his head was well down again, indeed until he had turned to go back, before striking. I knew then that I had him firm.'

Wind direction

A dry fly is almost weightless and, because of its wind resistant hackles, it is hard to cast upstream against a downstream wind. If you are only permitted to use dry fly, some assistance in extending the cast against the wind is given by a short 7½ft leader which should be 0.025in thick at the butt, tapering to a 0.006in (3-lb) point. An alternative, if allowed, is to fish the streamlined No. 14 Pheasant Tail Nymph which has some weight if dressed with fine copper wire.

If the wind is upstream, an idyllic day is ahead which may be made even better by the use of a 12ft leader. Hardy's Copolymer knotless tapered leaders are available in lengths of 7½ft, 9ft and 12ft.

Deceiving trout

From his position at the downstream end of the water to be fished, two courses are open to the angler. He can either cast to a selected rising trout, or fish all the likely places as he moves upstream in the hope of taking an unseen trout.

The first option brings the greatest satisfaction but cannot be put into practice if flies are not hatching and trout feeding. Let us suppose that blue winged olive duns are drifting down the river which is alive with rising trout. A trout discerned to be of keepable size, rising close to our bank, is selected. The cast is made upstream and the fly alights 1–2ft above the fish and drifts across the window of that trout. Only the fine part of the leader crosses his window, the fly line being below the area of vision, as is the angler who is keeping low by wading or kneeling on the bank. As the fly drifts back the angler must recover line at the same speed as the drift. If this is not done a loop of line will form downstream of the rod tip, delaying a strike or making one impossible.

Up comes the fish to suck down the fly. When should you strike? On raising the rod to hook the fish a few trout will always escape penetration by the point of the hook, departing in a flurry of water. My practice is to strike slowly into large fish (see Hills extract) but like lightning to 6oz moorland brown trout, which move as fast as flickers of light.

Of course, the trout may refuse the fly, in which case the angler may try another fish or lay seige to the original quarry. My advice is to continue for a while at the rejecting fish: try a smaller fly, finer nylon, cast to one side, or land the fly just behind his head. Experience is gained by persistence. It is possible that the trout has not seen your fly; if it is close to the water surface its window will be small and your fly may have alighted outside its circumference. Remember, when you whirl about at the sound of a heavy rise, the rings upon the water may have drifted 1–2yd downstream. Wait for a second rise to pinpoint the space in which to drop the fly.

The second course is to 'fish the water', adopting this option if trout are not rising. This manner of fishing does not have the long-established pedigree of 'fishing the rise'. However, in the rushed life of the present era one cannot expect an angler, with only one day a fortnight to fish, to sit on a bench for several hours waiting for a hatch of fly which may not materialise.

To fish the water, use a larger fly than when matching a hatch of small olives. Try to surprise a non-feeding fish into a knee-jerk take by the plop of a hairy meal upon the water. An excerpt from my diary:

> '2nd August 1997. River Test. 2 brown, 2 rainbow. Total 11lb 12oz. Best 4lb 4oz. Two on Tony's [my co-author] deer hair sedge, two by Lara on a Pheasant Tail Nymph.'

Flies failed to hatch on that hot sunny morning, whilst fish stayed low or in the shade. The water was so clear that a 3-lb point was chosen despite the presence of heavy trout. In the morning I dropped the sedge with a plop 1ft from the shady opposite bank where the water flowed beneath overhanging vegetation. This tempted the 4lb 4oz rainbow and a 3lb brown out. The other

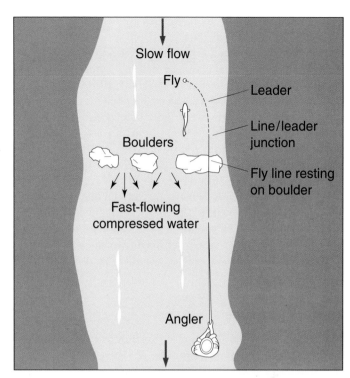

Drag avoidance in a fast-flowing rocky brook – dry fly. The fly line must be kept out of the gaps between the boulders, where the water is compressed and fast-flowing, or the line will be pulled downstream. This will cause the fly to drag, creating a wake which scares fish.

two fish fell to Lara's Pheasant Tail Nymph and were netted by Brian. (Lara's method will be described later.) In 'fishing the water' a cast should be made to all likely places: above the lip of a weir, beside a bed of trailing Ranunculus, in front of a boulder and on each side of a fast stream.

Now for a few words on 'pocket water'. Pockets are those small deep holes with a smoothly flowing surface, maybe only two yards wide, found between boulders on a moorland brook. Such sheltered safe havens are favoured by plump, experienced trout. Drop the fly upon the surface, the fly line resting on an adjacent boulder, with (probably) only the leader and fly on the surface of the pocket. Then lift off before the fly is swept away between the boulders. A swim of 1–2ft, in two or three seconds, is sufficient to tempt an edible half-pounder.

Nymph fishing

Two Pheasant Tail Nymphs are listed on page 101, one dressed with copper wire and the other with silk. The copper nymph enables one to fish for visible trout, which may or may not be feeding on invertebrates, 1–2ft below the surface; the silk-dressed pattern is for fishing at bulging trout taking hatching nymphs drifting in the water film.

The copper pattern is not acceptable on the waters of The Piscatorial Society on the Hampshire Avon, and if over-weighted becomes an unacceptable lure to those fishing with imitative intent. The weighted pattern may be used to 'fish the water', but greater enjoyment will be experienced by attacking an active fish which is feeding at a depth of about 2ft. Such a fish will be seen to swing from side to side and make an occasional dash downstream to take drifting nymphs. Cast the nymph several feet upstream of the trout, allowing it to drift back and sink until just above the trout. Then lift the rod tip to raise the nymph towards the surface. This movement is known as *induction*, and the trout's response as an *induced take*. The moment to strike is indicated by a twitch of the line or the opening of the trout's white lips. Polarised spectacles are essential in this style of fishing.

A silk-dressed nymph fishes in the surface film if fished off a leader greased to within 1ft of the point. If you wish the nymph to penetrate the surface, dose it with a lick of spit. This pattern enables one to take trout bulging in the water surface at nymphs, but not those that are sucking down drifting hatched flies.

Fishing wet flies

When fishing wet flies the angler may cast a wet fly upstream and retrieve at, or a little faster than, the speed of the current.

He may also cast downstream and across the current which will take hold of the line, swinging the fly across the river until it hangs below the angler. The former is difficult, but the latter easy to accomplish. In my opinion upstream wet-fly fishing is more skilled in practice, though not in understanding, than dry-fly fishing. The downstream wet fly is for use in a strong downstream wind when you are unable to cast upriver, and in a spate when all hope has been abandoned of imitative fishing.

Upstream fishing

I find little to persuade me that upstream wet-fly fishing differs from fishing a silk-dressed nymph in the surface of the water. It is a method of persuading trout that the wet fly they observe is an insect at the nymphal stage drifting downstream beneath the water surface, or a hatching fly struggling at the surface at the moment of eclosion. It follows, if you accept my imitative theme, that wet flies for casting upriver ought to be finely dressed on small hooks (in sizes No. 14, No. 16 and No. 18) as most insects in which we are interested are also small. Hackles,

Kneel when casting upstream.

representing the silk-thin legs and tails of an insect, take priority over wings in the dressings, and are sparsely applied and made of soft hen feather fibres which will move and sway in the water.

The cast is made upstream in the manner already described for dry-fly fishing. However, now a difficulty is discerned which, in my view, makes the upstream wet fly more difficult than the upstream dry: responding to a take. It is easy to spot a rise to a floating fly, but it is difficult to discern the movement when a mouth has closed on your offering beneath the surface. Sometimes there is the flash of a turning flank to prompt you to tighten, or the twitch of the line, or the forward jerk of the leader. Any of these trigger the raising of the rod to set the hook. If they are not noticed the fly will be ejected. To respond in time to takes, direct contact should be maintained with the fly by retrieving the line fractionally faster than the water flow.

Hooking is more effective than when casting downstream. When you are below the upstream facing trout, the hook is likely to be pulled back into the scissors of the trout's mouth. When casting downstream, with the trout facing the angler, the hook may be pulled out of the mouth. As with dry-fly fishing, the upstream method enables the angler to keep out of sight with ease, as he is fishing from behind the fish and from a lower level.

FLIES FOR UPSTREAM WET

I recommend the following wet flies for fishing upstream.

- Snipe & Purple
- Waterhen Bloa
- Partridge & Orange
- Black & Peacock Spider

Although the Blue Upright is a hackled West Country dry pattern, I find a ragged, well-chewed example which has not been waterproofed is always popular with moorland trout. One of my favourite flies is a No. 16 winged March Brown wet fly, with the wing trimmed to a stub by a pair of scissors to resemble the wing hump inside a nymphal case. The Invicta, a winged wet fly, is a useful pattern when sedges are hatching, and may be cast upstream or down. The laid-back wing resembles the roof-shaped wings of the natural fly.

If one wishes to use two methods at the same time, upstream wet and nymph, try a copper-wired Pheasant Tail Nymph on the point and a hackled wet fly on a single dropper. The nymph will fish at some depth below the surface, and the wet fly may be raised to trip across the top of the water when the moment has almost arrived to lift off into the back cast. For this system a rod of not less than 9ft is required.

Downstream fishing

This is the easiest way for a beginner to start fishing in a river, but the method is not allowed on the chalk-streams. The system should be employed in spate water conditions when the upstream method and small imitative flies do not suit the trout's poor vision through coloured water, and when the speed of flow is too great. One is also persuaded to cast downstream if there is a strong wind in that direction, making upstream casting tiring, frustrating, or impossible.

The cast is made down and across the river. It is easy to accomplish as the current straightens out both line and leader. The system suits those of little experience, as takes are indicated by a pull or pluck at the line – a benefit to those with poor eyesight. Casting is also less frequent than in the upstream method and thus the system is less tiring. A longer line is likely to be extended to assist in keeping the angler out of sight, and to slow the speed at which the fly travels across the river. Although the method requires less skill than upstream fishing, greater care is needed to keep out of the trout's area of vision.

Do not stand tall when fishing a wet fly downstream as the trout will see you . . .

. . . kneel instead.

The cast should not be made directly across the river because, on landing on the water, the line would be caught by the current and the fly swept downstream at high speed. The direction should be more down than across. Thus, if looking downstream and taking 12 o'clock to be the centre of the river, the cast should be made to 12 o'clock from the left bank, the current then moving the fly to 9 o'clock below the angler. If casting from the right bank, make the cast to 12 o'clock and the current will swing the fly to 3 o'clock. In this way the fly will fish slowly and thoroughly.

FLIES FOR DOWNSTREAM WET

These should be larger than those in use in the imitative upstream method. A spate water is usually more turbid than when low water conditions prevail, thus a fly needs to be larger to be noticed. Colour and stripes in the underwater fly are again of importance (see Chapter 'Trout Fishing on Still-waters'). The following are my choice of flies in hook sizes No. 10, No. 12 and No. 14.

- Invicta
- Peter Ross
- Mallard & Claret

Not only are these attractive to trout in a spate – you may find yourself attached to a salmon and land it, even on a 4-lb point! To this end, allow me to mention the Connemara Black, an Irish trout and sea trout fly of renown. The diary:

'20 August 1988. Grilse 6lb. Came upon a young man playing a salmon on a trout rod. 4-lb nylon. No. 12 Connemara Black. Hill Pool. 3.15 pm. Heavy water. His father had run back to the car for a large trout net, but I lent my 24″ Gye. He lost another on the same fly when nylon broke as salmon went into weeds.'

Playing, netting and handling trout

Playing and netting

The movement of raising the rod to hook the risen trout, commonly known as the strike, will lift the rod to at least 45° from the horizontal. It should be kept in this position to act as a

The author playing a trout on the River Test. Keep low when playing fish, and if possible out of sight.

shock-absorbing spring whilst the fish is being subdued. If the rod tip is lowered to point almost at the trout there will be no elasticity between the fish and the angler, and a break may result. Also, when the rod tip is close to the water surface and the trout is at a distance of 10–15yd, the water flow will cause drag on the submerged line. This pressure on the hook hold may enable the trout to break free.

The angler should do his best to remain opposite to or below the fish which will then have to fight both the pull of the line and the downstream pressure of the current. The fish which is allowed to fight downstream of the angler is helped by the current, and the hook may be pulled out of its mouth which is facing the fisherman.

A chalk-stream trout will commonly take refuge in a weed-bed. If this situation arises the angler should move downstream of the weeds, lower the rod point to water level and apply direct downstream pressure on the fish. After some moments, or even minutes, the trout may untangle itself and emerge.

If a trout is hooked in a channel on the far side of a weed-bed, it is sometimes possible to skate the fish across the top of the intervening weeds. This must be done before the fish recovers from the surprise of being hooked. Apply maximum lifting and pulling pressure, with the rod held high, as soon as the rod bends into the fish. If a trout leaps into the air, particularly in the case of a fish of over 1lb, I drop my rod

A trout net should have a telescopic handle.

point at once. This prevents the fish falling back on a tight leader, pulling out the hook or snapping the nylon.

On a rocky river when fishing upstream, a hooked trout usually dives into deep water on the upstream side of an intervening boulder. The angler must at once leap forward to a position from which he can exert an upstream pull. This movement is assisted by the use of a 9ft rod which can reach forward beyond the boulder, rather than an inadequate 7ft brook rod. I usually strand small moorland brown trout on a gravel bank or mid-stream boulder at water level, and do not carry a net in this situation.

When playing a chalk-stream trout the net should be left on the hang-all belt loop until the trout is played out. Lift the net off the loop, flick it open and extend the net beneath the water surface in a place where the current is slack. (It is difficult to net a fish in a strong current.) Trap the fly line beneath the fore-finger of the hand on the rod butt and draw the trout over the net which should then be lifted.

Releasing or killing

If the trout is to be released the process is helped if barbless hooks are used. Alternatively the barb can be pressed flat by a pair of snipe-nosed pliers. Lift the fish out of the water and place it on the grass whilst still in the net. Hold the fish through

There is more than one way to land a trout.

the meshes of the net with cold wet hands, then remove the hook with artery forceps. The fish is then returned to the water in the net and released by turning the net inside out. If fishing on a water where fish are normally released, the fish's scales are less likely to be damaged by a knotless net, as opposed to one with a knotted bag. If a fish is exhausted, and grayling tire to a greater

extent than trout, it should be held with its head to the current until it recovers and swims away.

If a trout is to be killed it should be dispatched at once by a couple of blows to the top of the head by the priest. It should then be placed in a wet fish bass which ought to be hung in a breezy position in the shade of a tree and wetted from time to time. The catch will be kept cool by the evaporation of water from the bass.

'Catch and Release'. Use barbless hooks, or press in the barb with snipe-nosed pliers.

Use of the priest 'to administer the last rites'.

The weighing scales

CHAPTER 20

SEA TROUT

Life history

A sea trout is a brown trout which migrates to the sea to feed when it is one, two or three years old, returning to the river in due course to spawn. No one knows why some brown trout stay in a river which has ready access to the sea whilst others go to sea. In their early river lives, before the first migration, the two types cannot be distinguished. When sea trout spawn in the river their eggs may be fertilised by the milt of native brown trout.

In the West Country of England a sea trout is called a *peal*, in Wales a *sewin*, in Scotland a sea trout, unless weighing about 10–12oz on their first return to the river in which case they are called *finnock*. In Scotland a salmon is called a 'fish', but this term does not apply to a sea trout.

Sea trout usually start to cut their spawning redds in the headwaters of rivers in early November, about two weeks before salmon begin to spawn. The hen extrudes ova, and the cock milt. The fertilised eggs, being heavier than water, sink to the bottom of the gravel redd. Hatching takes places after a period of time which depends upon water temperature, but three months may be taken as a general rule.

An *alevin* with a sustaining sac of yolk beneath its chin emerges from the egg beneath the gravel. After about a month when the yolk has been absorbed the alevin, now known as a *fry*, swims up through the gravel into the stream and starts to feed in April or May. As the fry grows to fingerling size it becomes known as a *parr*. After one to three years it becomes silvery in colour in April or May, and is known as a *smolt*. It then swims downriver to the sea at a weight of about 4oz. After feeding in the sea it is likely to return to the river in July, August or September of the same year weighing between 9–14oz.

These first-return fish are known as *school peal* in the south-west, as *herling* on the borders of Scotland and as *finnock* in Scotland. Some sea trout do not return in the same season but spend one or two years at sea before making a spawning run

---

The length and weight, and scale samples taken from the flank from beneath the knife blade, contribute to a life history and population survey of River Dart sea trout. The scales are sent in the envelope to be read under a microscope by Fishkill, Brecon, Wales.

into fresh water. The school peal, also known in some areas as a *schoolie*, may or may not spawn on their first return to the river, instead swimming back to the sea in winter. Of those which spawn on first entry many go back to the sea to feed again, then return a second time to spawn at weights between $1\frac{1}{2}$–$2\frac{1}{2}$lb in the following year. Third-visit spawners may weigh 4–5lb, and some manage fourth and even fifth spawning runs at weights of up to 10lb and above. These spawning visits to the rivers of their birth take place in declining numbers due to death by disease, predators, netting, rod catches and other causes.

Feeding habits in fresh water

Salmon do not feed in fresh water, but one cannot state this categorically in the case of sea trout. I have yet to find anything other than a single item, such as a beetle or an insect, in the stomach of a second or third-return peal. I have found many items of food in the stomachs of a small percentage of returning school peal. The consequence of this lack of sustenance in fresh water is that the fish lose condition, whilst their eggs or milt increase in volume and weight as a proportion of the whole body as they near the spawning months. A sea trout caught in the second half of September is rarely worth eating, the flesh being soft, pale and tasteless.

Night vision

The most exciting sea trout fishing takes place in rivers at night. I am often asked how sea trout manage to see the fly at night. In my opinion this is due to four factors: there is always *some* light; the body of a successful sea trout fly is usually of silver tinsel or coloured silver which reflects the light; the black colour of which the wing of many sea trout flies is comprised is in stark contrast to the starlight; and the eye of the fish makes better use of the available light than the eye of a human, due to mirror vision.

The lens of the sea trout eye focuses light on the retina. Unlike with the human eye, the light passes through to be reflected back to the retina by a mirror, the *tapetum*. The light is thus used twice. The fish eye does not have an iris to control the amount of light entering the eyeball, instead a pigment blacks-out the mirror in conditions of high light by day.

Distinguishing sea trout from salmon

The rod fishing open seasons of these two fish are not always identical. The salmon season on some rivers may open on 1 February or 1 March, whilst the sea trout season may be delayed to mid-March or 1 April. The salmon season may continue into October, November or even December, whilst the sea trout open rod season usually closes on 30 September. It is quite likely that a large sea trout of 5lb or above may be taken, and killed, in the autumn when a rod, thinking it is a grilse is fishing for salmon. It is, of course, illegal to kill a fish out of season but it may happen through mistaken identification.

Distinguishing physical details:

- The head – In salmon the back of the eye is level with the end of the maxillary. A sea trout eye is wholly forward of the end of the maxillary. A sea trout head appears shorter than the head of a salmon.
- The tail – School peal and finnock have forked tails. By the time a sea trout reaches 3–4lb, and could be confused with a grilse, the trailing edge of the tail is square and in a very large sea trout even convex. The trailing edge of the tail of a grilse, and of a two-sea-winter salmon, is concave.
- The scales – Count the scales in a line from the rear end of the adipose fin to the lateral line on the flank of a fish. A salmon has 9–12 scales, usually 11, whilst a sea trout has between 13–16 scales.

The fishing season

A few large sea trout enter some rivers in March and April. These are usually fish above 2lb in weight but may be substantially larger. May sees a considerable increase in the numbers of fish of 2–5lb, some of 10lb and a very few in the 'teens of pounds, and this continues through June. Heavy sea trout continue to enter the river throughout the rest of the season, but their percentage of the entry reduces as school peal start to arrive in July. A run of mixed weight fish continues until

Sea lice are visible above the anal fin of this sea trout caught in the River Dart in April four miles above the sea.

the end of the season. The greatest numbers of sea trout of mixed weight are taken in July, August and September. On a Scottish sea trout loch it is unusual to start fishing from boats before the end of June for sea trout, although boats may be out for salmon, the best period being mid-July to mid-September.

Fly-fishing tackle

Rods

Recently I purchased a Bruce & Walker 9ft 3in carbon fibre Powerlite Trout rod which takes an AFTM No. 7 line. It is expensive, but the quality matches the price – made in England at their Huntingdon works, it is a superb example of the rod builders' craft. Particularly desirable is the matt non-reflective surface of the tube. Bruce & Walker describe the rod as of middle-to-tip action and ideal for distance casting on small still-waters. I have proved this to be so and therein lies a financial saving – it is also suited to fishing for sea trout in rivers. The rod has power, yet it is not so stiff that hooks are pulled out of the soft mouths of fresh-run peal. It is also noticeably light in weight. Behind the reel mount is a 1¹/₂in built-on butt extension which supports the wrist when playing a heavy fish, and keeps the reel rim away from clothing and thus involuntary braking.

Reels and lines

In the Chapter 'Trout Fishing in Still-waters' I recommended the LEEDA Dragonfly 100 reel for still-water use, and this doubles as my night sea trout reel when fitted with spools holding the required fly lines.

The white AirCel Supreme double-tapered AFTM No. 7 floating line points towards the fly on dark nights when supported on the black surface of the water. However, it tends to flash in the air as it extends when cast across the water in bright moonlight which scares fish. The green AirCel floating line is suited to use on these bright nights. When fishing on a cold night early in the season, probably in May, I recommend a double-tapered slow sinking WetCel 1 Intermediate line. The green floating line and the intermediate sinker also find their place in daytime lake fishing for trout.

Behind each line should be approximately 100yd of 25-lb monofilament backing, sufficient to fill the reel spool, joined to the fly line by a needle knot.

Leaders

Leaders should be tapered, and may be home-made for wet flies and tube flies fished sub-surface. The line/leader junction differs from the braided loop/blood bight loop in use by day. This is because it is necessary to ensure that the line/leader junction can be wound smoothly through the rod tip, unseen by the angler in the dark, when netting a peal. To meet this need 1ft of 20lb nylon should be needle-knotted into the end of the fly line, the leader being blood-knotted to this extension. The leader may then be constructed of three sections of nylon blood-knotted together:

- 1ft of 20-lb BS nylon needle knotted to fly line
- 2ft of 20-lb BS nylon
- 3ft of 15-lb BS nylon
- 3ft of 8-lb BS nylon

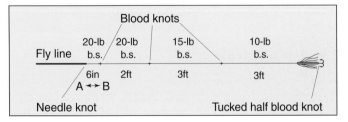

The final section of 8-lb fly line may be replaced by 10-lb if heavy peal are expected in spring, or 6-lb in the low, clear, warm water conditions of summer.

Flies

The beginner should not add a dropper to his leader. One fly is sufficient to catch fish and avoid tangles. Many flies are available; two will suffice for the first season. In low, warm, clear water in summer use a single hooked Black Lure:

> *Hook* – Partridge Code 01 Single Wilson No 8
> *Body* – Black floss
> *Rib* – No. 14 oval silver tinsel
> *Throat* – Black cock hackle
> *Wing* – Two black cock hackles
> *Silk* – Black Naples

This is also the best lure with which to start a night fly-fishing career, as fewer tangles will result than with the treble hook of a tube fly.

The Silver Stoat's Tail tube is a bulkier fly for use throughout the season when there is plenty of water in the river. To increase the length of the fly in cold water conditions, or if stoat's tail is not available, bucktail dyed black may be used for the wing. Bucktail is durable and longer-lasting than peacock herl which is used in another popular tube, the Alexandra.

> *Tube* – 1in Veniard Type B Slipstream, socketed
> *Hook* – No. 12 Partridge CS8 treble
> *Body* – Flat silver tinsel
> *Head* – Black varnish
> *Wing* – Two tufts of stoat's tail, one on each side, to reach
> to the end of the tube
> *Silk* – Black Naples

If the novice cannot obtain Silver Stoat's Tail tubes, the Alexandra is a fine fly as a replacement:

> Tube – 1in Veniard Type B Slipstream, socketed
> *Hook* – No. 12 Partride CS8
> *Tag* – Scarlet floss
> *Body* – Flat silver tinsel
> *Head* – Black varnish
> *Wing* – Peacock herl
> *Silk* – Black Naples

I do not suggest that the tyro fish dry flies as *wake lures* at the start of his sea trout career. Results are patchy and, if disappointing, may lead to the conclusion that he is fishing incorrectly.

Left: Home-made leader for night sea trout fishing
Section A–B is permanently inserted into the fly line by a needle knot. The leader is replaced by cutting at point B. Section A–B would originally have been 1ft, but reduces to 6in as leaders are replaced. When too short, a new 1ft section must be inserted.

Sea trout (ST) and salmon (S) flies
Top row, left to right:
Shrimp fly (S), Alexandra tube (ST), Peter Ross (ST)
Middle row, left to right: Black Dart tube (S), Black Lure (ST), Blue Zulu (ST dap), Black Pennell (ST).
Bottom row, left to right: Stoat's Tail (S), Silver Stoat's Tail tube (ST), Mallard & Claret (ST).

Miscellaneous equipment

The still-water trout net may be used, but ought to have a white-painted bowframe of not less than 20in. It should be suspended from the waist by the hang-all belt loop when the angler is wading. Other requirements are:

- Sink-mix
- Two torches, one with a flexible neck extension
- Priest on a cord about the neck
- Scissors on a cord about the neck
- Spool of tippet nylon
- Midge cream
- Spare car keys
- A bag suspended from the waist into which fish may be placed whilst the angler is wading.

Fly-fishing at night

I am often asked why it is necessary to fish for river sea trout at night. My explanation is practical: placing a pupil by day where he may observe a shoal of resting peal, I creep downstream of the fish, and cast a fly on a long leader up to them. Nine times out of ten, the shoal is seen to fade from sight into deep water. Sea trout are shy and as the majority do not feed in freshwater this shyness is not overcome by hunger. They can be caught by day on a wind-ruffled loch, and in a spate on a river. (These approaches are revealed on pages 117–119.) In low water river conditions they overcome their shyness on dark nights to take the fly. Why they do so is a subject for conjecture, but curiosity and distant memories of feeding in the sea, and in the river in their juvenile years, spring to mind.

The daylight survey

The knowledge that sea trout are present in the pool being fished at night encourages the angler. Equally, it is a waste of time fishing a pool devoid of peal due to ignorance. A daylight survey using polarised spectacles will reveal the presence of fish. Whilst they are not always in the same lies at night as those occupied by day, at least you know they are in the pool. My fish-spotting reveals that by day the shoals are in deep shady areas; my fishing at night suggests that *some* of these fish move towards the tails of pools soon after dusk. Generally more sea trout are caught at night in the tails of pools rather than at the tops.

The moon and the weather

In my researches into sea trout fishing at night I have asked many experienced anglers whether they like to fish by moonlight. Their responses have invariably been that they prefer the darkest nights. Doubtless they are right, an opinion confirmed when one observes a fly line flashing across the water when illuminated by the moon. This frightens fish. Nevertheless, a full moon behind full cloud cover provides a diffuse illumination which is helpful, and a comfort to those of a nervous disposition. If fishing close to the sea, remember that high spring tides bring in fresh sea trout, and these tides coincide with full and new moons. I was very glad to have a moon on a recent night when fishing alone close to a monastery – a black-cloaked monk flitted along the river path.

The air cools rapidly on a clear starlit night until it becomes colder than the water – not a good condition for fishing. Such air/water temperature differences will be found to have occurred when the hand on the rod grows cold but registers warm water if dipped into a river.

Heavy rain reduces chances but a warm, drizzly, sticky night is an ideal condition. A windless night is better than one which is windy, particularly if the wind is cold and dry. It is dangerous to fish in a thunderstorm, a carbon rod is a good conductor.

When to start casting

It is sensible to prepare the rod outfit by day, making up the rod, line and leader, and knotting on a fly whilst the light is good. Then carry this to the river, or take the outfit in rod clips on the roof of the car.

At the waterside the first action should be to wipe the leader with sink mix and place the leader and fly to soak in the water. These actions ensure that the fly and leader will sink below the surface of the water when the first cast is made. The angler should then sit still on the bank to await the full darkness of night.

The shortest nights are in the second half of June and the first half of July. In this period it is rarely safe to commence fishing until 10.45 pm, or even later in bright moonlight. By the end of August it becomes sufficiently dark by 9.30 pm. These starting times alter from night to night, advancing on cloudy moonless evenings, and delayed by a clear sky and the moon.

I have asked experienced anglers how they judge the moment when it is safe to start fishing without scaring peal.

Tackle for night fly-fishing. Anti-clockwise from the right: fly box with spare home-made leaders, carton for damp sink mix cloth, red filter torch, spool of tippet nylon, flat torch to hold in the mouth, flexible necked torch, midge cream, Supafloat and solid Mucilin for surface lures, surface lures in box, priest on cord, Hang-All Belt Loop, Swiss Army knife on a cord.

They have stated that they commence when they cannot discern: the waterline under the far bank, or the leaves on the trees on the other side, or the colours of flowers, or when they have seen three bats or six stars. A distillation of these opinions should leave you in no doubt that impatience to commence fishing must be controlled. For myself I start when the line where the water meets the grass of the far bank has dissolved.

Where to cast

Start by casting a short line downstream close to your own bank, then slightly down and across, then at 45°, then almost straight across. On these casts the line may be allowed to swing towards your bank on the current. The cast directly across at 90° must be retrieved at a slow speed. The rate of retrieval then increases on the up-and-across casts to a rate greater than the flow of the current. Draw off another yard of line from the reel and repeat this casting arc, again commencing in the downstream direction. By this progression and gradual line extension the fly will cover fish before they see the line. This

At night sea trout favour lies under trees. Check the distance to cast to these places by day . . .

. . . and that there is clear room for the back cast.

simple process assumes a treeless bank, an unusual situation! The direction of casts is best worked out by day, and observations made of the required casting distance to cover fish lies and prevent the fly catching in bushes on the opposite bank. A useful method to ensure correct casting length is to go to the position by day, then count the number of arm-length withdrawals of line from the reel required to ensure the fly reaches only the desired area.

Whilst the down-and-across cast provides the most delicate and sensitive search of the water, the upstream rapidly recovered throw usually ensures a firm hold on a sea trout by the hook being drawn into the scissors of the mouth of the fish. There are many productive stands on gravel at the tails of pools, or on the stonework of a weir, where the upstream cast retrieved at a rapid speed is a great provider of fish.

Hooking, playing and netting
I fish with my rod point close to the surface of the water, but at a slight angle to the fly line. This ensures that the slightest pluck at the fly is felt, but there is also some give to a violent take. Experience enables the angler to distinguish between plucks by fish and tweaks to a floating line by insect-hunting

Right: Fish bag under the net, both suspended on the belt loop

bats which are attracted to line movement on the water by their radar. A pluck encourages one to continue casting to that area for a few minutes before continuing to search the river. Sometimes many plucks are experienced, pulls too, but few hooked fish. This is usually a sign that rain is on the way. The diary:

'1992. August 4. One peal 1lb 14oz. 1in Silver Stoat's Tail tube. Had four more splashy pulls in Abbots Mead and Caddaford Turn Pool where I also hooked momentarily a large peal or grilse which departed in a boil of water. I think the peal were playing about with the fly as rain was on the way. Continuous rain arrived later in the night.'

There is little one can do to ensure that plucks become firm takes, other than alter the fly from a single to a treble hook, or to a tandem, or a single with flying treble. A full description of advanced sea trout fly design is given in my book *Sea Trout – How to Catch Them* (Airlife, 1997).

The rod should be raised to an angle of at least 45° the

Unhooking a peal

moment a sea trout is hooked. This position brings the shock-absorbing spring of the rod into play and should be maintained until the fish is netted. The line must be kept taut to the fish at a reasonable pressure, and should be stripped in at speed if the fish runs fast upstream from below the angler. Stripped lengths of line resting as coils upon the water ought to be recovered onto the reel as soon as possible, certainly before the moment arrives to net the fish when they would be a hazard. I like to play a fish off the reel with the drag set light, applying extra resistance as necessary by passing the line beneath the forefinger of the hand on the butt of the rod. If the fish jumps I drop the point of my rod whilst it is still in the air. This ensures that the sea trout does not fall back onto a tight line, causing the hook to be pulled out or the leader to snap.

At the end of the fight (if wading), I lift the net off the belt loop, flick it open at the hinge, and net the fish as soon as it is seen to be lying on its side. Do not scoop about for a submerged fish, await the final surrender. When safely in the net, push the rod butt down inside the top of a thigh boot. Withdraw the priest from your trouser pocket and knock the fish on the head whilst it is over or in the net. Usually a single hook can be freed and the fish slipped into the bag suspended on the belt loop without returning to the bank. A treble may require the use of a torch, in which case turn your back on the area to be fished and remove the hook by the light of the flexible neck torch which should be permanently clipped to your chest. Fishing may then continue when the angler turns about, the position remaining unchanged.

Later, on returning to the bank, I take my peal out of the belt bag and place them in a plastic shopping bag inside a game bag.

Threading baler twine into the mouth and out of the gills to provide a handle to carry the fish back to the car.

A sea trout taken when salmon fishing in a spate.

Whilst wading do not throw fish onto the grass to your rear, they will attract hungry slugs or be stolen by mink. On reaching home the fish are placed in the refrigerator for the night. The next morning they are cleaned, scales taken from the flank for life-cycle analysis if required, and then eaten the same day if possible. A freshly-caught sea trout has a finer flavour than one which has been frozen.

Fly-fishing in daylight

Previously I wrote that to cast a fly upstream to a shoal of sea trout by day is a waste of time *nine times out of ten*. This is true, whether the fly be a dry pattern or a weighted nymph on a tapered 12ft 3-lb leader. Once in every four or five years a small peal has taken my fly on Dartmoor when the target has been brown trout. I know two fly-fishers who intentionally fish Gold-head nymphs, or weighted Partridge X2B treble-hooked shrimp patterns cast upstream on long leaders. From time to time they take a peal after allowing the nymph to sink to the level of a sleeping shoal.

The beginner would be well advised to confine his daylight sea trout fishing to the following situations and conditions:

- Intentionally in a river by day by wet fly in a spate
- By chance when fly-fishing for salmon in a spate
- By dapping and wet fly on a loch
- By upstream spinning

The last method will be covered in the next Chapter, jointly with salmon.

Wet fly in a spate

On a number of occasions I have taken sea trout by day from the tail of a pool as a spate fines down. The water must have cleared to the extent that you can see your feet when wading with the water up to your thighs. The fly, one of the three patterns mentioned in 'Fly-fishing at night', on a leader tapered to 6-lb point, may be cast down and across in the usual manner. A better direction in which to cast is up and across, followed by a rapid retrieve. The fly then speeds downstream with a belly in the line as it swings towards the near bank. Peal chase, take, and then turn back upstream in a rapid curve.

When fly-fishing for salmon
The diary:

'1997. June 26. Peal 2lb 8oz. 1¹/₂in Black Dart tube. In tail of Bridge Pool when after salmon in high water.'
and
'1997. August 6. Peal 2lb 0oz. 1¹/₂in Black Dart tube. In higher rising water in tail of Bridge Pool.'

On several occasions large sea trout in the 4lb category have taken my salmon fly, and my daughter Lara holds the family record of a 7lb peal by this chancy method. It is, of course, a matter of luck. Follow the salmon fly-fishing principles described in the next Chapter and, from time to time, a sea trout will take your fly. There is a difference between the two fish in the manner of taking the fly: salmon must be given time to turn down before the rod is raised and the hook set; a sea trout flashes up to the fly so quickly that it is out of sight, and hooked, before you can say Jack Robinson. The 1¹/₂in Black Dart tube is the longest fly I use

for salmon in summer – it is acceptable to peal by day in high water.

Dapping and wet fly on a loch
I would not, in the certainty of success, drive 600 miles north to Ross and Cromarty, or Sutherland, to fish a west coast river for salmon. While we in the South yearn for rain, the weather forecaster regularly sends the deluges north to Scotland, or so he claims. However, go there and you'll find the rain has not arrived, or the water has run away. There is truth in the saying 'You should have been here yesterday'. It is better for me, in Devon, to await a spate and then sally forth on my home river. Offer me a sea trout week on Sutherland's Loch Hope, connected to the sea by the 1¹/₂-mile Hope River, and I would not hesitate to accept.

Realistically, daylight fishing for sea trout (other than by

Sea trout dapping water on Loch Maree in Scotland.

maggot or worm) is only reliable on a loch, and then only if a wind ruffles the surface. But if the wind blows and you have chosen the right month when the fish are there, from July to September, you will catch them.

It is necessary to fish from a boat, ideally with a companion rod and a boatman whose knowledge of the loch leads to success. The best arrangement is for one rod to fish the dap and the other wet flies. If both are right-handed, place the wet fly rod in the stern, where he will cast with his rod outside the boat, and the dapper in the bows.

Both anglers should sit whilst fishing, and this calls for a longer wet fly rod than would be normal on a river. A 10-ft or 11-ft all-through action No. 6 weapon is ideal as almost all casting will be downwind. The extra length in the rod enables a dropper and a bob fly to be trickled across the surface of the water just before lifting off the floating fly line into the back cast.

Home-made leaders should be tapered to a 6-lb point as described in Chapter 18 in the 'Fly-fishing tackle' section. The wet flies recommended in that section are ideal for the point and dropper positions: Peter Ross, Black Pennell and Mallard & Claret in hook sizes No. 10 and No. 12. The bob fly should be a bumbly creation such as a Blue Zulu.

The Shakespeare Co market a 17-ft telescopic dapping rod in carbon fibre at the remarkable price of about £40. A fly reel of approximately $3^5/_8$in diameter is required, or a spare spool for a salmon reel may be used. The spool should be filled with 20-lb monofilament to the end of which is knotted about 10–12ft of undressed floss line to blow out in the wind. The dapping fly is then suspended on 4ft of 10-lb nylon tied to the end of the floss.

Dapping flies are bulky palmered creations on lightweight hooks of size No. 8 or No. 10 such as Loch Ordie, Blue Zulu, Fore & Aft, Black Pennell or a couple of artificial Daddy-long-

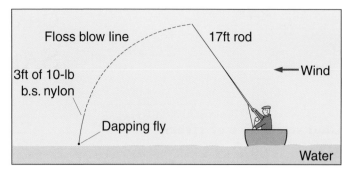

Dapping from a boat
A wind is essential to blow out the floss line in front of the boat. The buzzy waterproofed fly should be skidded across the surface of the loch whilst just touching the water. The nylon on which the fly is suspended should not touch the water.

legs. The flies must be thoroughly soaked in Supafloat. The practice of dapping is simple. Allow the floss line to billow out in the wind, the nylon to hang down almost vertically without touching the water, and the fly to drag across the surface. Sooner or later a pair of jaws the size of a mouse-trap will clamp shut on the offering. If the fish misses the fly, or solely inspects it, the dap should be swung away from the wet fly rod who should cover the area with his flies at once. The dap is a great method of raising fish from the depths.

Boat fishing on a sea trout loch makes for a relaxing daytime holiday in fine scenery, and the systems described allow a change of method. It is tiring to the eyes to watch a dapped fly for long periods and the change from bow to stern, and dap to wet fly will renew interest and vitality. If a boatman is not available I suggest one rod fishes for an hour whilst the other handles the oars and controls the downwind drift, positions may then be exchanged on the hour.

CHAPTER 21

SALMON

Characteristics of rivers

All salmon rivers are fed by rain, but the time interval between the rain falling on the land and then entering the river from the catchment area varies considerably.

Small spate rivers

A spate is the rise and fall in water level in a river following rainfall in the catchment hills. The hours when the spate is in progress, particularly the first hour as the water commences to lift and during the period when the water level is falling following cessation of the rain, are the best, and often the only, chance of catching a salmon on these small rivers by fly.

Many salmon anglers whom I have taught to fish the fly have asked me to telephone them when a spate is in progress in the river adjacent to my house. As these persons are usually working in an office, often one to three hundred miles away, I am reluctant to give this information. The reason is that by the time they have cleared their desks and travelled, the water is likely to have run away down the valley to the sea. You have to live locally to a spate river to be able to fish on what may be the single day of extra water following a rainstorm. Living in Devonshire I would not regularly book holidays to fish a Scottish West Coast small spate river. This is because the chances of arriving during a spate would be small.

The quality of the spate water is important. After a prolonged drought of several weeks the first spate is likely to produce turbid acid water if the run-off is from moorland and forestry plantations, resulting in poor fishing. The second spate,

A typical spate river in low water and . . .

... one hundred yards upstream in spate.

if after a short interval of one or two weeks, will be cleaner and produce a much better chance of catching a fish.

The actual rise in water level may be rapid during and after heavy rain. My home river may rise 1ft in an hour, or even by 3ft in a night. The fall is at a slower rate and produces one day of fishing in the headwaters and two days in the lower reaches. Salmon rarely run upstream in these small rivers other than in a spate, although grilse sometimes struggle over the stones in company with sea trout.

The large river

Salmon are able to run upstream in a large river at almost any time. Consequently the opportunities for fishing are greater than in a small spate stream. Because the size of the catchment area of such a river is considerable, the rise after prolonged rainfall may be substantial.

These rivers run for considerable distances through agricultural lowland areas. The run-off from cultivated fields carries mud into the river, turning it a muddy-brown colour which renders it unfishable. The river may then take several days to clear, starting at the top, but is then in good condition for many days. This is the type of river on which to book a holiday for there will almost always be fishing. Even if the water

Below: A tree trunk stranded by the last spate in the headwaters of this river.

The River Spey in Scotland

takes a long time to clear there is the chance of a fish if spinning and worming are allowed in high water.

The chalk-stream

These rivers, such as the Test, Itchen, Frome and Hampshire Avon have more stable flows during the summer than the two previous categories. This is because rain falling on the hills of the two types already mentioned runs *down* into the river; rain falling on the chalk hills of a chalk-stream downland catchment area soaks into the chalk sponge or aquifer and rises *up* into the river through springs. The river level may vary little during the season and there is always the chance of a fish. Even so, rain excites salmon and catches temporarily improve when the river is freshened by rain.

In the last twenty years the runs of salmon into the chalk-streams have reduced due to a number of adverse factors, critical amongst these is the reduction in the rate of water flow down the valley (see Chapter 18). On one major chalk river a friend and I caught thirty-two salmon between us in one season in the 1970s out of an estate catch in the region of 250 fish. In the 1990s the total estate catch for the many rods sometimes fell below our joint figure of 25 years ago.

The reduced flow fails to clear silt from salmon spawning beds, leading to the atrophy of ova in the redds which have

been cut by a much smaller run of fish. At the same time the deposition of silt has increased due to water run-off from ploughed land close to the river. Much dedicated work has been in progress for several years to clean the river-bed, and to restore the runs of salmon by the introduction of smolts raised under controlled conditions from stripped native fish. The

The River Test. Bernard Aldrich, retired head keeper, fishes this chalk-stream for salmon with a double-handed fly rod at Broadlands.

chalk-streams are not normally holiday rivers, fishing usually being confined to season rods fishing one day a week or fortnight.

The beginning – salmon on a spawning stream leap at dusk in mid-winter.

Juvenile electro-surveys in June, after the smolts have departed to the sea, ascertain the population of young salmonids in a spawning stream.

The life-cycle of salmon

Spawning and juvenile life

In the final week of November and the first two weeks of December the moorland streams which feed the rivers Dart, Tavy, Taw and Teign are alive with spawning salmon. In some other rivers spawning may be delayed until Christmas and later.

The female cuts a redd on a bed of gravel and small stones, usually at the run-off of a pool where shallow compressed water flows quickly, washing the river-bed clean. The redd is a small trough, usually about 6–12in deep, 2ft wide and 3ft in length, in water 2–3ft deep. A cock and a hen in the redd may be seen to curve in muscular spasms as eggs are released through the urino-genital pore by the hen and fertilised by the shed milt of the cock fish. The fertilised eggs sink to the bottom of the redd where they become covered by scoured gravel and small stones through which a flow of oxygenated water may pass. The parent fish, now wasted and thin and known as kelts, usually die in the river as they attempt to swim back to the sea. Very few succeed.

Beneath the gravel the *ova* hatch in about three months, depending upon the water temperature. *Alevins* are released

A grilse (one-sea-winter salmon) may be lifted by gripping it across the top of the head and pressing in the gill covers.

The 'kype' of a cock salmon found dead near a spawning bed and . . .

. . . the tail of the same fish. The noose of a tailer should settle in front of the gristle swellings at the base (wrist) of the tail which is concave.

from the split ova skin and are sustained for about one month by a yolk sac attached beneath their chins. They then swim up through the gravel to take their place in the stream. At this stage they are called *fry*. This little fish spends one to three years in the river, becoming known as a *parr*. The parr lives and feeds in the manner of a wild brown trout from which it may be distinguished as follows:

- trout – the anal fin has a thick white edge, and the adipose fin is brown, black or red
- parr – both fins are transparent

The marine period

After the river years the parr, now weighing about 4–5oz, takes on a silvery colour. It is now called a *smolt*, and in April and May swims down the river to the sea. After a minimum of 13 or 14 months it may return in the summer of the following year as a one-sea-winter fish, commonly known as a *grilse*, weighing between 3–7lb. If it spends two winters at sea it may enter the river of its birth at any time from very early spring to October, in some rivers as late as December, and on average will weigh 9lb. Fish of two-sea-winters, in my own knowledge from scale readings, may weigh between 8–24lb. Those of greater weight are now rare and are likely to have spent three or more winters at sea.

Sea lice and gill maggots

Sea lice are small suckered lice of about $\frac{1}{2}$in in length which attach themselves to the flanks, back and anal areas of the fish at sea. They fall off after three or four days of river life and thus, if seen on a salmon, denote a very fresh fish.

Gill maggots may be seen on the gill filaments of kelts and are sometimes claimed to identify kelts moving downstream in early spring from salmon on their way up the river to spawn. This is not reliable. In examining salmon in summer on their way up the river, gill maggots are sometimes in evidence.

Salmon lies

From the time a salmon returns to the river until it dies after spawning, it does not feed. Let us suppose a 10lb hen fish starts to swim up the river in April carrying two roes totalling 7000 very small eggs inside its body. If the fish is caught in September it will be found that the eggs are now large and fill the body cavity. Yet, the fish has not eaten! From this may be deduced that the egg mass has enlarged at the expense of body flesh. Body weight has also been consumed by the energy required to swim the many miles up the river from the sea to the spawning area, and to live for seven months. In the result the fish, which previously weighed 10lb, will weigh about 6lb as an emaciated kelt.

From the above it is apparent that the fish must make every effort to keep energy expenditure to a minimum. Therein is the key to the lies salmon occupy in a river: places where there is an oxygen-providing flow of fresh water, security through depth and an area where little energy expenditure is required to maintain position. A salmon will not lie where it has to swim hard to maintain its position.

In a salmon pool the speed of the current at the surface is greater than that close to the river-bed, thus a salmon likes to have four or five feet of water over its back. In a spate this may be available at the tail of a pool where a salmon may rest for a short time after struggling up through rough water, but in low water the required depth may only be available at the head of the pool. So these are the areas to fish in those conditions, for fish will move from the tail to the head of the pool as the water level falls and the spate recedes.

In detail, a lie may be only the length and width of a child's cot mattress. It will usually be found where an obstruction diverts the water flow over the head of the fish, or to either or

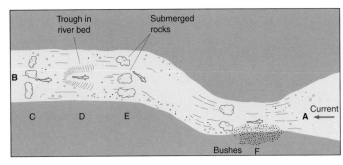

A spate river salmon pool
The deep head of this pool is at A, with the shallow tail or run-off at B. In high water salmon lie in front of the rocks at C for a rest after fighting their way up the fast stickle below the pool. As the spate recedes, fish move into trough D, which is a depression in the river-bed where the water speed is slower, the fast current passing over their heads near the surface. A further reduction in water flow will cause them to swim forward again to rest in front of the rocks at E. Finally, as the water level drops to low they take refuge in the deep turbulent throat at F, preferably beneath bushes or trees, and where they are invisible under the disturbed water.

both sides. Favourite places are: a trough in the river bedrock, in front of the rising bed of gravel or chalk at the tail of a pool, in front of a boulder and, in low water, beneath the turbulence at the narrow neck of a pool. Salmon are rarely found in the turbulent, disturbed water behind an obstruction.

There is truth in the saying by salmon anglers, 'It is the man who moves his feet who catches the fish'. The explanation of

Fish in the evening and at dawn in low water.

The River Tamar at Gunnislake is a substantial West Country river. Below this weir the river is tidal.

this cryptic comment is that in one mile of river there may be twenty salmon. Of these non-feeding fish, two may be slightly interested by the angler's fly in the rare arrival of extra water. As they occupy two lies, each 6ft in length in the 1760yd of the angler's beat, he must move his feet to find them!

Reasons for taking a lure

I am often asked, 'Why do salmon take a lure if they do not feed in freshwater'. The answer must be, 'Well, most of them don't'. Salmon lead a very boring existence in the river, with perhaps only twenty miles to swim from the sea to the spawning area, a distance which could be covered in one or two days but is spread over as much as six months. They must therefore spend many weeks in a static comatose state. Then it rains and the river lifts, a stirring excitement and change. Suddenly a Mepp spoon whirrs by across their window. Such an arrival is an extraordinary event and now, predatory instinct stimulated, one in ten fish will attack. In the case of a worm or prawn bait, there may be a freshwater juvenile or marine feeding memory.

Fly-fishing tackle

Recently I hooked, played and beached a $9\frac{3}{4}$lb cock salmon on the upper reaches of the River Tavy in Devonshire. A spate was in progress and thus my fly was a $1\frac{1}{2}$in Black Dart socketed

tube, with a No. 8 Partridge X3 straight-eye black outbend treble hook. I used an untapered 15-lb Maxima Chameleon leader, $3\frac{7}{8}$in Hardy St John reel, No. 9 AirCel Supreme sink-tip line and a 15-year-old 12ft Hardy graphite salmon fly rod. The river is narrow in that place and could be leaped by a roe deer, but as trees line the river preventing movement along the bank you have to hang on to a fish. If this outfit is considered it will be remarked that each item has considerable strength: 15-lb nylon, No. 8 treble hook, and a powerful rod. A small river does not mean fine nylon, but it may require a short single-handed rod with a butt extension if there is an overhead canopy of trees. On the whole I am not in favour of single-handed rods for salmon, they are a limiting factor in playing fish, working the fly and mending the fly line.

Rods

On a great river nothing better will be found than a 15ft Bruce & Walker No. 10 Speycaster. We don't have such rivers in the south and south-west of England and thus, for Tamar, Wye and other rivers of that size the 14-ft No. 9/10 Bruce & Walker (B&W) is my choice. For small to medium rivers, such as Dart, Tavy, Taw and Dovey the 12ft 4in No. 8/9 Speycaster is ideal. These rods have authority and the tube has a matt non-reflective finish.

When wading under a canopy of trees in a little river, a single-handed rod is forced upon one. Don't forget that in order to draw a fish to the net it is usually necessary to raise the rod to the vertical, thus a short rod is required to keep the tip beneath overhanging branches. All really good rods are expensive – you could save some outlay by using the 9ft 3in B&W Powerlite with 1½in butt extension which I recommended for sea trout. Such a rod will deal with grilse, but lacks strength for a 10lb fish in heavy water. Recently I received a 10ft 6in Powerlite No. 6 which would be better matched by a No. 7 line for short distance casting. This rod has all the power needed in the described conditions and has a built-on butt extension to support the wrist and keep the reel rim away from the clothes.

My own double-handed rods are:

- 14ft B&W Speycaster No. 9/10
- 13ft Normark Norboron No. 8/9
- 12ft Hardy Salmon graphite No. 9
- 12ft Sharpe's spliced impregnated split cane

All the above are in three sections.

Reels and fly lines

A 4¼in reel is necessary to accommodate the No. 10 or No. 11 lines and backing needed for a 15ft rod. For the first three rods listed above I have two Hardy St John 3⅞in reels with one spare spool. These hold:

- AirCel DT9F
- AirCel Supreme DT9F/S (sink-tip)
- WetCel 2 DT9S

In each case they hold about 100yd of 25-lb monofilament

backing. The St John reel has a long pedigree, I purchased my first from the Hardy Pall Mall shop in 1958. The reel is still in production.

At the end of the season run the lines off the reels, make sure both reel and line are dry and then evenly rewind the line. Then remove the spool, clean the inside and oil the spindle, ratchet and cam.

The nostalgic outfit

My first salmon rod was a 12-ft Hardy AHE Wood No. 2 split cane with a steel centre. (In those days the No. 2 did not refer to the line weight which was categorised differently.) This killed so many salmon that it grew tired after twenty years and had to be retired. Still, at times, ancient memories enter my mind and I take up the Sharpe's 12-ft spliced split cane. To this is fitted a reel of the same era, a 3⅞in wide drum Hardy Perfect. I have only one of these reels and thus only one line, an AirCel Supreme No. 8 sink-tip, for you cannot have a spare spool for such a Perfect. This rod is taken to the river in clips on the car roof. The slow action is a pleasure, as is the sure sweet steady wind of the reel. These reels are no longer in production in large sizes and are heavy by modern standards. Good second-hand models fetch about £150 at auction.

Leaders

Many salmon are landed on 10-lb leaders – and not a few are lost! The risk of breakage in a 10-lb leader depends upon the river. If there are many obstructions such as weed-beds and an abundance of boulders trouble lies ahead.

My leaders are of Maxima Chameleon, untapered and

The author fishing with a double-handed salmon fly rod.

Fishing tackle and rod racks in the author's garage. Left to right: thigh boots, sea trout fish bag, salmon tailer, trout net, 25in Gye type net, sea trout fish bag, 24in Gye net, fish bass, wading staff, trout net, game bag, fishing waistcoat, weighing scales. Above are double-handed salmon fly rods, and spinning rods.

straight off the spool. No. 6 single and double hooks, and the small Partridge up-eyed No. 10 and No. 12 X2B trebles, and those of smaller size are well matched by 12-lb Maxima. For 1in, $1^{1}/_{4}$in, $1^{1}/_{2}$in and 2in tubes the nylon should be 15-lb Maxima to ensure good turnover of the fly at the end of the leader.

I do not taper my salmon leaders, which have a blood bight loop tied on one end and are attached to the fly line by a double sheet bend. The spool is then unwound to a length of about 9–10ft. This bulky line-leader junction knot will never be wound up to the dangerous position of the top ring of a long rod when landing a salmon, as the leader is 2–4ft shorter than the rod. The knot itself is absolutely safe and has the advantage of acting as a visible indicator of the depth of a fish being played.

If using the 9ft 3in single-handed rod a needle knot line/leader junction must be used as described for night sea trout fishing, as the junction may be wound into the top ring of the rod.

When fishing, the leader should be inspected at regular intervals for wind knots. An unpicked wind knot produces a curl in the nylon which may cause it to be held visibly on the water surface film. In this case a new leader should be put into use.

Flies

These may be dressed on single hooks, doubles, trebles and as treble-hooked tube flies and Waddingtons. The Waddington is a fly dressed on a wire shank which passes through the eye of a treble hook at one end – it need not concern the beginner. I always use treble hooks with short shanks in preference to doubles and single hooks.

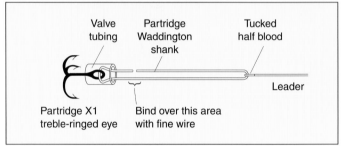

Partridge Waddington shank for a salmon fly

If the hook is damaged a new hook may be fitted provided the dressing materials are not taken over the gap in one wire of the shank. Rubber cycle valve tubing keeps the treble hook in line with the fly body. It is much easier to replace the hook of a tube fly.

If in the mood a salmon will take a thin slice of orange peel, but the length of the slice should vary from $^{1}/_{2}$–2in according to water conditions. Notice the colour orange. Remember also the colour vision capacity of fish: red, orange, yellow, and black with silver or gold tinsel ribbing.

To catch salmon you only need five flies, three of which are different lengths of the same pattern, the Black Dart, which is my own design to take account of the colour vision of fish. This is the fly which hooked the fish recorded at the beginning of this section on page 126. How to fish these flies will be described in the 'Fly-fishing' section of this Chapter.

THE BLACK DART

For spates and cold water.

Tube – 2in, $1^{1}/_{2}$in, $1^{1}/_{4}$in Veniard Type B Slipstream socketed
Hook – Black Partridge X3 outbend No. 8 treble for all lengths
Tag – No. 16 oval gold tinsel

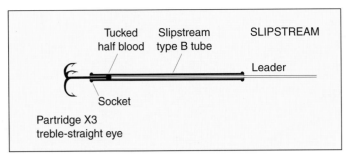

Tucked half blood | Slipstream type B tube | SLIPSTREAM

Leader

Socket

Partridge X3 treble-straight eye

Veniard Type B Slipstream socketed polythene tube for salmon and sea trout flies. A Partridge X3 straight-eye treble hook may be used, or the X1 round-eye if a firmer grip is required in the socket.

Body – Black floss over close turns of fine lead wire. The lead is stopped short of the head where the bucktail wing is to be tied in

Rib – No. 16 oval gold tinsel

Wing – Orange bucktail

Cheeks – Jungle cock or jungle cock substitute. A long feather, three-quarters the length of the tube, one on each side

Head – Black varnish

Silk – Black Naples

Stoat's Tail

For warm clear water.

Hook – Partridge X2B up-eyed black treble No. 12

Body – Black floss silk

Rib – No. 16 oval silver tinsel

Wing – Stoat's tail or black Labrador dog

Head – Black varnish

Silk – Black Naples

Shrimp fly

An alternative to Stoat's Tail in warm, low coloured water, and as a dropper.

Hook – Partridge X2B up-eyed black treble No. 10 or No. 12

Body – Red floss

Rib – No. 16 oval silver tinsel

Throat hackle – Hot orange

Cheeks – Two small jungle cock feathers, or jungle cock substitute

Wing – Orange bucktail

Head – Red varnish

Silk – Black Naples

If you do not possess any salmon flies but own a black dog, cut some hairs from his tail and tie directly around the shank of a single or double hook.

Fly-fishing tactics

There are rivers where fly-only is the rule; fortunate are those who fish such waters. I am not a fly-only purist, taking my turn with spinning artificial baits, and trotting a worm or prawn if conditions suggest such methods and they are excusable and allowed. Nevertheless, to be on a fly-only river where other anglers have not pestered salmon in a pool with a prawn, or plopped in a Flying 'C' ahead of your fly from the opposite

---

Dressing salmon flies.

Selecting a fly.

bank, is a rare privilege. I commend the fly to you for the simplicity of the terminal tackle: a spool of nylon and a box of flies. You are free to walk the banks, instead of clattering along weighed down by boxes of spoons, minnows, weights and worms which will sink you if you fall into a strong, deep river.

The water and the fly line

The temperature of the water governs the depth at which the fly should be fished. In cold water, below 45°F (7°C) or there-abouts, salmon are cold and thus lethargic. They will not jump weirs or rise to take a fly fished off a floating line. You must therefore take the fly down to them. In practice this requires a fast-sinking fly line to be fished from the opening of the season in January, February or March until the beginning or middle of April. Such a line may also be needed in late autumn and early winter when the water has cooled after the summer.

As the water warms to above 45°F (7°C) salmon become more active and will rise up to take a fly fished off a sink-tip line or a floater. This situation continues throughout late spring, the summer and early autumn. A heatwave, as with still-water trout fishing, might suggest a trial with a sinking line if the river is sufficiently deep for the fly not to snag on the bottom.

For many years I only fished a floating line in the summer, relying on the weight of my Black Dart fly to ensure it fished just beneath the water surface and did not skate in a fast current. In recent seasons the sink-tip has handsomely rewarded my efforts in strong, warm spate water. However, the fly catches on too many rocks if this line is used in low water.

Size of fly

Fish a large fly if the water is below 45°F (7°C), heavily-coloured or high. In warm water, clear water and a low river, fish a small fly. These situations are catered for by the 2in, 1½in and 1¼in tubes already described, and in warm, clear and low water by the Stoat's Tail and the Shrimp.

These suggestions can only be a general guide. In June I have taken fish on a 2in tube. In April, with frozen hands, I have lured 12lb and 15lb springers to a No. 6 Low Water single-hooked Hairy Mary fly 1000ft above the sea. These were exceptions. The conditions of water colour, temperature, height and rate of flow appear in so many combinations that you must juggle these in your mind to reach a correct decision. In my opinion a spate in summer overrides any regard to water temperature – the higher the water level the larger the fly, even if the water is at 65°F (18°C).

The diary:

'June 30. 10½lb salmon on a 1½in Black Dart. Air 74°F (23°C), water 65°F (18°C). River showing its bones previous afternoon. A night of rain. Dustbin lid full. 10 am river high and thick brown. By 2.30 pm had cleared and fallen 4in. Lara took the fish in tail of Black Hole. A spate overrides water temperature which would otherwise indicate a small fly.'

The inverted dustbin lid outside my kitchen window is a rather agricultural rainfall gauge. If full there is likely to be sufficient water when we arrive at the river which is ten miles from my house. I like to fish in warm drizzly rain, but not in a thunderstorm which is dangerous when holding a carbon fibre rod.

Air-water temperatures

Other than in a heatwave the air needs to be warmer than the water for the angler to meet success. This is also the case when fishing for trout and sea trout. A thermometer should be carried by a beginnner, but the experienced angler will judge the relative temperatures by his hand in the water and the air. The hatching of insects at the water surface from underwater nymphs also indicates a rising river temperature.

The diary:

'1992. September 24. Dart. 2 grilse. Total 12lb 8oz. 1¼in Black Dart and 1¼in Hairy Mary. After photographing Brian's 10½lb sea trout at noon. Started to fish down the river at 1 pm after he had fished down and back in the morning, but saw no fish. Water on 4 on the gauge. Took 6½lb cock on Hairy Mary on way down in main stickle above Stoney Pool. On way back another of 6lb on Black Dart between Chloe's and Ben's Pools. Water on 3 on the gauge on return. These fish took on falling coloured water. Air warming as north wind dropped in pm, flies hatched and trout rose.'

Brian is a very good angler who has detailed knowledge of the river. We fish the same lies. His lack of a grilse was due to the cold north wind; my two grilse came when olives started to hatch, indicating a warming of the air and, subsequently, the water.

Time of day

In March and April, if the air is at 55°F (12.8°C) at 10 am and the water at 46°F (7.8°C), the water temperature is likely to rise to 47°F (8.3°C) by lunch-time. The best period that day is likely to be between 1 pm and 4 pm at which time the air will start to cool. In May, June and September you should fish throughout the day.

In hot weather in July and August the first two or three hours after dawn are best. This is because the air and the water will have cooled overnight, but at dawn the air temperature will rise faster than the water temperature. This provides a short period of correct relative temperatures. You should also fish at dusk when the sun is off the water.

Working the fly

In cold water the fly should be worked slowly; in warm water the speed may be increased. Speed is hard to define. Imagine you are casting down and across in early spring. The requirement then is to slow the passage of the fly by casting a long line at a narrow angle and then making an upstream mend of the line (see diagram).

In summer an upstream mend is usually inappropriate as the current will glide the fly steadily across the river. In fact, it may be sensible to increase the speed of passage by stripping-in line, or even by 'backing-up' (see diagram). These actions create a fast passage of the fly which salmon must take at speed or miss the chance. Backing-up is an effective persuader of fish. Start at the tail of a pool, casting straight across instead of down and

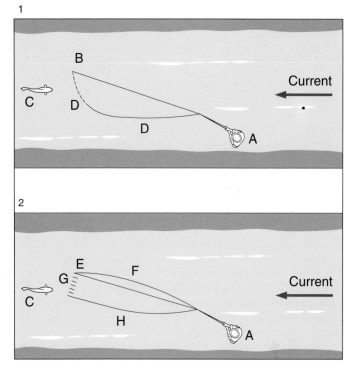

An upstream mend

1. An angler casts from A to B hopng to rise the fish at C. The current presses on the fly line and sweeps the fly away too rapidly in curve D.
2. The angler casts to E and at once mends the line over to F without moving the final yard of the line, the leader and the fly, which remain at E. The fly will then swim slowly in path G across the front of the fish at C whilst the current is straightening the upstream curve F to almost straight line H. Mending is used to counteract the pull on the line of fast water – it is not necessary to mend in slow sections of the river where the requirement may be to speed up the fly, as in backing-up.

across. Take two steps upstream and strip in the line, the fly following in a pronounced curve at speed. Fish often take in a determined fast surge. This method is particularly effective in a wide pool where the wind is blowing upstream to produce rolling waves as it pushes against the current.

The diary:

'1982. September 28. Dart.
10.30 am Top of Bridge Pool. 7½lb. 1in Copper Dart.
2.00 pm Sycamore Hole. 7lb. 1¼in Black Dart.
3.30pm. Middle of Firs Pool. 8½lb. 1¼in Black Dart
There was a strong east wind blowing up Firs Pool which created big waves. Hooked and lost two fish backing-up in same place within two or three minutes of each other and then, at once, the fish of 8½lb which was landed.'

The wind was very strong and blew my hat into the river. Cast as I would I could not hook it as it drifted away down the river. Despite the loss of this and other hats I would rather fish on a windy day than a calm one.

Movement of the fly in short upstream and downstream draws in line with the current has tempted many fish. I arrived

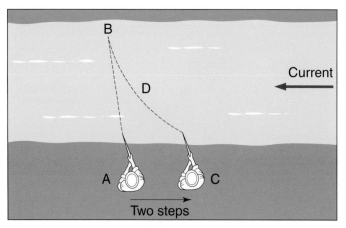

Backing-up the fly
Angler at A casts straight across to B in the wide slow tail of a pool. He then takes two steps upstream to C, retrieving line at the same time. The fly and line will come across in the fast curve D. Continue to the head of the pool. The best results are achieved when an upstream wind creates waves on the water surface.

one day beside a small pool to find an old friend seated beside the river at lunch-time. We shared my sandwich and tin of beer. 'There's a salmon over there' he said, pointing to a tiny smooth area about 2ft wide and 6ft in length in front of a boulder. 'I've risen him. Now I'll take him home.' Gilbert is now as ancient as his tackle was then, the fly line cracked, the rod brass ferruled. But in his day he was a master angler.

He dropped the fly into the top of this little run. The fish came up with closed mouth, then sank away. Three times the salmon rose. 'I'll have him yet,' smiled Gilbert. He cast the fly into the tail of the pool and, with horny hand, drew it one foot upstream and let it wash back three times. On the third upstream swim the salmon took. I netted the fish, Gilbert tied it head-to-tail with a length of binder twine and toddled home to Princetown and his tea.

Hooking fish
The actions to be taken depend on whether you are fishing a sinking or a floating fly line. You are unlikely to see a fish come to the fly fished off a WetCel 2 fly line and thus possibly a foot beneath the water surface. Your aim is to hook the fish in the scissors at the angle of the upper and lower jaws. To this end it is ideal if the salmon takes the fly and turns down or away before pressure is applied to drive home the hook. To achieve this on the WetCel, set the reel to the lightest drag. With the rod low and pointing down the line, fish off the reel. To fish 'off the reel' means that there is no resistance to the fish pulling line off the reel other than a lightly set adjustable drag. When line is drawn from the drum by the unseen fish, the angler should sweep up the rod without touching the line. The delay is sufficient for the fish to turn down, and the drag of raising the rod is enough to set the hook in the scissors on most occasions.

When fishing a floating line the movement of the fish to the fly is rapid. If an unseen fish gives me a pull, I pull back. If the fish is seen to rise I drop my rod point to allow slack line to give the fish time to turn down. Then I raise to hook the fish at the moment it disappears beneath the surface. The timing should be slow, and the tightening is best described as 'feeling for the fish'. This steady unexcited movement will not frighten a fish which has not taken the fly – the salmon may well try again. The best advice to a beginner at the start of a floating line day is, 'If you see a salmon come to your fly, do nothing. Let it hook itself.'

The trout man is at a disadvantage, being in the habit of striking or raising the rod to the risen fish at once. This habit is hard to break. Many fish are lost by the excited automatic strike to an up-curving fish, which may not have even reached the fly.

The reluctant taker
A salmon may rise, take a look, and then sink from sight without touching the fly. I usually give it two more casts in the same style. If it does not respond I move upstream for 25yd and fish down on it again, possibly with a smaller fly, putting the fly two or three times over the lie. If the fish responds but does not take I continue to put the original fly over it so long as interest is shown. As soon as the fish fails to respond it is best to carry on down the river, then return in two or three hours to try again. If the fish is not there another fish may have occupied the lie. At the end of all this you may not have a salmon, but you have tucked under your belt knowledge of a new lie, or confirmation of one already known.

The stealthy angler
You must be more cautious when fishing for salmon than when after trout. Because the beginner cannot spot a salmon on the river-bed in five feet of water he may imagine the salmon cannot see him. This is a great mistake. The adverse vision factors are: the salmon is looking upstream at the angler who is fishing downstream (instead of upstream as with trout dry fly); the salmon at a depth of 4ft has a window 9ft wide, whilst the visible trout at 1ft has a window 1ft 3in wide; the angler is high on the bank or, at least, at a vertically higher level on the river-bed whilst wading than the downstream fish; he has a long rod which may flash in the sun – one reason for eschewing false casting. Kneel, keep back from the edge of the bank, face the sun rather than be silhouetted from behind and throw your shadow on the water. Do not stumble on the bank, or thump with studded boots on the river-bed – vibrations carry.

Playing and landing

Playing
When a salmon takes a fly or spinning bait it is unaware of the angler at the other end of the line, all it knows is that something is pulling at its mouth. The longer the angler remains out of sight the better, for as soon as the fish sees him it will make an extra effort. Therefore keep low and take advantage of cover.

On hooking a salmon, which usually takes place downstream of my position, I like to move down opposite to the fish which then has to fight both the pull of the line and the push of the current. If the salmon takes the lure upstream of your position (as in upstream spinning), it then has to fight both pressures together, an ideal combination and position. It is a mistake to allow the fish to remain static downstream of the rod, where the helpful pressure of the current cancels out the pull of the line.

Having moved opposite to the fish a steady upward pressure should be applied to make the salmon bore nose-down towards the river-bed. This might be described as static heavy energy expenditure. If continued for two or three minutes much steam will be taken out of a 10lb fish. Then it is time to move the rod to a sideways position to create a pull from across the river. The salmon counters this by facing towards the far bank, the river pressure increases on its flank and it must swim forward. I describe this as 'stirring up the fish'.

It is possible at almost any time to make a salmon jump by applying excessive pressure. The jump is a risky moment and should be avoided. A two-sea-winter salmon gives about two seconds notice of its intention to leap by dramatically accelerating, whilst a grilse can erupt without notice. There is controversy about the immediate action to take whilst the fish is in the air; I drop my rod point to allow the salmon to fall back onto a slack line. If the line is kept tight during the leap the violent movement may pull out the hook.

Ideally, as stated, the fish should be persuaded to fight opposite to or upstream of the angler, but the fish has its own ideas and may dash away downstream. If the fight is in a small pool from which, due to bankside trees, the angler may not follow, rapid and courageous action must be taken well before the salmon reaches the pool run-off. Slacken the line entirely by stripping two or three yards off the reel, and lowering the rod point at the same time. In four cases out of five the fish, feeling released, will turn to face upstream. The line may then be tightened and the fish worked up to the centre of the pool.

In a long pool, if a salmon persists in a downstream swim until twenty-five or thirty yards below the angler, slacken the line to turn the fish. It may then be 'walked-up' away from the dangerous tail of the pool. To 'walk-up' a salmon, drop the rod tip close to the water with the rod straight out at 90°C from the bank. Without winding the reel, gently increase the almost direct upstream pull on the salmon until it starts to slide forward through the water in line with the current. Step by step the angler progresses towards the head of the pool, with the fish following. A grilse may take five minutes to land; a 10lb fish twice as long. All fish are more difficult to land in a fast current.

Landing methods

Landing salmon is more readily achieved if the fish can be brought to an area of slack water, as it is difficult to secure a salmon if a fast current runs beneath your bank. If using a net it may be impossible to hold it out submerged against the flow. Additionally, a salmon loses direction in a slack area, particularly if vision is impaired by muddy water which at times may be stirred up by the angler's boots for this purpose.

BEACHING

This is only possible if a sandy, stony or muddy bank slopes gently into the water. The salmon must be played out, then drawn head first to the bank, pressure being maintained by the rod lowered over the land. As soon as the head of the fish rests upon the bank the angler, maintaining the rod pressure, should move behind the fish and push it onto the land by a grip in front of the tail.

THE HAND

Tailing is only safe with two-sea-winter-salmon which have a gristle swelling at the wrist of the tail, in front of which the

Beaching a salmon.

Netting a salmon.

hand may achieve a grip. The grilse tail lacks these swellings and the hand will slide off over the tail. Before taking hold it helps if the palm of the hand is roughened by wiping it across sand to increase the friction between fish and hand. Now grip the wrist of the tail firmly by the ring of the thumb and the first two fingers, with the little finger towards the trailing edge of the tail. This grip will lift a salmon from the water.

A grilse may be secured by hand by placing the open palm over the top of the fish's head, thumb and forefinger towards the nose. Then with fingers on one side and the thumb on the other, press in the gill flaps to secure a firm hold beneath the bony skull. It is then easy to lift the grilse out of the water. This should not be done if the grilse is to be returned as the gill filaments may be damaged.

THE NET

The best net is the 24in Gye with a sliding handle and shaft. This is carried on the back, held in a peel sling, and should remain there until the salmon is played-out. With one hand on the rod, the peel sling can be released by the other hand which then grips the net handle. With one foot pressing the net ring onto the ground, the handle may be pulled to draw out the shaft. This may sound complicated, but with practice becomes a swift, easy movement.

The salmon should be persuaded upstream of the angler, then swum back head first into the net. It should not be netted by trying to sweep it up tail first because it can swim forward out

of the net. Neither should it be pulled upstream from below the angler to the net. This puts a strain upon the hook hold, and the first item to reach the net rim will be the leader and, possibly, part of a treble hook exposed on the edge of the fish's mouth.

A salmon may be drawn across the water to a submerged net, but this should be done in water which is at least of knee depth so that the net is mainly underwater. If the angler is standing in water which is only a few inches deep, the fish has to be pulled over the net rim where the risk of one of the hooks of a treble protruding and catching in the meshes of the net is considerable. This would pull out the whole treble, releasing the fish. I always carry a Gye net because it is the safest system where beaching is impossible, and one never knows that a beach will be available.

THE TAILER

Whilst this is an excellent piece of equipment for losing fish I must describe the actions necessary to try to secure a salmon. The system relies upon a wire noose like a rabbit snare, but on the end of a thick wire cable, settling around the wrist of a two-sea-winter salmon's tail above the gristle swelling. It is a very risky business to attempt to tail a grilse as these fish have a slim tail. The device should be carried, noose in a bow, over the back.

When a fish has been played to a standstill, slide the brass ring at the end of the thin wire to the end of the metal shaft. Together with the thick wire cable, withdrawn from the hollow handle, a bow will be formed which may be placed over the tail. Move this noose up the body to just behind the dorsal fin, then pull sharply at right angles to the salmon's body. The noose

The tailer in use.

should slide back down the body, tightening as it goes, settling just above the tail. If the noose slides over the tail you are left with a long handle, a long cable at the end of which is a circular wire noose, and no fish. To re-set is a problem with only one hand, the other being on the rod.

THE GAFF

This is a sharp, pointed metal hook. The flank of a salmon is penetrated, the fish lifted onto the land, and there it must be killed. I will not write more about the gaff which is a cruel instrument illegal on many rivers, and which may become illegal nationally.

Returning salmon to the river

Salmon are scarce compared with the populations of twenty years ago. Increasingly, fish are being returned unharmed to the water. At the back-end of the season hen fish heavy with eggs and cock fish with milt sacs must be returned. The fish should be brought to the bank or net as rapidly as possible and must not be in an exhausted state from a prolonged fight. It is well if the net has a smooth knotless bag, now a legal necessity to prevent damage to the scales of fish. Artery forceps usually enable rapid hook removal. The fish should then be held with its head to the current until it recovers and swims away. At no time should a fish be touched with dry hands, and thus all releases should take place with the fish remaining in the river.

Spinning for salmon and sea trout

There are two effective directions in which to cast to catch salmon on a spinning bait. In cold water cast down and across, then retrieve slowly whilst the bait traverses the river close to the bottom. In warm water cast upstream and then retrieve at a speed greater than the flow of the water with a large bait 2–3ft below the surface. Alternatively, fish down and across with a smaller bait at mid-depth.

Rods

I have two Hardy Fibalite spinning rods, one is 10ft in length and the other, my favourite, is the 8ft 6in model. The 10ft rod is the better length for worming and prawning, and for spinning in a wide river.

Spinning reels and lines

My co-author, Tony Allen, suggests a Mitchell 300 fixed spool reel for pike spinning (see his 'Rods and Reels' Chapter), and this is also my choice for salmon and sea trout. This reel comes with two spools which I suggest, in common with Tony, be loaded with not less than 100yd each of 18-lb and 12-lb Maxima monofilament. The 18-lb nylon should be used at all times for salmon; the 12-lb when pursuing sea trout and unlikely to encounter salmon. The spools should be filled to within $1/10$in of the rim. If underfilled they will not cast far, but if overfilled coils of line will come off the reel in a tangle.

The fixed spool reel is ideal for use in both open and restricted casting spaces, little rod swing being required to flick out a bait between trees. The other type of reel available is the multiplier, but this is less versatile and mainly suited to casting heavy baits in open spaces. This is because a wide swing of the rod is required to overcome the inertia of the drum, and keep it revolving. Overruns are a hazard with multipliers due to the revolving drum line, whilst fixed-spool reels do not revolve and therefore cannot overrun. A beginner only needs one reel – a fixed spool.

Weights, swivels and traces

A swivel should be tied to the end of the spinning line. Between the swivel and the bait is the trace, a 2ft 6in or 3ft length of nylon of lesser strength than the reel line. The 18-lb reel line should have a 15-lb trace; the 12-lb reel line a 10-lb trace. Lesser strengths risk breakage.

It is illegal to use lead weights between 0.06g and 28.35g. In my opinion the best weight design for spinning is the banana-shaped Wye which is made of a legal alloy metal. This lead-free design should be carried in weights of 7, 14 and 18g. The

Wye weight attachment
The reel line must be tied to the wire loop at one end of the Wye, the trace to the swivel at the other end. Both knots are tucked half-bloods.

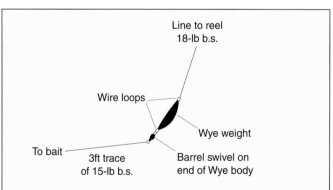

Line to reel
18-lb b.s.

Wire loops

Wye weight

To bait

3ft trace
of 15-lb b.s.

Barrel swivel on
end of Wye body

Spinning in March. This angler carries a 30in net.

Wye has a wire loop at one end to which the reel line is knotted, and a swivel at the other end to which the trace is attached. If a weight at the line-trace junction is not required, a barrel swivel may form the joint, or a 'BB' ball-bearing swivel. The 'BB' is expensive, but the best on the market. All line to-weight, weight or swivel-to-trace, and trace-to-bait knots should be tucked half-bloods.

Artificial baits

A great variety of baits is available for purchase: metal and wooden Devon minnows, plugs, Tobies, spoons of many styles, and even one to frighten any fish, the River Runt Spook! The beginner need only select two in different sizes or weights, the Flying 'C' and the Mepp Aglia.

The Flying 'C' comes in combinations of silver or gold blades, together with rubber tails in red, brown and white. Gold and red is a good mix in 10g and 15g weights.

The Mepp Aglia, one of many Mepp designs, is a fast revolving spoon in which a large size is suited to upstream casting where the retrieve is with the current. You will be well rewarded by the gold colour in the large size No. 4 for upstream use, and the smaller No. 2 for downstream fishing for salmon. The No. 2 may be cast upstream in low water for sea trout.

Cold water spinning

When the water temperature is below 45°F (7°C), as described in 'Fly-fishing tactics' on page 130, salmon must be sought close to the river-bed. This situation is likely to apply from the opening of the season until the first or second week of April. It will also be necessary to spin at considerable depth in November and December if the river is still in season.

The Flying 'C' is the best bait to use in the deep sections of the river. Whether to use the 7g or 15g 'C', and which Wye weight, or possibly just a swivel, can only be decided when you

have knowledge of the speed of flow and depth of the river, and the snags to be avoided on the river-bed. The speed of flow will vary from day-to-day with the height of the river, thus a judgement of weight can only be made on arrival at the water. Obviously the stronger the flow the greater the weight required to keep the bait down to the river-bed when casting downstream.

The cast should be made 'down and across'. In a wide river the near half should be fished first, casting halfway across and retrieving with the rod held at about 45° to the horizontal. The far half should then be fished with the rod held high to keep most of the line out of the water, thus allowing the bait to track slowly across the river. If the rod is held low, too much line will be in the water, and the bait will be pulled across at high speed by the drag of the current on the line. If the river is at a low level and the water is clear, I have found the No. 2 Mepp Aglia an excellent bait, usually in conjunction with a 14g weight.

A salmon will not normally be seen to take the lure – the line will just stop. You will soon know there is a fish at the other end, and should then follow the instructions on playing fish set out in the 'Playing and landing' section on pages 132–133, with this difference, the fish must be 'pumped towards you'. The fixed spool reel has an adjustable drag and slipping clutch. The salmon may pull off line against this drag whilst the clutch slips and the spool revolves. To increase pressure on the fish you must either adjust the clutch by tightening, or put your finger on the spool rim to either slow it, or stop it revolving. To pump the fish towards you, place the forefinger of the hand adjacent to the reel on the spool rim to stop it revolving and giving line to the fish. Now raise the rod tip almost to the vertical, then lower the rod tip whilst winding in the line.

The reward of upstream spinning with a No. 4 Mepp Aglia in June.

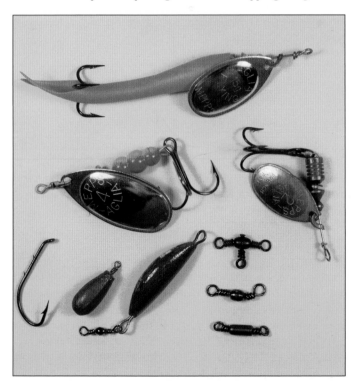

Warm water spinning

As this takes place in late spring, summer and early autumn you are just as likely to attract sea trout as salmon. The most productive condition is likely to be a warm August or September spate when there will be plenty of fish in the river and the flow is slightly coloured. Now is the time to cast upstream with a 7g Wye and the No. 4 Mepp Aglia. I can assure you that the large size of this spoon does not deter fish – they go for it at speed.

A long cast is made upstream. When the spoon hits the water there should be a pause of two or three seconds to allow the bait to sink one or two feet, then reel back at a moderately fast speed. If you retrieve slowly the spoon may catch on the riverbed and the fish may not be shocked into an instinctive grab at the bait. Even in low clear warm water under a sunny sky I have taken salmon by spinning upstream with the No. 4 Mepp Aglia. In these conditions it is also worthwhile casting the No. 2 Mepp Aglia upstream on the 12-lb line over a visible shoal of sea trout, for one will sometimes follow, although they rarely take.

Releasing snagged baits

When casting downstream and the bait snags on the bottom, do not react by pulling on the line. Instead open the bail arm of the reel, allowing 25yd of line to run off the reel to form a loop downstream of the bait. Close the bail arm and with the finger on the spool rim, strike hard. This manoeuvre will usually pluck the bait free by a downstream jerk. If this does not work, pull from all directions. If you have to pull and break it is likely that the weaker trace will part rather than the reel line. The underwater bait is not likely to fly back at you if it is released by this pulling.

If the bait catches in the branch of a tree a dangerous situation has been created. The line is elastic, and the tree branch becomes a catapult. The bait and Wye weight act as bullets, and you are the target. In this situation move back 20yd from the river bank, wrap a handkerchief around one hand and take two turns of the reel line around the handkerchief. Put up the collar of your coat, turning your back and lowering your head, then pull until something breaks. The Wye weight will usually fly across the river and hit the bank. On one occasion a Wye hit and penetrated my waxed jacket.

Prawn, shrimp and worm fishing

If these baits are allowed on a river salmon are likely to be harried into a permanent nervous state. Fish may be caught on

Left: Salmon and sea trout artificial spinning baits, hooks, weights and swivels.
Top: 15g Mepp Aglia Flying 'C'.
Middle row, left to right: No. 4 Mepp Aglia, No. 2 Mepp Aglia.
Bottom row, left to right: sliced worm hook, Arlesley Bomb, Wye weight, swivels (3-way, barrel swivel, BB ball bearing swivel).

large prawns in cold water, on small prawns and shrimps in warm water, and on a worm in warm high, coloured water. There is no rest for the fish. For the angler more pleasure may be gained by fishing the fly than by spinning, and by spinning than bait fishing. I suggest the beginner examines the reason why he fishes for salmon. If it is that he wants to eat fish in quantity, then farmed salmon may be purchased. If he wishes to catch more salmon than his neighbour, then natural baits will involve him in much digging in the garden if he chooses the worm, or visits to the harbour for prawns followed by cooking them in the kitchen. But if he fishes for the joy of fishing and with conservation in mind he should fish the fly, or spin in those rivers unsuited to fly-fishing. If you catch many fish the achievement of each is diminished; if you take a small number on the fly each rise will quicken the pulse and be remembered.

The prawn and the shrimp

In low water salmon may be spotted resting on the river-bed if the angler wears polarised spectacles. If he can arrange for a prawn or shrimp to sway in the current one foot in front of the salmon's nose, the fish may open its mouth and engulf the bait. He should then strike, and if his hook arrangements are suitable the fish is likely to be hooked and grassed. To this end the following equipment is required, some of which will already be possessed for spinning:

- 10ft Hardy Fibalite rod
- Mitchell 300 reel with 18-lb monofilament
- Spools of 15-lb and 8-lb monofilament
- $^3/_4$oz and 1oz Arlesley Bomb weights
- 3-way swivels
- 1in, $1^1/_2$in and 2in Partridge T2 prawn and shrimp pins
- Fine copper wire, preferably orange
- Partridge X1 or X3 No. 8 trebles for prawns and No. 10 for shrimps

The terminal tackle may be made up for fishing using the Paternoster system (see diagram).

To mount a prawn, first snap off the spear at the head, as it may deter a salmon from taking hold at this end of the prawn where the treble is partially concealed by the prawn's whiskers. Then twist off the tail flaps which can cause the prawn to twist and spin in an unnatural manner. A Partridge T2 barbed prawn pin should be inserted under the tail and up through the straightened body. The pin has an eye at the end which is now under the tail of the prawn. Pass the 15-lb trace through this eye, knot on the treble hook and press one of the three hooks into the head of the prawn beneath the whiskers. The trace should be led back between the legs under the body, and the whole held in place by a few turns of very fine orange-coloured copper wire. The same mount may be applied to the shrimp with a shorter T2 pin and the No. 10 treble, or two small double hooks mounted one behind the other (see diagram).

A prawn may also be spun across the river on a vaned mount obtainable from tackle shops. This method does not appeal to me as the action of the prawn appears unnatural.

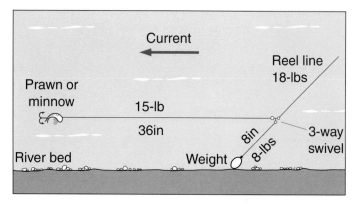

A Paternoster
This system is used to fish a worm, prawn, shrimp or artificial bait. The weight, normally between $^3/_4$ and 1oz, either pear-shaped or Arlesley Bomb, will rest on the bottom whilst the bait sways in the current. The weak nylon leading to the weight will break before the trace if the weight snags. The angler is able to 'feel' his way over the river-bed by raising and lowering the rod tip as the weight will be felt to thump on the bottom. The method is suited to fishing an area very slowly.

Fresh, tough small English prawns, lightly cooked and thus not softened, are better than large over-cooked soft, stale specimens. They may be obtained from the harbour in summer, cooked by the angler until pink, and frozen in packets to provide a supply for the season, or next season. The shrimp is a delicate creature which may easily be broken. It should not be cooked, but used in the natural, brown state.

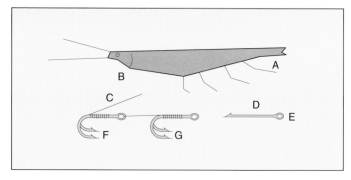

Shrimp mount
Wire C is whipped onto the shank of hook F and inserted into the shrimp at point B. Shrimp pin D (Partridge D2) is inserted forward into the shrimp at A. The nylon trace from the rod passes through pin eye E and is tied to the eye of the hook G.

The worm

The worm is a warm water summer bait which may be fished in the Paternoster system in high water. A more delicate method is upstream worming in low water. Worms may be purchased from tackle dealers or worm farms, dug out of the garden, or collected at night from the damp grass of mown lawns and cricket pitches. They should be kept in damp moss for a week or so to toughen their skins before they are used.

Two large lob worms make a good mouthful. They should be mounted on an eyed Partridge No. 4 FW3 sliced beak hook. This hook has two upward-pointing slices in the shank to prevent the worms sliding down to the bend. Two worms should be slid up the shank to cover the whole hook including the point, and the two ends of each worm should hang free. The Paternoster system of fishing is illustrated. (In this cast the worms replace the prawn.)

For upstream worming the 10ft rod is required and the Mitchell reel with 18-lb nylon. At the end of the reel line, knot on a barrel swivel and then the 15-lb trace leading to the worms. Some extra weight may be required in the form of one to three Thamesly lead-free SSG Sure-Shot. These should be squeezed on to the reel line above the swivel.

The worms are cast upstream, up and across, or across. With the rod held high the worms are trotted across the river-bed. If you can see a resting salmon, place the worms before his head and react to his visible attack. Salmon may not be visible if the water is deep or murky, forcing you to fish by touch. The line usually stops and trembles when a salmon takes. On these indications do not strike, but allow the line to become slack and, if the fish immediately swims away with the bait, feed line to the fish with the bail arm open on the reel. After about twenty seconds the salmon will have had time to swallow the bait – click shut the bail arm and strike.

Worming has the disadvantage that if you strike too soon the worms are likely to be plucked out of the fish's mouth; if you allow plenty of time the salmon may swallow the worms and then be impossible to unhook if it is desired to return a gravid fish to the river. Successes and disappointments attend worm fishing. Salmon love a worm, but so do trout, slippery eels and other fish. The system has much in common with the bran tub lucky dip.

Freezing salmon: The two centre sections of the fish will be frozen in separate polythene bags. Note the concave tail (a sea trout's tail edge would be straight), and the back edge of the eye in line with end of the maxillary (a sea trout's eye is wholly forward of the end of the maxillary).

Appendix I

Further Information

Rod licences

An Environment Agency Rod Licence must be obtained from a Post Office or distributor prior to carrying and fishing with a rod in England and Wales. In addition the permission of the owner of the fishing must be obtained. A Rod Licence is not required in Scotland.

A salmon licence allows the holder to fish also for sea trout, trout and coarse fish. A non-migratory trout and coarse fish licence is available at a lower price. Licences are available for the season and, regardless of the date of purchase, expire on the following 31 March. Eight-day, one-day and concessionary licences are available. The Concessionary Licence is granted to:

- Junior anglers aged 12–16 years inclusive
- Senior anglers aged 65 years and above
- Disabled anglers.

A child under the age of 12 years does not need a licence.

Waders

These are available as thigh boots, waist waders and chest waders. Neoprene waders keep you warm in cold water. Felt soles provide a good grip, but tungsten studs are better and available in the Ocean brand which I always use. Waders for children are difficult to find, but are made by Dunlop in sizes 3, 4 and 5, and may be purchased from Sportsmail Ltd.

Tuition and Safety

The Register of Experienced Fly Fishing Instructors, Schools and Guides (REFFIS)
Chairman: Charles Bingham, West Down, Warren's Cross, Whitchurch, Tavistock, Devon, PL19 9LD.
Secretary: Richard Slocock, Wessex Fly Fishing, Tolpuddle, Dorchester, Dorset, DT2 7HF
This organisation visits and assesses the facilities, game fishing waters, literature and knowledge of all members throughout Mainland Britain and Ireland, and in some distant lands. Many members let fishing. Addresses and details may be obtained in a Directory and Journal which is published each year and obtainable from the Secretary together with a leaflet 'Safety and the Game Angler' (Copyright Pat O'Reilly) on receipt of a stamped and addressed A4 envelope.

Gillies

Knowledge of a water is acquired through spending many seasons on a loch or river. The gillie or guide should have this knowledge (REFFIS Guides do) and the beginner should take advantage of their experience. Fish where he suggests with the fly he recommends, at least to begin with. If success is lacking then try your own fly, he will be happy enough if you catch a fish. I would always employ a gillie on a strange water, at any rate for a day or two, otherwise much time is wasted finding fish lies and fruitful areas.

Cleaning and freezing fish

Fish caught on a hot day ought to be placed in a bass which should be kept wet and hung in a breezy place. Evaporation of the water will keep the fish cool. Clean the fish the same evening, or early the next morning if they are sea trout caught

Cleaning a fish at the river in April.

at night, pack in polythene and freeze.

In the case of grilse I not only clean the belly of the fish, but also cut out the gill filaments, the grilse then being frozen whole. For salmon above about 6lb it is convenient, after cleaning the belly, to remove the head and the tail. I then cut it into chunks of 2–3lb, freezing these separately. If a whole salmon of 10lb is cleaned and then frozen in one piece it has to be defrosted in one piece, or chunks cut off with a hacksaw which is a messy and difficult business.

Single-bank fishing

The question is often raised whether an angler fishing a single-bank beat may cast over to the far bank in a river which may be fully covered from both sides. I am unable to advise on the law, but courtesy will go a long way towards an amicable arrangement.

On arrival at a pool being fished from the opposite bank wait until the occupant has ceased, and then follow him down. On no account start in front of him. In this way neither will cast under the feet of the other. It is incumbent on your opposite number to move on steadily down the pool and then on down the river, and not to fish back up for a second go at the best places. He could, of course, start in behind and follow you down if he wished to cover the water for a second time.

Also, do not wade out more than one third of the width of the river. If the angler on one bank is fishing the fly and the man on the other bank is spinning or fishing a natural bait such as worm or prawn, it would be courteous to allow the fly man to cover the water first, for he is likely to cause less disturbance.

A satisfactory arrangement is to divide the beat into top and bottom halves. One bank fishes the top half in the morning and the lower section in the afternoon, and vice versa, the change-over being at lunch-time.

Author's note

The Environment Agency and anglers are increasingly concerned by the reduction of salmon spawning population particularly those of two or more sea-winters. These heavy fish tend to enter rivers in the early months of the season. On 18 November 1998 the Agency proposed the following measures for 1999 to protect salmon stocks in England and Wales.

(Scotland is not included.) Of the measures proposed the hook restrictions also apply to anglers fishing for sea trout. If these measures are confirmed, readers using the hooks suggested in this book should carry a pair of snipe-nosed pliers to press in the barbs of singles, doubles and trebles. Even if the proposals are not confirmed the author recommends the release of all multi-sea-winter salmon.

Proposed National byelaws
NETS

Delay the season until 1 June for the salmon and sea trout fishing. A small number of sea trout fisheries will be exempt to avoid disproportionate economic loss (e.g. Anglian, Northumbrian T & J nets, Seine nets in the Twyi, Dart and Teign estuaries). Any salmon caught before 1 June would have to be released.

RODS

1. Mandatory catch and release of all salmon on all rivers before 16 June.

2. Only flies and spinners to be used before 16 June for salmon fishing. Anglers would still be able to fish the worm for other species (i.e. sea trout, non-migratory trout and eels). However, the hook restrictions (see below) would apply to sea trout.

3. Not more than one barbless hook (single, double, or treble) to be used for salmon or sea trout with a maximum gape of 8mm. The 8mm gape would allow most hooks size 6 and smaller. The byelaw will not preclude the use of a team of flies.

The byelaw on the size of hooks on a fly, spinner or other artificial lure will not come into force until 2000, in order to allow the tackle trade to adjust. The other restrictions on hooks, including the size for use with natural baits will come into force immediately. Barbs can be flattened to comply.

In addition to the above I suggest that anglers be encouraged *throughout the season* to release all salmon over 8lb. A copy of the Environment Agency leaflet 'Catch-and-release: a guide to careful salmon handling' is available from Agency Customer Service Centres (telephone 0645-333111).

Appendix II

Glossary

Adipose fin – Small fin on the back of a game fish between the dorsal fin and the tail

AFTM Scale – Defines the weight of a fly line

Alevin – Fishlet with yolk sac which hatches from an ovum

Aquifer – Chalk stratum underlying the hills and valley of a chalk-stream

Arlesley Bomb – Weight incorporating a swivel (used as part of Paternoster system of fishing a bait)

Artery forceps – Used for extracting hooks from fish

Backing – An additional length of strong thin line joined to, and beneath, the fly line on a fly reel

Backing-up – Method of fishing a salmon fly in a fast-moving curve whilst the angler moves from the tail to the head of a pool

Baggot – Hen salmon swollen with eggs which it has been unable to extrude

Bail arm – Part of a fixed spool reel which gathers and winds the line on to the spool

Bait thrower – Appliance similar to a sling for dispensing groundbait over a distance

Bank (in boat fishing) – Area of shallow water in a loch

Bank (of a river) – Looking downstream, the right bank is to your right, the left bank to your left

Bite detector – Device over which the line passes emitting a sound to indicate a bite when coarse fishing

Bivouac – Tent to provide cover at the water's edge for carp fishermen

Blow line (Floss line) – Undressed fluffy line blown out by the wind from the tip of a long dapping rod, to carry the fly out, over, and onto the water when dapping from a boat

Bobbin – Ball of dough, wood or plastic on line to indicate a bite when coarse fishing

Boilie – Proprietary mix sold in small balls for carp fishing

Bread punch – Tubular punch to cut small slugs out of a slice of bread for bait

Burn – Small Scottish stream

Butt (of leader) – Thickest part of a tapered leader where it joins the fly line

Butt (of rod) – Handle end of a rod

Caddis – Another name for a sedge fly

Casters – Maggots which have turned into a chrysalid state and are used for bait

Centre pin – A reel in which the drum revolves on a centre pin, and the line is wound on by rotating the drum

Chironomid – A midge

Close season – Spawning period of the year when fishing is prohibited for certain species of fish

Collar – Short length of thick monofilament needle knotted to the end of a fly line and to which the leader is attached

Crane fly – Daddy-long-legs

Dangle (on the) – Position of fly, or taking salmon, when straight downstream of the angler

Dead bait – Dead fish, or portion thereof, attached as bait to the line by one or more hooks

Disgorger – Instrument for extracting hooks from fish

Dropper – Second or third fly fished on a leader above the point fly. The top dropper is sometimes called a 'bob'

Dry fly – Artificial imitation of natural fly, or coloured attractor, which floats on the surface

Dun – First aerial stage in the life cycle of flies of the order Ephemeroptera

False cast – When fly-fishing this cast is made in the air to extend the line, check distance, or dry a floating fly

Finnock – Small Scottish sea trout on first return to the river after marine excursion

Fish – In Scotland refers to a salmon rather than a sea trout or a trout

Fixed spool reel – Line is drawn off the front of the spool which does not revolve

Flake – Morsel of new bread from the crumb of a loaf. It is pinched on to the hook

Flight (hook mount) – Treble hook, wire (sometimes nylon) and swivel passing through the hollow centre of a Devon minnow

Float – Device made from feather quills, reed, or plastic to suspend a bait in the water at desired depth

Floss line – see Blow line

Flotsam – Dead weed, bits of wood or rubbish washed into the river

Fry – Small fish (after the alevin stage)

Fly line – Plastic (used to be silk) floating or sinking line for casting a fly or lure

Gaff – Pointed barbless hook on a shaft for landing salmon (often illegal)

Gape – Defines the width of gap between the point and shank of a hook

Gillie – A person who should have detailed knowledge of a river or loch and who is employed to assist an angler

Gravid – Description of a hen fish with well-developed roe

Grilse – A 'one-sea-winter' salmon

Groundbait – Mix of various materials to attract fish to the area being fished

Gye net – Large salmon or sea trout net carried on the back

Hackle – Neck feather used in dressing flies: cock bird for dry flies, hen for wet flies

Herling – Small sea trout

Hook link – 12in or 18in of nylon of weaker breaking strain than the reel line. Looped at one end for attachment to reel line; the hook is tied to the other end

Jack pike – Small pike

Keep net – Long tubular net suspended in the river to hold caught fish which are to be returned

Kelt – Spawned fish

Kype – Upward hook on lower jaw of cock fish

Lead Shot – Round bullet or other weight made from a metal substitute for lead

Leader (historically called a 'cast') – The length of nylon (used to be gut) joining the fly line to the fly

Ledger – Weight used to suspend a bait when ledger fishing

Lie – Place where fish rest in a river

Lure – General term embracing spinning baits, artificial flies, plugs etc

Marrow spoon – Narrow long spoon used to withdraw the stomach contents of a dead fish to ascertain its diet

Mend – To move the fly line on the water, after the initial cast, by switching upstream to decrease the speed of passage of a fly across the river to the angler's bank

Mepp – A revolving spoon bait

Milt – Male seminal fluid emitted by cock fish to fertilise female spawn

Monkey climber – Type of bite indicator attached to the line between the reel and the first rod ring

Monofilament – Single strand nylon in various breaking strains for casting a bait or fly to fish

Neck (of a river pool) – Narrow entrance where the river runs into a pool

Nymph – Underwater stage in the life-cycle of some insects

'On the fin' – Position of feeding river trout close to the water surface and waiting to take passing, floating, natural flies

Otter – Device to release baits caught on the river-bed when spinning

Ova – Eggs of a fish

Parr – Small fish in the early stage of its life-cycle

Paste – Bait made from white crumb of a stale loaf soaked in water then squeezed to doughy consistency, or a mix of flour and water

Paternoster – Method of fishing an artificial or natural bait slowly and close to the river-bed

Peal – West Country term for a sea trout

Peal sling – Quick-release harness by which a Gye net is carried on the angler's back

Pharyngeal teeth – Teeth at the back of the throat of some species of fish for masticating food

Plug bait – An artificial vaned bait, usually fish-shaped, sometimes jointed, which moves in a wiggly manner when retrieved by a spinning reel

Plummet – Pear-shaped weight with a cork insert in the base for checking depth of water

Point fly – The fly at the end of a leader

Pole – A fishing rod of one or several tapered plastic tubes which slide into each other

Pole float – Specially designed float for pole fishing

Priest – Short truncheon with which to kill fish by hitting them on the head (administering the last rites)

Pupa – Immature stage of some flies

PTFE – Plastic material with a very slippery surface over which a line or elastic can flow with little friction

Quiver tip – Attachment to the top joint of a ledger rod to indicate a bite

Rapala – Type of plug bait

Reaving – A method of straightening the line when the current makes it drift away or beyond the float

Redd – Depression cut in gravel or small stones by fish in river-bed, into which the female deposits ova, which are then fertilised by the milt of the cock fish

Rod rest – A 'V' shaped or 'U' shaped rest on which a rod is placed instead of being held in the hand

Roller rest – A special padded roller or rollers on which a pole is rested

Run-off – The downstream, tail end of a river pool

School peal – West Country term for small sea trout on their first return to the river in summer from the sea

Scissors (to be hooked in the) – Description of the point of the angle between the upper and lower jaws of a fish

Sea lice – Suckered lice found on the flanks and backs of salmon and sea trout when they enter the river from the sea (denotes a fresh fish)

Sea trout – Migratory brown trout

Sewin – Welsh term for a sea trout

Shoot (to) – When false casting, and making intermediate or final throws, the extra line which passes out through the rod rings to obtain additional distance

Shouldered bung – A plastic bung inserted into one of the joints of a pole to which the elastic is attached

Silk weed – Weed found growing on sluice walls rich in snails and invertebrates

Skate (skid) – An artificial fly crossing a river, or drawn over the loch or lake surface, creating a wake

Slider – A float which is free to slide on the line to a predetermined depth

Smolt – An immature salmon or sea trout migrating downriver in spring to make its first entry to the sea

Sneck – A hook with a reverse bend

Spade-end hook – A hook with a portion of the shank flattened to facilitate the attachment of nylon with a spade knot

Spate – Rise and fall of water level in a river following rain

Spawn – Eggs laid by the hen fish

Spinner – Metal, wood or plastic bait which revolves when retrieved

Spinner (natural fly) – Second aerial and egg-laying stage of flies of the order Ephemeroptera

Split cane – Rod of hexagonal cross-section formed of six planed strips of cane, bonded by glue or wrapped together with silk

Spoon – Bait which wobbles or darts when retrieved

Spring tide – High tide occurring at full and new moons

Stale fish – A salmon or sea trout which has returned from the sea and been in fresh water for some weeks, most common in the autumn, usually returned alive to the river

Stick float – A fishing float made from balsa wood or plastic on which a baited hook is suspended when float fishing

Stickle – Shallow section of a river between two pools

Stop knot – Special knot tied onto the reel line to stop a sliding float at a predetermined depth

Swim feeder – A plastic cage, usually round, with holes in the side to release a filling of groundbait gradually into the current. Groundbait is moulded around a wire cage feeder

Tailer – Wire noose to land salmon. It grips the fish at the 'wrist' just above the tail

'Taking on the drop' – Fish taking a bait suspended from a float or freeline when descending through the water to reach the set depth. Also applies to weighted fly lures as they sink towards the bed of a lake

Toby – Type of long spoon bait

Trace – About 3ft of nylon or wire, between the swivel at the end of the line from a spinning reel and a natural or artificial bait

Trotting – Allowing a float suspending a bait to float freely with the current

'Unibung' – Patented name for a plastic plug to secure elastic in a pole

Waggler – Type of float made from balsa wood, plastic, or quill, to suspend a bait

Walk-up – Method of persuading a salmon to move upstream by gentle pressure, and follow the angler as he walks up the river bank towards the head of a pool

Wide-gape – A hook with extra width between the point and the shank

Wind knot – Knot formed unintentionally in the leader when casting a fly. The knot weakens the leader, which must be replaced or the knot removed.

Wye weight – Weight used in salmon and sea trout fishing by artificial or natural bait. The weight has a loop at one end for reel line attachment, and a swivel at the other to which the trace is attached.

Appendix III

Useful Knots

DOMHOF KNOT

This knot is suitable for spade-end and eyed hooks. Thread the line through the hook eye or over the spade end. Lay it along the shank and form a loop. Take eight turns round the hook and the loop and pass the end through. Then moisten and pull the line tight.

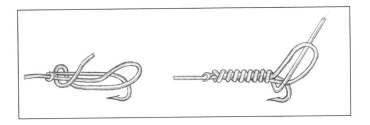

SPADE-END KNOT

This knot is suitable for spade-end hooks. Make a loop along the hook shank with one turn round the hook shank at the spade end. Make another turn passing the loop over the shank. Make a total of six turns round the shank, passing the line end through as arrow. Moisten and pull the line tight.

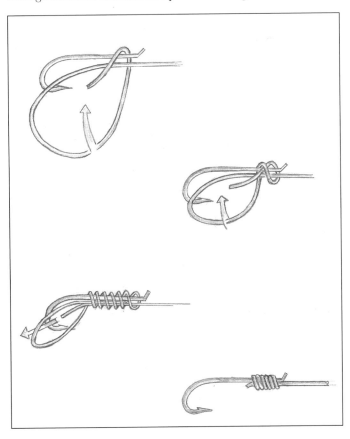

STOP KNOT

For use with a sliding float.

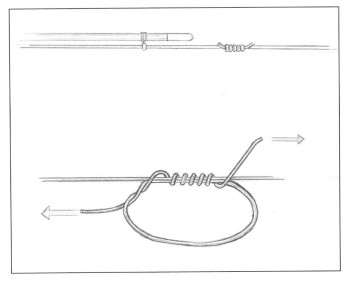

Reel to backing

ARBOR KNOT

This knot is suitable for both monofilament and braided backing.

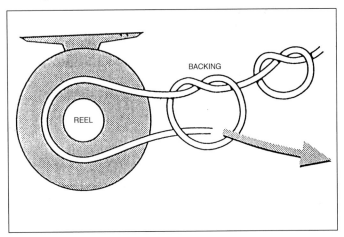

Backing to fly line

ALBRIGHT KNOT

Used to join braided backing to the fly line. This is the bulkiest of the three alternative knots in this position, and is one reason why monofilament backing is preferable.

ALBRIGHT KNOT

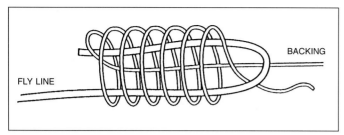

NEEDLE KNOT

This can only be used for monofilament thin enough to pass into the core of the fly line. Use 20-lb monofilament, cutting the end on a slant to ease introduction into the fly line. The diameter of needles needs to be chosen with care, but the needles do not need to be heated to establish a suitable hole. This is the best and smoothest knot, passing without disturbance through the rod line guides. In sea trout fishing it is also my choice for joining the fly line to the butt of the leader.

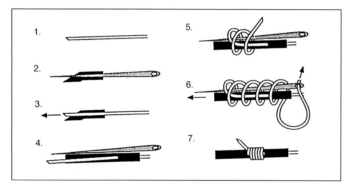

NAIL KNOT

For use when the monofilament backing is too thick to pass into the core of a thin fly line. A fat needle is required. The result is not as smooth as the needle knot.

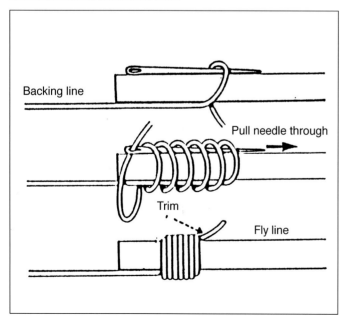

Fly line to leader

NEEDLE KNOT

Already described. Pass 1ft of 20-lb monofilament into the core of the fly line; join this with a blood knot to the butt of the leader. This is the most desirable line/leader junction for sea trout fishing in the dark.

LOOP TO LOOP

For joining a braided loop on the end of the fly line to the blood bight loop on the butt of a knotless tapered leader, or homemade sectional leader. An inferior choice in sea trout fishing to the needle knot, but good for daylight fishing when one is able to see that the junction is kept outside the top of the rod. Good for trout fishing and the rapid changing of leaders.

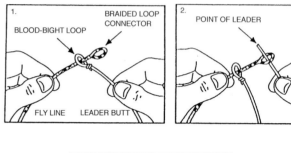

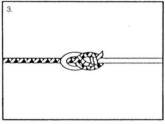

Leader construction and droppers

BLOOD BIGHT LOOP

To form a loop on the butt end of a homemade leader in order to join 'loop-to-loop' with a braided loop on the end of a fly line.

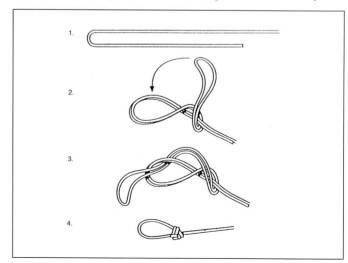

WATER KNOT

For making tapered leaders and joining lengths of nylon where one length is short. One end, the upper, may be left about 4in long, and pointing upwards towards the rod tip, to form a dropper.

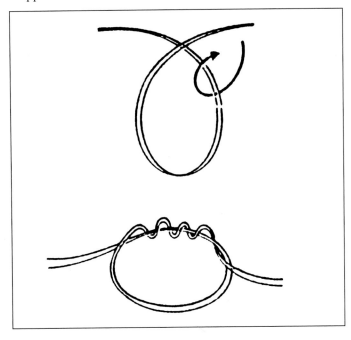

BLOOD KNOT

Used to join sections of nylon when making leaders. Lengths to be joined should not be of widely dissimilar diameters or the knot will not tighten. To add a dropper, leave one end of the knot extending a few inches after construction, whilst trimming the other end close to the knot. The end to be left as a dropper should be the continuation of the section above the knot; in the unlikely event of the knot coming undone whilst playing a fish, the quarry would still be attached. The knot should be moistened in the mouth before tightening.

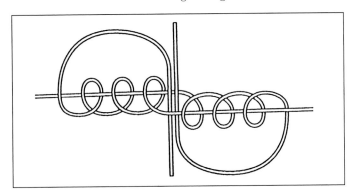

Leader to fly – eyed

TWO-TURN TURLE

The best knot for eyed flies. The loop, passing around the shank of the hook immediately behind the eye of the fly, keeps the fly

in line with the leader. When tying eyed flies there should be left a small neck behind the eye to accommodate this loop. Too many dressers wind their tying silk thickly right up to the back of the eye of the fly – this prevents use of the Turle.

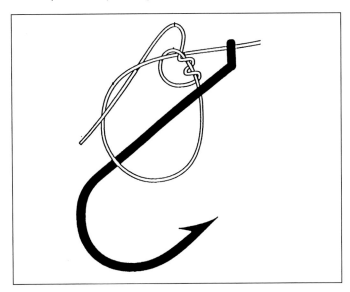

Leader to fly – tube fly and spinning baits

TUCKED HALF-BLOOD

This should not be favoured for eyed flies as the knot can slide around the perimeter of the metal eye of the fly. This may cause the fly to fish at an angle to the leader. It must be used to attach the 'in line with the shank' eyes of treble hooks used in tube flies, or where the dresser of the fly has not left a neck to an eyed fly to take the loop of the Turle.

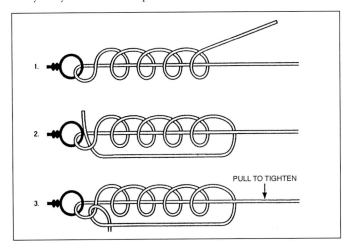

WIND KNOT

A wind knot is a single turn formed unintentionally in a leader whilst casting. It reduces the breaking strength of nylon by about 50%. The faulty section of the leader should be replaced or, at the least, the knot snapped with a jerk and the ends joined with a blood knot. The specialised knots illustrated do not reduce the breaking strength of nylon by more than 20%.

Index